Implementing the Convention on the Rights of the Child

IMPLEMENTING THE CONVENTION ON THE RIGHTS OF THE CHILD

Resource Mobilization in Low-Income Countries

Edited by
James R. Himes
Director,
UNICEF International Child Development Centre,
Florence, Italy

unicef
United Nations Children's Fund

MARTINUS NIJHOFF PUBLISHERS
THE HAGUE / LONDON / BOSTON

A C.I.P. Catalogue record for this book is available from the Library of Congress.

ISBN 90-411-0090-3

Design: Bernard Chazine
Phototypesetting: Bernard & Co. – Siena, Italy

Published by Kluwer Law International,
P.O. Box 85889, 2508 CN The Hague, The Netherlands.

Sold and distributed in the U.S.A. and Canada
by Kluwer Law International,
675 Massachusetts Avenue, Cambridge, MA 02139, U.S.A.

In all other countries, sold and distributed
by Kluwer Law International,
P.O. Box 322, 3300 AH Dordrecht, The Netherlands.

Printed on acid-free paper

Kluwer Law International incorporates the publishing programmes of
Graham & Trotman Ltd, Kluwer Law and Taxation Publishers,
and Martinus Nijhoff Publishers.

Printed in the Netherlands

CONTENTS

Tables

Figures

FOREWORD

Thomas Hammarberg

The message of the United Nations Convention on the Rights of the Child can be summarized in four words — *Children should be respected*. This means that:

- children's survival, protection and development should be given priority;
- their best interests should be a primary consideration whenever decisions are taken that affect them;
- their views should be heard and given due weight; and
- these principles should apply to all children without discrimination of any kind.

On the basis of these key principles, the Convention defines substantive provisions on how children should be treated in the different areas of their lives. Some provisions relate to the family environment or alternative care; others describe measures to guarantee children a meaningful education and access to health care. Special measures are required to protect vulnerable groups of children or children who are in dangerous situations. The Convention adopts a rights approach; it is in fact a human *rights* instrument for children.

It took the United Nations Member States 10 years and a good many meetings to produce the Convention. Since its adoption by the United Nations General Assembly in November 1989, almost all of the countries in the world have pledged to adhere to its principles and implement its provisions. (By March 1995, 170 countries had become States Parties to the CRC by ratification, or accession, acceptance, or succession). An international committee has been set up to monitor progress in realizing children's rights.

Is it all worthwhile? Does the Convention actually lead to improvements for children? Does it add anything to the international efforts already under way in development programmes?

These questions can now be answered. Four years have passed since the United Nations Committee on the Rights of the Child was elected. It has now evaluated and discussed more than 30 reports from States Parties and has adopted concluding observations on how the Convention has been implemented.

On the whole, the record is impressive. Perhaps the most important achievement is that governments have been encouraged to give children's issues political priority. A number of countries have undertaken comprehensive reviews on the overall situation of children. Almost all countries that have submitted reports to the Committee have amended relevant pieces of legislation to conform to the Convention. Several countries have decided to establish Ombudsmen for Children or other structures to monitor independently how the authorities treat children. International organizations as well as many governments have focused on vulnerable groups such as child labourers, child prostitutes and children in armed conflicts. Furthermore, non-governmental organizations have begun to take on an important role, adding considerably to both the debate and the practical work on children's rights.

Without the Convention's human rights approach, some of these developments would probably not have come about as explicitly and quickly as they have. The fact that the Convention is a legally binding instrument has also proved to be valuable. A government that ratifies the Convention is legally committed to implement its articles. Supportive measures for children are therefore seen as *obligations*.

The commitment of political leaders at summit meetings or the decisions of governing boards of the World Bank or the specialized agencies of the United Nations can of course have enormous impact. But a duly ratified international convention adds a further dimension in that it represents a long-term commitment, one that outlasts shifting patterns of political control at national and subnational levels of society.

There is no contradiction between a rights approach and development strategies. The Convention itself specifies that development efforts are essential for the implementation of the Convention. Within the United Nations family, nonetheless, a divide still exists between human rights and development approaches, both in programmes and structures. This division is in part due to the slow recognition of economic and social rights as genuine rights. Things, however, are beginning to change. There is a growing awareness that the purpose of development work is to promote and to protect human rights — or more specifically, civil, cultural, economic, political and social rights. An especially positive sign is the current discussion about the 'right to development'.

In this book on implementing the Convention, a group of experienced development practitioners, not human rights lawyers or specialists, take the firm position that addressing basic issues of children's well-being, including their education, health and nutrition, from a rights perspective, as well as — not instead of — a more conventional development approach, strengthens rather than detracts from the earlier strategies that have guided child-oriented programme efforts for decades.

A key proposition underlying their conviction is that working effectively for children's rights involves many of the same strategies and implementation methods that have proved successful in numerous development efforts throughout the world. One of the main strategic elements of both a rights and a development approach to working for children in developing countries is a systematic concern for resource mobilization. In low-income or otherwise resource-poor societies, neither approach will prove successful if innovative and sustainable ways are not devised to overcome the formidable resource constraints that are faced.

This book deals primarily with the obligations of States to implement the Convention, concentrating on children's basic economic and social rights in developing countries. Article 4 is the main 'umbrella' provision of the Convention regarding implementation, requiring that "States Parties ... undertake all appropriate legislative, administrative, and other measures for the implementation of the rights recognized in the present Convention". A key sentence in the Convention then follows: "With regard to economic, social and cultural rights, States Parties shall undertake such measures to the maximum extent of their available resources and, where needed, within the framework of international co-operation."

Article 4 describes obligations of conduct rather than of result; the emphasis is on what efforts States Parties make in promoting the implementation of the Convention. States Parties should review their legislation and ensure that laws are consistent with the Convention. This process of legal harmonization is relevant not just for civil and political rights but also for many of the rights usually described as economic, social and cultural. Laws are needed, for instance, for the protection of children against exploitation in the formal or informal labour market and to ensure compulsory education. In the fields of health and social welfare as well, most countries have developed legal norms to establish certain principles and guarantee non-discrimination.

The "administrative and other measures" could include a range of steps to make implementation effective. One is to establish mechanisms at national and local levels to coordinate policies and to monitor the implementation of the Convention, including through ombudswork. Non-governmental organizations form part of the national commissions for children established in a number of countries. Of course, political decision-making is in itself crucial. What procedures are there to ensure that child matters are taken seriously in both the national legislature and in local assemblies? Are there opportunities for children themselves and their representatives to make themselves heard?

Another aspect that the Committee on the Rights of the Child has raised in this context is the importance of collecting reliable and relevant information on the situation of children. With precise data the discussion about remedies can be better informed and focused. Improvement of the capacity of a national statistical office can therefore be an essential contribution to the implementation of the Convention.

One important means towards the genuine realization of the Convention's goals is the education and training of the people who work with children: teachers, child psychologists, paediatricians and other health personnel, police officers, social workers, and others. A clearer understanding among these professionals of the concept of children's rights can be immensely important.

The second part of Article 4 deals with the problem of *resources*. What is meant by the commitment that governments make to implement economic, social and cultural rights "to the maximum extent of their available resources"?

Obviously, this wording is prompted by a concern that some countries will not have sufficient resources, at least not in the short term, to assure the full implementation of all of the Convention's provisions. The possibility that resource problems could arise is also explicitly stated in some of the substantive articles; for instance, in Article 23 where the provision of special care for the disabled child is made "subject to available resources". The Convention deals with this crucial aspect with an innovative approach.

First, it recognizes that some of the more resource-demanding changes cannot take place overnight. It specifies, for instance, that the rights to health care and education can be achieved "progressively" (Articles 24 and 28).

Second, it makes clear that, although the formal responsibility will always be placed on governments, there is also an international duty to assist. Indeed, a significant phrase is found at the end of Article 4 (following the wording about available resources): "and, where needed, within the framework of international co-operation".

Third, although some rights can be implemented progressively and with international assistance, governments still have immediate obligations. Rich or poor, they should allocate the maximum extent of their resources for the implementation of the Convention. They should, in other words, give priority to children. Poor countries should at least endeavour to fulfil a defined set of minimum core obligations, making every effort, as a matter of priority, to use their limited resources to meet these minimum requirements. Devising strategies and programmes and monitoring their effectiveness are obligations whatever the starting point is.

The authors of this book emphasize the importance of a broad interpretation of societal "resources", going well beyond the severely limited finances of governments in most developing countries. This interpretation needs to extend both to the international (official and non-governmental) levels and to the expanding civil societies of these nations. In addition, "resources" must be broadly defined to include human, technological, cultural and organizational capabilities as well as conventional economic resources. Traditions, culture and political maturity are other important factors enabling societies to tackle their problems. Values such as tolerance, mutual respect and a spirit of solidarity can also be seen as "resources". Furthermore, although implementation must necessarily be "progressive" in view of pervasive resource constraints, clear targets and strategies are seen as a critical means to keep the process on track.

"Resources", moreover, should not be seen as static. There is a dynamic dimension, which is of interest not least of all for the long-range perspective: increasing and broadening the mobilization of resources over time. Although the authorities are directly responsible for the implementation of the Convention, the resources of the entire society matter, including those in the 'civil society'. For this reason, governments need to be open to and encourage the initiatives and action of non-governmental groups, recognizing that this process takes time.

The thematic chapters of this book give many examples of human, organizational and economic resources being effectively mobilized for children. Some of the most promising of these involve the active participation of actors that the development and the human rights worlds conventionally define as 'non-traditional'. They include 'ordinary citizens' acting through community groups, women's associations, cooperatives, youth groups, religious organizations and trade unions, to mention just a few, as well as professionals such as journalists, doctors and lawyers.

Most importantly, some of the most exciting initiatives involve the active participation of children themselves, providing both young children and youth with opportunities to begin to develop the experience and skills needed for responsibly exercising their participation rights, which are formally recognized, often for the first time, in this Convention.

When the Convention was drafted, the developing countries were led to understand that their support for the Convention would improve their standing in the international community. The aim was to create procedures that are constructive rather than punitive or 'finger-pointing'. It was suggested that the Committee on the Rights of the Child could, as it considered appropriate, transmit to "the specialized agencies, the United Nations Children's Fund and other competent bodies" requests for technical advice and assistance (Article 45.b).

Similar provisions were included in the decisions made at the World Summit for Children. Its Plan of Action states that "many developing countries, particularly the least developed and the most indebted ones, will need substantial international co-operation to enable them to participate effectively in the worldwide effort for child survival, protection and development".

What obligations are tied to the Convention's clauses about international cooperation? For the donor countries the question is what priority — and direction — child-related programmes should have in their overall development aid policies. Similarly, developing countries should clarify what room they intend to give children's rights in their cooperation programmes.

Some donor countries, notably Sweden and Norway, have in fact reviewed their development cooperation programmes in the light of the Convention, but they seem to be exceptions. Developing countries, on their side, have more frequently discussed their aid needs when reporting on the Convention and the follow-up to the World Summit. Vietnam and Namibia are good examples.

However, development aid is not the only aspect of international resource mobilization. Other types of cooperation in the economic arena were discussed at the World Summit, including the foreign debt problem:

> Debt relief for children, including debt swaps for investment in social development programmes, should be considered by debtors and creditors. The international community, including private-sector creditors, are urged to work with developing countries and relevant agencies to support debt relief for children.

Efforts to bring the Convention and the State Party reports into the macro-economic discussions on individual countries that take place at World Bank aid consortia meetings and elsewhere have not as yet been successful. Suggestions to that effect have been left largely unheeded.

In recent years, aid and debt relief have been extended to developing countries on the condition that they undertake 'structural adjustment'. There is no doubt that economic adjustment reforms in a number of countries have had dire consequences for children, especially vulnerable groups of children. When discussing this problem with States Parties, the Committee on the Rights of the Child has taken a similar approach to that adopted by the World Summit, which called for adjustment measures that "promote world economic growth, particularly in developing countries, while ensuring the well-being of the most vulnerable sectors of the populations, in particular the children".

A responsible — and future-oriented — economic policy is naturally in the interests of children. For them it is desirable that space is created for necessary investments and that foreign debts are reduced. This ought not to be controversial. The problem relates to the present priorities and to how the cutbacks and savings are being made. UNICEF and others have discussed structural reform with a "human face", the intention being to create safeguards against the severe social consequences of decreased government funding of basic services.

The emphasis by the United Nations Development Programme and others on "human development" has contributed to wider awareness of the importance, including the economic importance, of investing in people. Primary education and access to basic health services are often cited as key examples. The World Summit for Children emphasized the principle of "first call" for children. Such priority setting fits well with the wording in Article 4 urging governments to undertake child-oriented implementation measures "to the maximum extent of their available resources".

The Convention is of course not only about the mobilization of resources for children in general. An important feature of the human rights approach to development is *non-discrimination* and equity (as specified in Article 2). That aspect is not always emphasized in conventional development cooperation programmes. Lately, with the prevailing tides of private-sector-driven economic development, there is in fact a growing concern in many countries that the current patterns of development, heavily supported by the main international financial actors, are exacerbating disparities and inequities, particularly to the disadvantage of the poorest families.

Many national and international development agencies, moreover, whether intentionally or not, are perpetuating myths about social progress by paying too much attention to highly aggregated measures of gains made. We are impressed by the statistics showing success in extending the benefits of prenatal care, immunization and primary schooling. But too rarely do we focus attention on who are the children and mothers not being reached and why? Is it because of their ethnicity or race, gender, religious or social origin? When this is the case, even in the context of the inherent realities of achieving rights "progressively", then national and international agencies and actors concerned with children's rights need to take vigorous action. Such discrimination is simply wrong — and it is illegal.

The Convention on the Rights of the Child was not intended — nor is it equipped — to be an instrument to address all the major political issues of distributive justice and social equity in today's inequitable world. But it can become, with time, an effective additional instrument for dealing with many of the inexcusable failures of society to address the most basic survival, protection, development and participation needs of children. The lack of an adequate excuse relates fundamentally to the underlying theme of this book: We do have "available" the resources, ranging from human ingenuity to new technologies. The challenge is to use these resources to put an end to child poverty and deprivation, and to ensure that the rights of children in every part of the world are indeed respected.

Contributors

JO BOYDEN, a social anthropologist and free-lance consultant, has worked extensively with UNICEF, ILO and NGOs such as Rädda Barnen at both a policy and programme level. She has carried out assignments in the Andean region, the Horn of Africa, Bangladesh, India and Burma. She is author of several publications on especially disadvantaged children and families, among which *Combating Child Labour*, with A. Bequele (ILO, 1988); *Children of the Cities* (Zed Press, 1991); *Families* (Gaia Books, 1993); and 'The Relationship between Education and Child Work', *Innocenti Occasional Papers* (UNICEF International Child Development Centre, 1994). Her current interests include the generation of indicators for monitoring the Convention on the Rights of the Child, children in areas of conflict and child work.

FRANK P. DALL, until recently Senior Adviser for Primary Education at UNICEF Headquarters in New York, is now based in Amman, Jordan, where he serves as UNICEF Regional Education Adviser for the Middle East and North Africa. Before he joined UNICEF, his career in international education took him to East and Central Africa with the Overseas Development Administration (United Kingdom) and to Central and Latin America with the United States Agency for International Development. From 1987 to 1990 he directed an education policy research project at the Harvard Institute for International Development. Among his publications are 'Non-formal Education and National Development: A Critical Assessment of Policy, Research, and Practice' (Praeger, 1984) and 'Basic Education: An Investment in a Better African Future' (UNICEF/Organization of African Unity, 1992). He is co-author of the forthcoming *Guidelines for Implementing Primary Education for Countries in Transition* (Al-Kutba/UNICEF, Amman, Jordan), which will be published in English and Arabic.

THOMAS HAMMARBERG, Ambassador and Special Adviser on Humanitarian Issues at the Ministry of Foreign Affairs, Stockholm, has been a member of the United Nations Committee on the Rights of the Child since 1991 and the Committee's Vice-Chair since 1993. A graduate of the Stockholm School of Economics, he was a journalist and foreign editor of the daily *Expressen* from 1972 to 1977 and worked at the Swedish Broadcasting Company from 1976 to 1978. He was Chairman of the International Executive Committee of Amnesty International from 1976 to 1979 and its Secretary-General from 1980 to 1986. He served as the Secretary-General of Rädda Barnen from 1986 to 1992. He has written a number of articles on human rights, the rights of the child and humanitarian affairs.

JAMES R. HIMES is the founding Director of the UNICEF International Child Development Centre in Florence, Italy, which is UNICEF's main facility for applied research and policy analysis on issues of improving the well-being of children and families. He joined UNICEF in 1981, serving first as Chief of the Americas Section and then as Director of the Planning Office. Earlier he served as the Ford Foundation's Representative for Colombia and Venezuela (1972-1977) and Head of the Latin

American and Caribbean Programme (1977-1981). He holds a master's and a doctorate degree in development studies from Princeton University. He has written on numerous topics concerning economic and social development, most recently on children's rights.

URBAN JONSSON is Regional Director for UNICEF in South Asia, based in Kathmandu, Nepal. As Chief Adviser on Nutrition at UNICEF Headquarters in New York from 1990 to 1994, he led the work of the preparation, promotion and implementation of UNICEF's new Nutrition Strategy. During this period (1990-1991), he worked with Prof. N. Scrimshaw in the World Hunger Programme, United Nations University, Tokyo. Prior to that, he was the UNICEF Country Representative in Tanzania for eight years. He started his work in developing countries as the Chief of Planning, Tanzania Food and Nutrition Centre (1976-1980).

ROBERT J. LEDOGAR is Senior Planning Officer at UNICEF Headquarters in New York. Prior to his headquarters appointment, he served for 10 years with UNICEF in Central America in various capacities; was Field Director for the American Friends' Service Committee in Lusaka, Zambia; and worked with the United Nations Centre for Housing, Building and Planning during the lead-up to the 1976 Habitat Conference in Vancouver. He has co-authored several articles on Sentinel Community Surveillance. His book *Hungry for Profits* (IDOC North America, 1975), an investigation of the impact of multinational food and drug companies on consumers in Latin America and the Caribbean, was also published in Spanish and Portuguese. He holds a doctorate degree in theology from the Institut Catholique de Paris and a master's degree in city planning from the Massachusetts Institute of Technology.

DAVID PARKER is Regional Economic Adviser for UNICEF in South Asia, based in Kathmandu, Nepal. He served previously at UNICEF Headquarters as Senior Adviser for Health Financing, and subsequently in the Office of Social Policy and Economic Analysis. In these different capacities, he has carried out and contributed to a number of studies on the design and financing of social-sector programmes. Prior to joining UNICEF in 1987, he carried out research and policy analysis at WHO, Georgetown University, the University of Ibadan, Nigeria, and other institutions. His publications include articles and reports on health economics, evaluation and management, and he is co-editor of a WHO training manual on cost analysis for primary health care. He holds a master's and doctorate degree from Princeton University, and a master's degree in public health from Harvard University.

VICTORIA RIALP is based in Amman, Jordan, where she serves as the UNICEF Area Representative covering Jordan, Syria, West Bank and Gaza, and Djibouti. Since joining UNICEF in Manila in 1981, she has been involved in urban development projects and in programmes dealing with street children and working children in the Philippines, in Brazil and, prior to taking up her current assignment, in New York where she was project officer for children in especially difficult circumstances. She undertook preparatory work for the Urban Child Project carried out by the UNICEF International Child Development Centre, Florence, and was a member of its consultative group. She has written numerous UNICEF documents on street children and working children and has also written on this subject for ILO, WHO and NGO publications.

DIANA SALTARELLI, a free-lance editor/translator, works primarily with UNICEF on children's rights and urban child issues. Based in Italy, she has held various positions within the United Nations system, first with the FAO/World Bank Cooperative Programme in Rome (1975-1986), and then with the UNICEF International Child Development Centre in Florence (1988-1991). She is a graduate of Smith College.

CLAUDIO SEPÚLVEDA, currently UNICEF Representative to Turkey, joined UNICEF in 1985 as Senior Regional Planning Officer, East Asia and Pakistan region. From 1977 to 1984, he was posted in Bangkok, first as Health Programme Coordinator at the United Nations Asia and Pacific Development Institute, and subsequently with the United Nations Economic and Social Commission for Asia and the Pacific. Earlier, he worked for WHO in the South East Asia (1974-1977) and Pan American (1973) regions. From 1970 to 1973, he was Director-General of Planning and Programming of Chile's National Health Service. He has published numerous books and articles on basic community services, primary health care, pharmaceuticals and children in national development. A Doctor of Medicine, he holds a master's degree in public health planning from the University of Chile.

ABBREVIATIONS

ARI	Acute respiratory infections
BRAC	Bangladesh Rural Advancement Committee
CDD	Control of diarrhoeal diseases
CEDC	Children in especially difficult circumstances
CRC	Convention on the Rights of the Child
EPI	Expanded programme on immunization
EU	European Union
FAO	Food and Agriculture Organization of the United Nations
GDP	Gross domestic product
GNP	Gross national product
HIV	Human immunodeficiency virus
IBRD	International Bank for Reconstruction and Development
IFAD	International Fund for Agricultural Development
ILO	International Labour Organisation
NGO	Non-governmental organization
NFPE	Non-formal primary education
NPA	National programme of action
ODA	Official development assistance
ORT	Oral rehydration therapy
PHC	Primary health care
PEOC	Primary education for older children
SFA	Schooling for All
UNDP	United Nations Development Programme
UNESCO	United Nations Educational, Scientific and Cultural Organization
UNFPA	United Nations Population Fund
UNICEF	United Nations Children's Fund
USAID	United States Agency for International Development
WFC	World Food Council
WHO	World Health Organization

Introduction

James R. Himes

1. The Convention on the Rights of the Child: A Historic Opportunity for Action – or Inaction?

The potential importance of the 1989 Convention on the Rights of the Child (CRC) for organizations concerned with the rights and well-being of children would be difficult to overstate. The United Nations Centre for Human Rights has recognized this widely ratified covenant as "the most comprehensive statement of children's rights ever made". A document for UNICEF's 1991 Executive Board asserted that the CRC, in addition to its comprehensive approach to children's rights, may also be "the most innovative human rights instrument to be drafted by the international community".[1]

By early 1995, 170 countries had either signed the CRC or had become States Parties to it by ratification or accession. *No other international human rights covenant has been ratified so quickly* by so many States. A number of countries are well advanced in the task of examining the implications of the CRC in terms of their own legal norms and, sometimes, actual practices.[2] Comments on the CRC not only from child rights activists but also from world political leaders have been almost embarrassingly enthusiastic. The CRC has been described as nothing short of "the cornerstone of a new moral ethos for children", possibly a "milestone in the history of mankind", and an instrument stressing that "respect for and protection of children's rights is the starting point for the full development of the individual's potential in an atmosphere of freedom, dignity and justice".[3] Somewhat more cautionary notes have also been struck, including in UNICEF circles: the CRC represents "not only a historic opportunity for practical action but also an extraordinary challenge not to allow this set of international commitments to go the way of far too many noble declarations and solemn covenants in the global arena of human rights".[4]

Even as committed a promotor of the significance of the Convention on the Rights of the Child as the former Norwegian Ombudsman for Children, Målfrid Grude Flekkøy, has written that "laws, national and international, are, after all, words on paper. They may codify attitudes, but the real results depend upon how they are implemented, what is done to follow up and to reach the ideals". In some countries, she notes, "there is either a distrust of the efficacy of legislation as a useful instrument or a tradition of disregarding the fine principles stated in law".[5]

The Chairman of the United Nations Committee on Economic, Social and Cultural Rights, Philip Alston, has provided a frank assessment of the limited results of much of the United Nation's work in human rights in a challenging article entitled 'Revitalising United Nations Work on Human Rights and Development'. Among his conclusions is the sobering statement that "the United Nations Commission on Human Rights has expended an enormous amount of time and energy on matters of marginal importance ...".[6]

□ 1.1. OBSTACLES TO IMPLEMENTATION

This chapter examines two of the many obstacles that could stand in the way of effective implementation of the CRC. Primary attention is devoted to the critical issue of "available resources", as included in Article 4:

> States Parties shall undertake all appropriate legislative, administrative, and other measures for the implementation of the rights recognized in the present Convention. With regard to economic, social and cultural rights, States Parties shall undertake such measures to the maximum extent of their available resources and, where needed, within the framework of international co-operation.

In terms of the history and politics of the CRC process, the reference in Article 4 to the "maximum extent" of "available resources" was included, as in other United Nations instruments,[7] especially to allay the fears of official representatives that governments would be held responsible for achieving standards of children's well-being that are 'unrealistic' in terms of resource availability and specific time limits, especially in lower-income countries. Several other articles of the Convention emphasize the resource constraint point, as will be discussed in greater detail in the chapters that follow. Notable among these are references to "the highest *attainable* standard of health" (Article 24.1, emphasis added) and to "the right of the child to education, and with a view *to achieving this right progressively*" (Article 28.1, emphasis added). The history of the inclusion of these qualifying phrases, as well as a 'common-sense' interpretation of their meaning, has raised fears that they could become convenient excuses for justifying implementation performance falling well short of what might be reasonably expected in terms of *accelerating* progress towards meeting children's basic needs, as well as in promoting and protecting their rights as set forth in the CRC.

Rather than allowing the "available resources" provision and related clauses of the CRC to become a justification for poor performance, the United Nations, other agencies and non-governmental organizations (NGOs) concerned with the implementation and monitoring of children's rights should turn these clauses into opportunities for promoting and assisting governments and non-governmental partners to undertake the 'step-by-step' financial and human resource planning required to ensure that the *progressive achievement* of children's rights represents real progress in meeting the challenging goals of the CRC.

The development of a useful and positive interpretation of the "available resources" reference in Article 4 requires that we address a second and closely related issue: the nature of the obligations of States Parties in terms of the Article 4 requirement that they "undertake all appropriate legislative, administrative, and other measures for the implementation of the rights recognized in the present Convention". The issue of the "obligations of States" is viewed here as a potential obstacle because of:

(a) the vagueness of this concept both in international law and in development theory and practice; and

(b) the tendency to limit recognition of these obligations to the formal agencies of the State, especially at the national level, at the expense of a broader and more decentralized concept of the public sector, which more explicitly recognizes the potential of governmental and non-governmental cooperation, including — or especially — at the community level, in achieving social objectives, such as those of the CRC.

□ 1.2. HUMAN RIGHTS AND HUMAN DEVELOPMENT

There are a number of initial efforts under way seeking to narrow the gaps both in action and in understanding between those in recent decades who have been concerned with the advancement of human rights and those concerned with development. One especially significant expression of this trend is the work of the United Nations Development Programme (UNDP) in its annual *Human Development Report*.[8] In spite of these efforts, very little practical work has been undertaken to bridge the enormous gulf foolishly separating the achievement of 'human rights' (or 'human freedom', as some prefer) from the fulfilment of development, especially 'human development', objectives. "[T]he reality is", as Alston notes,

> ... that until the end of the 1980s international development agencies and policy makers were only very rarely prepared to address themselves directly to human rights questions. While the importance of such questions was sometimes grudgingly acknowledged, that recognition almost invariably was accompanied by the assumption that human rights matters were appro-

priately dealt with by other bodies or agencies. As one report has noted, '[g]overnments have sought to confine humanitarian concerns to the periphery of international relations ...'.[9]

On the human rights side of this 'gulf', it is noteworthy that the 'mainstream' independent human rights organizations, based largely in Europe and the United States, have tended to avoid the sort of activism and practical work in the area of social and economic rights ('development' concerns) that have characterized their involvement in the protection of civil and political rights. In some cases, of course, notably the traditional position of the United States Government, there is a strong denial "that there is any such thing as an economic, a social or a cultural human right".[10]

It is hoped that this book will represent a contribution to the bridging of these gaps between 'human rights' and 'human development' policy concepts, leading to the development and application of practical tools for coordinated action on both fronts.

■ 2. The Concept of "Available Resources" and Their Mobilization in the Context of the CRC

□ 2.1. A BROAD DEFINITION OF "RESOURCES"

How is the concept of "available resources" to be interpreted? Is there any likelihood of finding significant common ground in this regard between the human rights and the development communities?

As applied in the human rights field, there appears to be little conceptual work on, and often an unduly limited set of assumptions about, the nature of a society's "resources". Among parts of the development community, moreover, there is sometimes a tendency to identify resources only with economic — and then typically with financial — resources. In general, however, development theory and practice, especially that concerned with human and people-oriented development, comes closer than the human rights community to having a set of definitions needed to ensure practical and constructive interpretations of the various references, direct and indirect, to "resources" in the CRC.

In the drafting history of the CRC, and to a lesser extent in the forthcoming *Commentary on the Convention on the Rights of the Child of 1989*,[11] an impression is created that the inevitable references in such legal documents to "States Parties" and their "available resources" will tend to concentrate attention on *national-level, public-sector funding* required for the implementation of the CRC. It is relevant, however, that the *Commentary* does cite an important reference in the Plan of Action of the September 1990 World Summit for Children: "Action at the community and national level is, of course, of critical importance in meeting the goals and aspirations for children and development" (the remainder of the citation drawing attention to the need for "substantial international co-operation").[12]

The *Commentary* also cites an important issue reviewed by the United Nations Committee on Economic, Social and Cultural Rights regarding the "minimum core obligations" of States, an issue to which we will return. In a *General Comment*, the Committee concluded that:

> In order for a State Party to be able to attribute its failure to meet at least its minimum core obligations to a lack of available resources it must demonstrate that every effort has been made to *use all resources that are at its disposition* in an effort to satisfy, as a matter of priority, those minimum obligations (emphasis added).[13]

The phrase "at its disposition" appears to be too vague to serve as a guide to an interpretation of "available resources" that can maximize the opportunities for this phrase to facilitate rather than inhibit full and effective implementation of the CRC. We will leave to the lawyers the question of how much flexibility and justifiable potential there may be in the interpretation of phrases of this sort. From a 'human development' perspective, however, it is clear that a broader and clearer interpretation is needed regarding:
(a) the various types of resources available in a society for the survival, protection, development and participation of children;
(b) the different levels of society, including the 'civil society', and the various levels of government at which these resources are available; and
(c) the key political issues of who controls these resources and makes the decisions regarding their allocation or reallocation.

There have been many formulations by economists, planners and others of the various concepts and types of resources that have particular relevance for human development, including for children's well-being. Building on earlier work, especially by Moseley and Chen,[14] Cornia and others[15] developed a comprehensive framework illustrating the most important causal linkages among the various social, economic and biological factors influencing child survival and development. Three sets of resources were used in that framework:
(a) real resources in cash or kind at the household level, especially subsistence production and money incomes;
(b) government expenditures for services such as health care, education, child care, water and sanitation; and
(c) family and community characteristics, notably the time, health and skills of the parents, especially of the mother.

This framework was developed importantly in an attempt to indicate the channels through which economic decline adversely affects child welfare and to attain a clearer understanding of the actions necessary to prevent such deterioration. Although it has been difficult, especially given data limitations in developing countries, to fit empirical information into this framework, it is a useful model to gain a better understanding of the complex relationships involved, over time, in addressing issues of children's welfare, especially in the areas of health, nutrition, education and child labour, as discussed in later chapters.

In an effort to develop a somewhat less complex framework, which might be especially useful in this process of encouraging better communication between the human rights and development communities, we have drawn on another formulation being applied in UNICEF.[16] Accordingly, we have classified "resources" as follows:

- *human resources* — physical and mental health, knowledge, creativity, self-confidence, time availability, and skills (interpreted broadly to include important abilities such as child-rearing, teaching, leadership, managerial and political skills);
- *economic resources* — income (in kind or cash, of individuals or enterprises), assets, natural resources (especially land and water), credit, government revenues and expenditures;
- *organizational resources* — family and household structure, extended family or clan relationships, community structure and organizations, cooperatives, political movements, trade unions, religious organizations, the media, governmental organizations, other public- or private-sector institutions and managerial arrangements, technologies (to the extent not 'embodied' in human or economic resources).

Having suggested this classification, we should quickly add the customary qualification concerning the rather arbitrary nature of all such rough divisions. There is considerable overlap and interaction among and within these three very general categories. Economic resources such as family income or tax revenues can be allocated to purchase or improve human or organizational resources. Organizational resources, such as a well-functioning network of community volunteers, can greatly enhance or multiply the productivity of other human resources, such as trained midwives or other health care workers. Improved organization, management and control can substantially increase the cost-effectiveness of economic resources through the reduction of waste, inefficiencies and corruption. There is, moreover, nearly always some degree of substitutability among these different types of resources.

It may be useful, as well, to mention the economist's distinction between stocks and flows of resources, which will be discussed in greater detail by Parker in Chapter Two. Stocks (such as assets, infrastructures and capacities) establish the range of opportunities for change over time. Flows (such as wages, labour inputs, budget allocations and organizational decisions) are what the majority of decision makers are most immediately concerned with in the short run. The references in the CRC to the progressive achievement of children's rights, as well as the necessity of ensuring sustainable achievements, should serve as a reminder of the need to be concerned with strengthening 'stocks' (that is, investments in capacity-building and in the creation of infrastructures) as well as with mobilizing 'flows'.

Most analyses of resource utilization for development concentrate on economic resources and, to a lesser extent, human resources. Often neglected, in part since they are difficult to quantify, are a society's 'organizational resources', even though most development practitioners have a general impression that the failures of policies and programmes can often be attributed to organizational, managerial, political and cultural factors. Only rarely does the development literature include the structure and organization of the family as a significant factor relating to resource availability. The family, in its multiple forms in different cultures, is the most hidden of all resource bases. This situation must be changed in any serious analysis of resource availability and mobilization for fulfilling children's rights.

Considering the importance for the rights of children of mobilizing political leadership (or 'political will') behind the CRC, one could develop a separate category of 'political resources'. We have chosen, however, in this book to consider political factors as one important element either of human or organizational resources. The human-resource dimension includes the creativity, commitment and certain skills, such as communications and leadership capabilities, essential for 'good politics'. The concept of 'organizational resources' also relates directly to the capacity of households, communities or political entities to stimulate 'social mobilization' or generate increased political commitment to children. Regardless of the semantics of classification, the politics or political economy of children's rights must be a key part of the analysis of the implementation of the CRC, including its resource implications.

□ 2.2. MANY LEVELS OF SOCIETY

Crucial to any treatment of "available resources" or resource mobilization issues is the clear recognition that resources are "available" at all points of society, public and private, from the individual or household level to the national and international levels. As emphasized earlier, for purposes of developing strategies for work on child rights, the neglect of resources at the individual/household/family level is especially unfortunate. That is the level at which, by far, most of the relevant resources exist, including time and energy for child care, and where most of the critical decisions about resource allocation are taken — in favour of or against the interests of children. Even in areas such as health and education, where governmental contributions are especially important, private spending often exceeds that of the public sector.[17] And research on this subject generally does not attempt to quantify the human and organizational resources deployed by the household or family in favour of children. The time and organizational skills of the mother, grandmother or older sister spent in child-rearing and child care simply do not 'count' in most studies of costs and benefits of child development. There is also generally little recognition of the additional burdens on women — as opposed to men — implied by many attempts to 'mobilize' resources at the household level for more effective child care.

It is also a mistake to assume, often implicitly, that the 'State' has little or no influence on resource-allocation decisions at the household or community level. Positive incentives can be of various sorts, including but not limited to financial incentives. Appropriate sanctions can be powerful deterrents to violations of rights — such as the employment of children in hazardous occupations. Governments at different levels, including at the most local level they reach, have many options for encouraging the realization of children's rights, not only through the 'mobilization' of resources but also through resource 'recognition and respect', as described in a later section of this chapter. Indeed, many of the ways to increase the protection of children's rights and to facilitate opportunities for children make only modest new demands on hard-pressed governmental budgets. Conversely, excessive demands by governments on already overburdened family and community resource bases, at the lowest income levels, can discourage or inhibit the desired responses in terms of children's well-being, and result in serious social inequities.

Table 1.1 presents a framework for further analysis of the various types of resources existing in any society, with a summary of the different levels at which they are available and where decisions are made about their allocation

***Table 1.1.* - "Available resources" for implementing child rights**

Level of Society	Type of resources		
	Human	Economic	Organizational
Household	Health, knowledge, skills, time, etc., of family members, especially for child-rearing	Family income, assets, access to credit	Family structure, access to extended family, kinship or clan support
Community/ District	Management/leadership/ political skills, community self-reliance and solidarity, civic pride	Community financing strategies, communal lands and other assets, community credit and insurance arrangements	Community-based child care or other child services arrangements; water/sanitation cooperative arrangements; traditional forms of social security or conflict resolution; family courts
Metropolitan / Provincial / State	Management / leadership/ political skills; solidarity based on cultural and political factors at this level	Municipal- or state-level financing strategies, including taxing/user-charge authority as well as assets and access to credit in some systems	Municipal/provincial/state-level social services arrangements, especially relevant for education, health, housing and juvenile justice in some systems; judicial arrangements
National	Management/leadership/ political skills; national statesmanship and sense of citizenship	Principal public revenue-generating capability in most systems, including taxation and national or international credits; substantial natural resources and other assets	National planning, policy-making and public-sector coordinating capability; state enterprise arrangements; ultimate legislative and judicial authority in most cases
International	Management/leadership/ political skills, especially in human development and human rights organizations; international statesmanship; growing sense of global solidarity (on some issues)	Development cooperation (credit, grants, technical assistance) in fields of human development and human rights (other international economic relationships have strong influence on national-level resource availability)	International arrangements for child-related services, including actions to protect children from wars, commercial exploitation and other transnational abuses; monitoring of nations' human rights and human development performance

(though levels of availability and levels of decision-making are not always the same). The boxes or 'cells' in this table have been filled in largely by way of illustration for the purposes of this chapter, rather than as a complete list of all conceivable resources in a society. (It is worth recalling that there is considerable interaction among the resources listed in these various boxes.) The important point to stress here is that any approach to the CRC or other child rights instrument or strategy that restricts attention to just one or two of these 'cells' is unlikely to prove useful for public policy or other purposes. As noted earlier, there is a tendency to focus the implementation debate, including about Article 4, largely on the matter of the economic (especially financial) resources available at the national level; or for international agencies to concern themselves only with financial resources at that level available for transfer to the national level. In some areas closely associated with key substantive articles of the CRC, such as health, nutrition and education (and similar provisions in national constitutions and legislation), such an approach may weaken the effort — particularly as a child rights initiative — from the start, especially in many of the lowest-income countries.

□ 2.3. WHO CONTROLS THE AVAILABLE RESOURCES?

Those seriously concerned with mobilizing resources for achieving children's rights, especially at the national and subnational levels, will need to study and understand in some detail the patterns of control and use of resources in their societies: the political economy of child rights. To do so, they do not need to agree or disagree with the central tenet of prevailing neo-liberal orthodoxy, which is that open and competitive markets are the best means societies have for the efficient organization and distribution of goods and services. It is important to keep constantly in mind, however, that people and groups of people, not markets, make decisions about how public and private resources are allocated. And the decision-making power of individuals and groups is far from being distributed in a manner that assures 'open competition', let alone equity. Markets, when they function well, provide a set of necessary 'rules of the game', but the game is generally played on a very irregular surface, and the rules are often applied with considerable advantage to those who have power and wealth.

Even stronger criticism may be in order regarding attempts to replace markets with central planning and heavy governmental intervention in most areas of the economy. Since the dominant political and economic thinking in the world today, however, tends strongly towards the 'market-friendly' side, analysts and advocates of children's rights are well advised to direct much of their attention to issues of resource control and use in market-oriented economies. At the same time, it is also vital to recognize that millions of people in many developed countries, living in absolute poverty, are largely untouched by the relatively modern markets that assume primary concern in much of the 'development' thinking and action.

Fortunately, a critical reassessment of the roles of the State and the market and ways in which they can be more complementary — and more favourable for human development and human rights — is already under way. Even as 'market-friendly' a development organization as the World Bank calls for a "large and irreplaceable" role for government, going well beyond the need simply to "let domestic and international competition flourish":[18]

> At the same time, governments need to do more in those areas where markets alone cannot be relied upon. Above all, this means investing in education, health, nutrition, family planning, and poverty alleviation; building social, physical, administrative, regulatory, and legal infrastructure of better quality; mobilizing the resources to finance public expenditures; and providing a stable macroeconomic foundation, without which little can be achieved.[19]

The UNDP is more blunt when it comes to reviewing global markets:

> If global markets were truly open, they would allow capital, labour and goods to flow freely round the world — and help equalize economic opportunities for all. But global markets are neither free nor efficient. At a time when national markets are opening, global markets remain greatly restricted. The developing countries, with some notable exceptions, are finding it difficult to exploit fully the potential of these markets. This reflects the weakness in their policies and the restrictions on global markets.[20]

The UNDP report adds that markets are means not ends, and "they are of little value if they do not serve human development".[21]

Moving from the global level to the other end of the spectrum we are concerned with, we find that households and families, in addition to being affected by market or governmental 'imperfections' at all other levels, are also subject to considerable internal inequities, which influence how their resources are controlled and used.

Of particular concern is the fact that in many cultures the low status and weak decision-making role of women and female children is a formidable barrier to the full realization of both women's and children's rights.[22] Women are largely responsible for child-rearing in most societies (a cultural pattern that will undoubtedly have to change, but probably very slowly in most developing countries), but their control of the resources available in families and communities rarely corresponds to the weight of this responsibility. In low-income, female-headed households, furthermore, women may have more control over household resources, but this resource base may be so weak that it barely suffices to ensure family survival.

A useful example of this issue of household-level decision-making is provided in the case of child nutrition, as summarized in a 1992 UNICEF publication:

> The World Bank and other organizations have argued that increasing income to the poor is the most efficient long-term strategy for reducing malnutrition. More recent studies ... indicate that food purchases of the poor

> may increase less than previously thought with increases in income. One reason ... is that control of income affects how it is spent. ... [Women] may have responsibility for child-rearing without control over the resources to perform the responsibility. Control of resources *may* be greater if the woman earns the income, although this is not always the case. ... A few studies have shown that women who earn an income have more household decision-making power than those who do not work. ... A number of correlational studies have shown that income in the control of women is more likely to be allocated for the immediate benefit of children, such as the purchase of food, than is income earned by men.[23]

This is not the place to attempt a more thorough analysis of the locus of decision-making in resource allocations, the many inequities in the control of societal resources, and the multiple imperfections in the workings of markets or governments. Much of that work, in any event, needs to be carried out at the level of countries and communities. Our main point here is simply to draw attention to the enormous range of options — public *and* private — societies have as they confront the very real limitations that "available resources" pose for the achievement of the objectives of the CRC and other goals for children in the years ahead.

Fortunately for the child rights community, there is an important opportunity at hand for linking forces, nationally and internationally, with those concerned with 'human development' — or people-oriented development — who are further advanced in analysing the complex issues relating to the control, allocation and utilization of resources for achieving individuals' and societies' objectives. Some of the work is highly technical, often economic and statistical. Social and political studies are also important, including on who controls resources at all levels, starting with families and households.

A good example of the type of political study needed is Myron Weiner's book on *The Child and the State in India*.[24] It examines the political forces, as well as values and belief systems, inhibiting universal primary education and the prohibition of child labour in India. These issues are reviewed more briefly, and from a historical perspective, in several other developing and industrialized countries. This type of analysis is well worth encouraging in many areas relating to children's rights, as a way to suggest practical strategies for dealing with issues of adverse patterns of control and allocation of resources, as well as an unduly limited concept of the obligations of the State and society in relation to children's rights.

It is to this issue of "obligations" that we now turn.

■ 3. Obligations of Society Created by the CRC

□ 3.1. A BROAD DEFINITION OF "OBLIGATIONS"

Any discussion of resources available for implementing the CRC (or other international or national instruments concerning children's rights) raises the complex issue of the obligations of the State and the broader society in relation to such an instrument. For many lawyers, as noted in the *Commentary*,[25] this subject generally requires drawing attention to the distinction between 'obligations of result' and 'obligations of conduct'. In the CRC, Article 2.1 creates an obligation of result (to "ensure the rights set forth ... without discrimination"), while Article 4 prescribes an obligation of conduct (to "undertake all appropriate legislative, administrative, and other measures for the implementation of the rights recognized in the present Convention").

Even lawyers sympathetic to the concept of "economic, social and cultural rights" (not to mention others who refuse to recognize these as 'human rights') find considerable difficulty with these and other distinctions that have been developed in an attempt to define a State's obligations in these areas. In an article on the "right to food", for example, a past president of Amnesty International Canada has written that the "... scope and nature of state duties are not clearly set out in the international instruments which establish the right to food",[26] and he adds that the "fluidity of these obligations has caused great difficulty in measuring state compliance".[27] A former Special Rapporteur of the United Nations Economic and Social Council has noted the difficulties attached to "the vagueness flowing from economic and social rights", including the "unsatisfactory guidance given to States on how to report on the realization of these ... rights. States have not been and cannot be given precise guidance unless their obligations are clarified."[28]

Seen more from a 'human development' than a legal perspective, what appears to be needed is a definition of the obligations created by the CRC and other such instruments that explicitly recognizes duties (as above, with regard to "available resources") at all levels of society — from the individual or family/household level to the national and international. Limiting obligations to those of national governments will not prove useful for the fulfilment of children's rights. Again, we must leave to the law reviews and the courts debates regarding the nature of legal obligations created by national constitutions, legislation or international covenants for individuals, parents, 'communities' and other groups such as indigenous peoples or ethnic minorities. A clause in the new Brazilian Constitution is interesting, not to say ambitious, in stating that "it is the *duty of the family, society and the State* to guarantee the child and the adolescent, with absolute priority, the rights to life, health, food, education, leisure, professional training, culture, dignity, respect, freedom, family and social life, and to protect them from all forms of negligence, discrimination, exploitation, cruelty and oppression"[29] (Article 227, emphasis added).

With regard to the CRC, there are two key provisions that clearly recognize that families and parents (and in some cases the 'community'), as well as States, have duties regarding children. The first such reference is in one of the key 'umbrella' articles of the CRC, Article 5, which provides that:

> States Parties shall *respect* the *responsibilities*, rights and *duties* of *parents* or, where applicable, the members of the *extended family* or *community* as provided for by local custom, legal guardians or other persons legally responsible for

> the child, to provide, in a manner consistent with the evolving capacities of the child, appropriate direction and guidance in the exercise by the child of the rights recognized in the present Convention (emphasis added).

Article 18 adds that:

> States Parties shall use their best efforts to ensure recognition of the principle that both parents have common *responsibilities* for the upbringing and development of the child. Parents or, as the case may be, legal guardians, have the *primary responsibility* for the upbringing and development of the child. The best interests of the child will be their basic concern (emphasis added).

Regardless, however, of the results of legal interpretations at the international and national levels of these and other references to "obligations", "responsibilities" and "duties", from the perspective of development planning and practice it is abundantly clear that "obligations" must be broadly defined to include families, households, communities, the private sector and other participants in the 'civil society', as well as all levels of government. In some countries, it is becoming increasingly common to specify certain obligations of non-governmental and private/commercial organizations, working in partnership with the State in key areas concerning human development (for example, the role of subsidized private education in Chile or the United Kingdom, public/private vocational training in Germany, or private health insurance and other health plans in Mexico, the Republic of Korea, Thailand and many other countries). Some of these new partnerships have ancient roots, including for example in medieval Europe. To some extent, this broader definition of obligations simply provides appropriate recognition of the vital role (as well as the limitations) of the family and community in ensuring children's well-being. A greater recognition is also implied of the importance of public/private-sector partnerships for social development. But clearly this broadened concept of the obligations of 'States' is essential to the task of developing both equitable and cost-effective strategies for mobilizing the additional resources (human, economic and organizational) needed to achieve the rights included in the CRC.

The next chapter will address the difficult subject of 'equity and efficiency' and other issues that inevitably arise when one begins to broaden the concept of "obligations" beyond those of the State, and especially to include the family and community level, as well as the private sector.[30] With regard to resources and obligations relating to CRC implementation, suffice it to say, however, that the matter of resource mobilization to achieve child rights raises many complex issues of how the costs and benefits of such mobilization are distributed within a society. These issues are of considerable importance in the context of the CRC for many reasons, including the key 'non-discrimination' principle in Article 2 and the principle of progressive achievement of universal coverage for child 'development' rights such as health and education.

There may be a tendency to assume that the more orthodox notions of a State's obligations, largely relating to the policies and responsibilities of national-level governmental agencies, tend to lead to the most equitable, if not always the most efficient, provision of the social benefits, services or entitlements corresponding to the rights of the child in question. This may be particularly the case if the central government has a strong redistributive mandate. But that assumption needs to be examined carefully on a country-by-country basis and sometimes also at subnational levels, especially in federal States. Such an analysis must look not only at the distribution of the benefits but also at the distribution of the costs of providing the benefits (through taxation, fees, borrowing, public-sector pricing policies, cost-sharing arrangements, for instance). Especially when public services rely heavily on borrowing, or simply printing money, the distributional and other consequences of the resulting inflation must be considered.

It may be useful to cite one example from the CRC where the definition and more precise specification of the nature of the States Parties' obligations may raise difficult questions in low-income countries, especially if those obligations are interpreted too narrowly and mainly as obligations of national governments. Article 28 is of prime importance to organizations concerned with human development largely because of its key reference to making primary education "compulsory and available free to all" (para. 1.a). Furthermore, it refers to the right to education "on the basis of equal opportunity" (para. 1) (which may be especially important, for example, for the girl child and children of ethnic minorities). Other clauses in Article 28, however, specify the State's obligation to make "higher education accessible to all on the basis of capacity by every appropriate means" (para. 1.c) and cite "the introduction of free education and offering financial assistance in case of need" (para. 1.b) as a way of encouraging universal coverage of secondary education. Especially in countries where there is currently very limited access to higher education and traditional secondary education, and particularly in countries with a highly regressive tax system (and these two situations often go hand in hand), efforts to direct attention to the national government's obligations under the CRC with respect to higher and secondary education could well be at the expense of that country's achievement of its obligations to provide compulsory and free *primary* education. These efforts could paradoxically also result in low-income but tax-paying workers subsidizing the costs of university education for the children of the élite.

Difficult questions of this sort regarding priorities and appropriate resource-allocation strategies will inevitably face those who are seeking to implement the CRC. The point stressed here is that it will be less difficult to meet these challenges if a broader and more analytical approach is taken to assessing both resource availability and the nature of States' obligations than is customary, certainly in most of the human rights literature as well as in much of the literature regarding development. This is not to say that those charged with monitoring the implementation of the CRC, including the members of the Committee on the Rights of the Child, will have the time or the expertise to delve deeply into all the complexities of these sorts of analyses concerning the economic and social policies of the States Parties. But these considerations do lend weight to the importance of increased communication and collaboration between the human rights and child rights communities on the one hand, and the human development planners and practitioners on the other.

☐ 3.2. OBLIGATIONS: TO RESPECT, PROTECT AND FULFIL

Returning now to issues related more to the legal interpretation of States' obligations, we could usefully look at one of the formulations that, building on other studies,[31] was set out by the Special Rapporteur to guide the work of the United Nations Committee on Economic, Social and Cultural Rights. A threefold division of obligations has been proposed and applied to the case of food security and the right to food.[32] The obligations the State is required to undertake are to respect, to protect and to fulfil. More specifically:

> (a) ... States must *respect* the freedom of individuals to take necessary actions and use the necessary resources, either alone or in association with others, to facilitate the fulfilment of their needs. It is in regard to associative action that collective or group rights become important: resources belonging to a collective group, such as indigenous populations, must be respected if such groups are to satisfy their needs by the use of their resources;
> (b) ... States also must *protect* individual freedom of action and use of resources as against other more assertive or aggressive subjects [including protection against fraud, unethical behavior in trade and contractual relations and the marketing or dumping of hazardous products];
> (c) ... States have an obligation to *fulfil* the expectations of all to enjoy [certain rights].

This last obligation is described as taking two forms: to *provide opportunities* for those who lack them; or to *provide directly* for the fulfilment of the right (for example, by providing food to disadvantaged or marginalized groups or during disasters; or by providing the resources necessary to acquire the food).

In an imaginative application of this set of definitions to problems of food security and nutrition, the authors develop:
(a) a framework for relating factors conditioning the improvement of nutrition (food security, adequate care and adequate prevention and control of diseases) at all levels of society from the individual to the global; and
(b) a "food security matrix" which relates the three levels of state obligations (respect, protect and fulfil) to a number of key guiding principles for achieving food security (such as the sustainability of food supplies, nutritional adequacy and cultural acceptability).

They note, furthermore:

> This matrix could serve as a tool in national and local analysis of, and planning for, food security. It would help operationalize the right to food in given contexts, as a guide for the direction of State policies and thereby also clarify constraints on State action to help realize the right to food. Collecting, organizing, and analyzing information according to the logic suggested

> might enable policy makers and technical personnel to better comprehend the complexity of a system of State obligations *taken together*, and help them become aware of how and where specific obligations, defined with regard to *content and degree of State involvement*, might fit into their unique situations. Such exercises, where necessary and desired, can be supported and assisted by international agencies, universities and NGOs.[33]

The application of this framework to the issue of children's rights to adequate nutrition is discussed in more detail in Chapter Five.

A variation on this type of framework, which would appear to be especially useful for our present purposes, is presented in Table 1.2. (As in Table 1.1, the entries in the boxes are intended to be illustrative rather than all-inclusive.) There we have shown four rather than three main categories of States' obligations. The purpose is to emphasize the importance of the distinction, regarding the State's obligation to *fulfil*, between:

(a) enhancing opportunities of individuals or groups within a society; and
(b) the direct provision by the State of benefits or services.

In many societies, there appears to be a growing conviction, crossing some traditional ideological debates, regarding the importance of opportunity-enhancing or empowerment strategies, especially to assist disadvantaged, vulnerable or marginalized groups. In terms also of the objective of achieving greater recognition through the CRC of the importance of children's rights to participation, it appears useful to have a separate category for actions of the State that enhance opportunities, as opposed to providing services directly.

From the vantage point of the challenge of mobilizing available resources for the implementation of the CRC, it should be useful to analyse jointly the frameworks presented in Tables 1.1 and 1.2. To be used as planning tools, of course, these frameworks would need to be developed with a time dimension, projecting especially economic and demographic trends, and linking the analysis to specific and more operationalized goals than most of those included in the CRC, as well as to target dates for achieving the goals (points taken up in the next section). Whatever tools are used, however, organizations concerned with child rights and the CRC need to move forward towards a more operational approach to determining States' obligations and for the mobilization of resources under conditions of severe resource constraints, such as those prevailing in many developing countries. 'Social planning for achieving children's rights' might be one way to describe what is needed. 'Public policy and children's rights' — or well-being — may be more appealing. Regardless of the language one prefers, however, one key to success will be planning and management by objectives.

Table 1.2. - **Framework for analysis of governmental obligations for implementing child rights**

Level of governmental authority	Nature of the obligation			
	Respect	Protect	Facilitate	Fulfil
Community/District	Respect participation and other rights and relevant individual or community initiatives	Protect individual and community initiatives, assets, etc., from illegal or anti-social use; protect rights as appropriate and feasible at community level, especially of vulnerable groups including working or minority children	Organize and empower community-based opportunity-enhancing initiatives, especially for information, education and training; facilitate credit and cooperative initiatives, particularly for women	Provide access to communal lands, other assets or services, especially to vulnerable members of the community, e.g. females heading households, street children, disabled children, etc.
Metropolitan/Provincial/State	(similar obligations at these levels, with significant revenue-generating and managerial capacity in decentralized systems)			
National	Generally the ultimate legislative, executive and judicial responsibility to respect individual and group rights, respecting children as a primary consideration	Protect all citizens (without discrimination) from human rights abuse or other forms of illegal action, with the "best interests of the child" as a primary consideration	Plan, organize and implement policies, laws, regulations, etc., to increase and equalize opportunities, including educational, cultural and other opportunities for children; encourage empowerment at subnational levels	Plan, organize and provide and/or finance benefits or services, generally not easily or traditionally provided at other levels of government
International	Respect national initiatives; independent monitoring of respect for rights at country level	Protect children from wars, commercial exploitation and other transnational abuses	Facilitate international exchange of information, expertise and experiences	Promote development cooperation; provide assistance for child victims of natural disasters, wars, trans-national abuses; support national-level monitoring of human development/ human rights situations

4. Planning, Implementation and Monitoring of Child Rights by Objectives

4.1. EXPLICIT GOALS AND SPECIFIC TARGET DATES

When lawyers refer to 'obligations of result', they often seem to the development planner or public policy practitioner to be several steps removed from the question of actual impact on human beings. To "respect and ensure" the rights in the CRC "without discrimination of any kind" certainly suggests an important *result*. But in a world plagued by discrimination of every conceivable kind, often malicious even when directed at children, how do we convert such a broad principle into more specific goals and indicators to help plan, achieve and measure progress within specific time periods?

As we approach the more substantive articles of the CRC, it becomes clearer as to what needs to be done to ensure effective implementation and monitoring *not so much of the process as the actual outcomes for children* resulting, at least to some extent, from measures taken by States Parties. Article 28.1.e, for example, requires States to "take measures to encourage regular attendance at schools and the reduction of drop-out rates". Reporting on progress in complying with this provision should not only refer to policies adopted or steps taken to reduce drop-out rates, but should also specify what rate of reduction is seen as adequate compliance, within a given time period, and what rate has actually been achieved. Article 24.2.d refers to the right to "appropriate pre-natal and post-natal health care for mothers". How is "appropriate" to be defined and applied? One suitable way would be to monitor over time the reduction in low birth weights (2.5 kg or less), with the goal of achieving within a specified time period the rates of the world's or the relevant region's best performers in this regard.

In some areas, such as the prevention of child abuse and promoting children's participation rights, goals will be more difficult to quantify and progress more difficult to measure. But difficult does not mean impossible. More qualitative but still verifiable indicators can be and have been developed in many countries to assist in protecting children from abuse and providing social services or enhancing opportunities for children in need. A report on disadvantaged children in India,[34] for example, includes or refers to a considerable amount of information on street and working children, which can serve as baseline data and be useful in the development of indicators to assess progress during the coming years in facing the formidable challenge of achieving child rights in India.

In an introduction to a series of reviews on 'Adjustment with a Human Face – Record and Relevance', Jolly and van der Hoeven draw attention to an increasingly important process, marked by the World Summit for Children, "of managing human development by objectives through a system of formulation of explicit goals to be reached by specific dates".[35] UNDP's *Human Development Report 1991*[36] calls for national and global "compacts" for human development. The national compacts would be based on a four-point agenda:

(a) developing a "human development profile";

(b) identifying and costing human development targets;
(c) restructuring budgets to maximize expenditures on human development and strengthening the case for additional resources, nationally and internationally; and
(d) formulating a viable political strategy to develop a national consensus on the need for reform.

The development of improved data and better indicators of human development (including child and gender-related indicators) greatly facilitates this approach. Specific target-setting, furthermore, especially if linked to international monitoring and the promotion of international cooperation, can encourage the development of national capacities to collect and analyse data related to key goals. Most importantly, however, as UNDP emphasizes:

> Improved data on where human development stands today would make it possible to define more clearly the long-term (say, ten-year) goals for the high priority items — including education, health, nutrition, housing, water, sanitation and other basic social services — as well as significant economic targets, such as those for productive jobs.
>
> For each goal a realistic target should then be established and costed, with a list of alternative means of implementation. Investment and budget priorities could next be reviewed to incorporate these targets into policies at every level. And GDP growth targets could be worked out so that the human development goals are accommodated in the overall national strategy.[37]

□ 4.2. THE WORLD SUMMIT FOR CHILDREN AND NATIONAL PROGRAMMES OF ACTION

Jolly and van der Hoeven draw attention to several critical factors that have inhibited this "manage by objectives" approach to development in the past: most of the goals of the so-called United Nations development decades, for example, were "of a general character, often vaguely formulated with little consultation and with hardly any action program for the international bodies or national-level decision-making bodies".[38] In contrast, the goals approved at the 1990 World Summit for Children (see Appendix Two) were formulated through unusually broad consultations in various forums attended by virtually all Governments, the relevant United Nations agencies and a large number of NGOs. These were not the results of numbers-crunching by faceless technicians sitting behind desks in large bureaucracies.

Perhaps even more importantly, the Summit has been followed up by extensive further consultations and planning at the national and subnational levels. For most countries, National Programmes of Action (NPAs) have been developed that are attuned to the specific situations, needs and opportunities in each setting. In some cases, subnational or municipal programmes of action are being formulated.[39] Many of the NPAs are much more specific than either the Summit goals or the CRC in key areas of "protection" rights that are of critical importance to children in especially difficult circumstances, such as street and working children. Participatory approaches to planning are naturally more feasible in some countries than others. NGOs, professional associations, community organizations and the private sector have played an active role in developing NPAs in several countries. In general, substantial improvements are evident in comparison with earlier efforts at global or national 'goal setting'.

An immediate challenge is to link, especially at the national but also the international level, the processes of implementing and monitoring the CRC and the NPAs for children — as well as subnational programmes of action, where feasible. In many respects, there is considerable complementarity between these two endeavours. The CRC has, for example, the advantage of being a permanent and legally binding document for the States Parties. Reporting on CRC implementation — a public process — is also mandatory. Most NPAs, on the other hand, benefit from much more specific and time-bound objectives, especially in areas such as health, nutrition, water and sanitation, and basic education, which are of especially high priority for the majority of low-income developing countries. In fact, there is a strong argument to consider the Summit-related goals for children for the current decade, supplemented by the NPA goals at the national level, as a concrete starting point for the determination of the "minimum core obligations" of the States Parties to the CRC, as described earlier.

☐ 4.3. INTERNATIONAL COOPERATION

The principles of planning, managing and monitoring by objectives also need to be applied to the matter of "international co-operation" which figures prominently in Article 4 and elsewhere in the CRC. UNICEF, UNDP and others have been emphasizing recently how little international aid actually goes to meeting minimum human needs and advancing human development. The proportion of the industrialized world's "co-operation" directed at these objectives represents a mere 10-15 per cent of the total (less than 10 per cent by some calculations). Only about 4 per cent of aid goes to primary health care and 2 per cent to primary education.[40]

UNDP has provided useful guidelines for analysing international development cooperation. Four key ratios are formulated[41] and then applied to current patterns of aid:[42]

- *the aid expenditure ratio* — the percentage of a donor's gross national product (GNP) going to development aid;
- *the aid social allocation ratio* — the percentage of each donor's aid that goes to the social sectors;
- *the aid social priority ratio* — the percentage of social-sector aid committed to human priority areas; and
- *the aid human expenditure ratio* — the product of the three foregoing ratios, and thus the percentage of a donor's GNP going to human priority areas

in recipient countries. For aid donors as a whole, this is a tiny figure: 0.026% of their combined GNP.

One of the objectives of the international community concerned with the implementation of the CRC should be to join forces with others (NGOs, governmental and intergovernmental initiatives) seeking to establish and attain precise targets for international cooperation in areas of particular relevance for achieving the more 'resource-demanding' goals for children, especially in the lowest-income developing countries and those heavily affected by natural and man-made disasters and other adverse economic conditions.

□ 4.4. A FOUR-STEP PLANNING AND IMPLEMENTATION STRATEGY

Drawing on planning and programming guidelines widely used in the international development community, we would propose a four-step strategy as a basis for work on implementing the CRC, including the challenge of identifying affordable approaches and mobilizing the necessary resources. The strategy can be summarized as follows:

Situation analysis. The essential first step in developing an implementation strategy for work in child rights is "to ascertain, as precisely as possible, the nature of the existing situation with respect to each right, so as to identify more clearly the problems that need to be addressed and provide a basis for principled policy making".[43] Good baseline data, appropriately disaggregated (including by categories such as gender and ethnicity needed to identify patterns of discrimination), are essential to an effective system of monitoring compliance with the CRC provisions. Participatory planning approaches, especially important in the area of children's rights, need to involve households and communities in the situation analysis process. Children and youth can be effectively involved as well, helping them to develop their capacities to exercise responsibly their rights to participate as young citizens in society. An effective situation analysis should be an ongoing process over time more than just a one-shot data-gathering exercise. The situation analysis process is closely linked or even merges with the monitoring mechanisms described below.

Goal and standard setting. Effective planning for action in the human rights field, as in other areas of public policy, requires the setting of standards and agreement on goals; rights (especially economic, social and other rights requiring achievement "progressively") need to be converted into verifiable goals or objectives, achievable within agreed time-frames. Indicators to measure progress in achieving these goals need to be identified and accepted by the appropriate authorities. Some goals, such as universal primary school enrolment, can be quantified more easily than others, for example, eliminating "discrimination of any kind". But specific and sometimes binding standards (or indicators of progress) have been set by legislatures and courts even in the more difficult areas. Goals and standards are much more likely to be viewed as legitimate, and indeed as 'rights', if a broad and genuine consensus in society is reached regarding these goals. Once again, children should be a part of that emerging consensus.

Plans and programmes of action. Different countries have widely varying approaches to social or development planning, but most systems (including various international systems) have some capability to develop concrete plans or programmes for action to achieve agreed goals. Countries that have developed strong NPAs or subnational programmes of action following the World Summit for Children, including cost estimates and financial plans, have a good basis for implementing many of the key provisions of the CRC. Attention must be given to a broad array of legislative, administrative, judicial, regulatory and other measures *at all levels of government,* needed to achieve the goals or attain the agreed standards. For many of the objectives linked to the CRC, goals and concrete financial and other measures to achieve them need to be developed, whenever possible, at the municipal and other levels of local government closest to families and children. Plans can include an active role for the private or non-governmental sector. Realistic plans and programmes must recognize clearly that fulfilment of nearly all rights has significant resource implications. Feasible measures for the mobilization of all "available resources" — human, economic and organizational — need to be specified, including through international cooperation where required.

Monitoring compliance and enforcement. A mix of official and non-governmental monitoring mechanisms (national and international) are important to help ensure that goals are being reached and the legal rights and duties of all relevant parties are *recognized, understood and enforced.* Rights need to be understood at the level of communities, families and children. Monitoring, which must also reach those levels to be useful, is much more effective when based on widespread popular understanding of the relevant goals and rights. Especially at the international level, a non-adversarial 'constructive dialogue' among the relevant parties, led by the United Nations Committee on the Rights of the Child, is likely to be the most accepted form of monitoring. At the national and subnational levels, however, strong incentives, including financial incentives, for compliance, as well as significant penalties for non-compliance, will be essential complements to an effective system of monitoring progress. Finally, monitoring mechanisms need to include provisions for monitoring the allocation or mobilization of the resources necessary to achieve these objectives. Very few monitoring systems have adequate provisions for keeping track of the way resources are or are not allocated to meet governmental or broader societal obligations for the fulfilment of children's rights or human rights more generally. Filling this glaring gap deserves high priority on the agendas of both international and national human and child rights organizations.

5. The 'Resource-Related' Provisions of the Convention

It may be useful to return more specifically at this point to the CRC and examine briefly those provisions that bear directly on policy issues concerning resource requirements. A rough listing of the most relevant provisions is sufficient for our present purposes. (The full text of the main resource-related provisions of the CRC can be found in Appendix One.) The references that follow are not necessarily in order of likely importance, but are taken largely in the sequence in which they appear in the CRC.

As mentioned earlier, the reference in *Article 4* to "the maximum extent of [States Parties'] available resources" will attract much of the attention of those concerned with the resource implications of the CRC. But a potentially powerful and perhaps more positive provision is found in the first clause of *Article 2,* dealing with non-discrimination:

> States Parties shall respect and ensure the rights set forth in the present Convention to each child within their jurisdiction without discrimination of any kind, irrespective of the child's or his or her parent's or legal guardian's race, colour, sex, language, religion, political or other opinion, national, ethnic or social origin, property, disability, birth or other status.

In some legal systems, juridical or administrative proceedings have successfully challenged laws or public policies that have given rise to a highly inequitable distribution of public funds and other resources by building a case on non-discrimination provisions in national constitutions or legislation at various levels of government. These proceedings can be particularly important when discrimination based on race, ethnic or social origin compounds disadvantages vulnerable groups face due to poverty. Although much of the 'judicial activism' of this sort comes from industrialized nations, there are some useful precedents from the low-income countries, especially India.[44]

Clearly, however, not all national situations or legal systems will be conducive to an application of Article 2 to cases of discrimination, in public finance or other aspects of public policy, against minority or low-income children and families. Wherever possible, nevertheless, useful precedents could be set by seeking this sort of interpretation and application of Article 2 to reinforce whatever is legally feasible at the national (or subnational) level. Countries that have broadened the concept of *locus standi* — legal standing to address a court — to include professional groups and other NGOs have sometimes opened the door to 'social action litigation' in favour of underrepresented groups in society, including women and children. Again, a number of examples from developing countries have been cited.[45]

An especially important provision of the CRC is, of course, *Article 3,* dealing with the "best interests of the child". Whether intended or not, this article brings us back, albeit somewhat indirectly, to the matter of resource constraints and affordability:

> States Parties shall ensure that the institutions, services and facilities responsible for the care or protection of children shall conform with the *standards established by competent authorities*, particularly in the areas of safety, health, in the *number and suitability of their staff*, as well as *competent supervision* (para. 3, emphasis added).

This paragraph serves as a useful reminder that issues of local standard setting, suitability and competence will inevitably be conditioned by serious constraints of available resources, including organizational resources such as management and information systems. There are many other references in the CRC, not all of which we will cite, to "appropriate" or "effective" measures or guidelines, to the principle of "accordance with national law", or to "feasible measures" (as in *Article 38*). All of these terms have significant resource implications which need to be analysed with, it is hoped, a constructive approach aimed at overcoming resource-related constraints.

We come back now to *Article 4*, the 'centre-piece' for those concerned with the resource implications of the CRC, including the difficult questions of resource mobilization, feasibility and sustainability. The operative provision, for our purposes, is deceptively brief:

> With regard to economic, social and cultural rights, States Parties shall undertake such measures to the maximum extent of their available resources and, where needed, within the framework of international co-operation.

For reasons relating to rather ambiguous distinctions in human rights law, as well as the CRC's legislative history, the "available resources" qualification is applied only to the achievement of "economic, social and cultural rights" (as distinct, the assumption goes, from "civil and political rights"). These unfortunate distinctions (not otherwise raised by the CRC) should not lead us to the conclusion that significant resources (human and organizational, as well as economic) will not be required for the achievement of children's "protection" and "participation" rights, which correspond, though very loosely, with the "civil and political rights" category.

In fact, in terms of the priorities usually reflected in national or other governmental budgets and staffing priorities in developing countries for child-related programmes (heavily committed for education and health), one can expect considerable difficulty in mobilizing the substantial resources for effective *protection* from abuses such as exploitative and dangerous child labour practices (as analysed in detail in a later chapter), racially motivated violence or child prostitution, not to mention from unwanted teenage pregnancies or drug abuse.

As far as *participation rights* are concerned, an often-neglected point needs to be underscored — namely, that for children to be able to benefit significantly from these rights of democratic citizenship,[46] families and societies must be willing to invest the resources necessary:

(a) to prepare children to exercise these rights effectively (including awareness of their rights, as well as functional literacy); and

(b) to assist children to assume the civic responsibilities that go hand in hand with exercising their new 'freedoms'.

Accomplishing these enabling or empowering objectives requires the commitment of time, money, organizational skills and other resources. In the absence of such a commitment, efforts to stimulate children's participation can easily become "exploitative or frivolous" rather than reach the higher rungs of what has been described as the "ladder of participation" of children.[47]

The key provision in Article 4 relates to the obligation of States ratifying the CRC to undertake measures required "to the maximum extent of their available resources". An important question facing those concerned with the effective implementation of the CRC is: Who determines whether that requirement is being met? The *Commentary on the Convention on the Rights of the Child of 1989* answers that question in a formal way: "Resource allocation decisions remain the responsibility of the States Parties themselves."[48] As though realizing the potential problems created by that reply, the *Commentary* quickly adds: "However, the overall decisions taken by those States are not completely immune from scrutiny by the international body charged with supervising States Parties compliance with their treaty obligations."[49] There is then a reference to a process-oriented approach taken by the United Nations Committee on Economic, Social and Cultural Rights in connection with the corresponding Covenant suggesting, rather mildly, that States "might be requested to show that adequate consideration has been given to the possible resources available to satisfy each of the Covenant's requirements, even if the effort was ultimately unsuccessful".[50]

After the reference to the "minimum core obligations" of the States Parties, mentioned earlier in this chapter, the *Commentary* adds a point that could become of increasing importance to the United Nations Committee on the Rights of the Child and other concerned organizations, including NGOs: there is a clear obligation (deriving again from the analogies with the International Covenant on Economic, Social and Cultural Rights) to monitor the realization, "or more especially the non-realization", of these rights. Furthermore, the obligations "to devise strategies and programmes for their promotion are not in any way eliminated as a result of resource constraints".[51]

In sum, all States Parties have an obligation, regardless of resource constraints:

(a) to ensure at least some minimal essential level of each right;

(b) to plan strategies and programmes for the eventual fulfilment of all their obligations under the CRC; and

(c) to monitor both the fulfilment and the non-fulfilment of these obligations over time.

In light of the current economic crisis facing many developing countries, especially severe in Africa, it is noteworthy that the *Commentary* underscores the importance of another conclusion of the Committee on Economic, Social and Cultural Rights:

> ... that even in times of severe resources constraints whether caused by a process of adjustment, of economic recession, or by other factors, the vulnerable members of society can and indeed must be protected by the adoption of relatively low-cost targeted programmes. In support of this approach, the Committee takes note of the analysis prepared by UNICEF entitled *Adjustment with a Human Face: Protecting the Vulnerable and Promoting Growth*, the analysis by the UNDP in its *Human Development Report 1990*, and the analysis by the World Bank in the *World Development Report 1990*.[52]

Article 18 is very important for our purposes, since, together with Article 27, it raises, at least implicitly, the complex issues of:
(a) the financial responsibilities of parents "for the upbringing and development of the child" (para. 1); and
(b) the financial responsibilities of the States Parties to "render appropriate assistance to parents and legal guardians in the performance of their child-rearing responsibilities" (para. 2).
Article 18 also includes a significant provision, of considerable potential importance for work in early childhood development:

> States Parties shall take all appropriate measures to ensure that children of working parents have the right to benefit from child-care services and facilities *for which they are eligible* (para. 3, emphasis added).

Our present interest in this article relates both to the explicit recognition of the special child-care needs of working parents and also to the issue of eligibility for state-supported services in this area. It may appear that this clause is of relevance largely to higher-income countries. The experience, however, of a number of developing countries — both middle-income, such as Colombia, and low-income, including China and India — suggests considerable potential for a gradual extension of "eligibility" for early child-care and integrated child development programmes to increasing portions of those countries' low-income, working families, including situations where the burden of work on women is especially severe.[53]

There are three relevant resource-related aspects of *Article 27* concerned with "the right of every child to a standard of living adequate for the child's physical, mental, spiritual, moral and social development" (para. 1):
(a) the reference to the parents' primary responsibility for their children's development, "within their abilities and financial capacities" (para. 2), which explicitly recognizes a resource-limitation constraint at the family level;
(b) a reminder of the States' financial limitations and the need to establish eligibility requirements for programmes to assist parents:

> States Parties, in accordance with national conditions and *within their means*, shall take appropriate measures to assist parents and others responsible for the child to implement this right and shall *in case of need* provide material assistance and support programmes, particularly with regard to nutrition, clothing and housing (para. 3, emphasis added).

(c) a warning to parents (presumably aimed at non-custodial separated parents) that States "shall take all appropriate measures to secure the recovery of maintenance for the child from the parents or other persons having financial responsibility for the child, both within the State Party and from abroad" (para. 4).

A key public policy issue presented by this 'standard of living' article relates to the question of when parents' financial and other conditions are sufficiently perilous to require governmental assistance to ensure an "adequate" standard of living for their children. In addition to posing the problem of defining the inherently subjective term "adequate", this article also implies the need for further interpretation of the reference to the States' "national conditions" and what can realistically be expected "within their means".

Article 23, concerning disabled children, repeats the "available resources" and "the eligible child" qualifications for state assistance (para. 2), but then introduces the concept of the right to free services: "assistance ... shall be provided free of charge, whenever possible, taking into account the financial resources of the parents or others caring for the child ..." (para. 3). It may be of considerable legal as well as economic significance that the principle of providing free services appears only here and in two other articles of the Convention: the most significant being *Article 28* concerning education (see paras. 1.a and 1.b); and then *Article 40* in connection with the child's entitlement to the "free assistance of an interpreter", if needed, in cases involving alleged infringements of the penal law (para. 2.b.vi).

We will introduce here only a passing reference to *Article 26* on social security, including social insurance, since one can assume that most countries for which this provision is particularly relevant will generally have national laws that set higher and more detailed standards than proved possible in an international convention of this nature. In any event, this article includes a clear reference to the requirement of a full realization of this right "in accordance with national law" (para. 1). This article, therefore, appears to add little power to this area of public policy, however important it may be in an exhortatory sense. It is, nevertheless, relevant to cite its later language, which provides that benefits be granted "taking into account the resources and the circumstances of the child and persons having responsibility for the maintenance of the child ..." (para. 2). In the expanding number of countries[54] with social security legislation of direct relevance to children in need, this provision might be useful in helping to encourage the collection and monitoring of statistical and other information on the situation of children in poverty, or living in other especially difficult circumstances, particularly in otherwise affluent societies. It might also be used to encourage 'middle-income' developing countries to consider a variety of social insurance schemes in place in industrialized countries — highly relevant especially for protecting maternal and child health and nutrition — which combine features of efficiency, cost-effectiveness and equity.

Subsequent chapters will examine in greater detail the resource-related issues raised by two key articles of the CRC: *Article 24* (health and health services) and *Article 28* (education). Presumably because of the considerable weight of these two areas in government budgets in developing countries, it is not surprising that these are the principal 'sectoral' articles[55] that specifically commit the States Parties "to promote and encourage international co-operation" to achieve the realization of these rights, adding that "particular account shall be taken of the needs of developing countries".[56]

The reference in Article 24 to "the right of the child to the enjoyment of the *highest attainable standard* of health" (para. 1, emphasis added) provides not only another potential 'excuse' for poor performance but also an especially important opportunity to link the issue of "attainability" (or feasibility) to the specific child-health goals for the decade of the 1990s adopted at the World Summit for Children together with additional and/or more detailed goals included in the post-Summit NPAs. With reference to the particular issues of resources, affordability and feasibility we are concerned with in this chapter, it is also important to highlight the principles of primary health care (para. 2.b), the priority assigned to preventive health care (para. 2.f), and to the highly cost-effective child-health measures to which specific reference is made in Article 24, including prenatal and post-natal care, breastfeeding, hygiene, clean drinking water, environmental sanitation and access to basic knowledge of child health and nutrition. These are all measures essential to the achievement of the Summit and NPA goals for children. United Nations agencies, including UNICEF, and their allies, national and international, are engaged in concerted efforts to ensure the collection of baseline data and the monitoring of national performance on these health-related goals for children during the 1990s. Special efforts will be needed to ensure that the results of this work also become an integral part of the situation analyses and monitoring needed for the effective implementation of the CRC. Since work on primary health care cost analysis and financing is relatively advanced (including the availability of training manuals), this is an area that could be used to help pave the way for similar initiatives needed in other important fields covered by the CRC, including child development and basic education, as well as priority concerns in terms of "protection" and "participation" rights.

We conclude this section on the main clauses of the CRC relating to resource issues by turning to those provisions covering education (*Articles 28* and *29*). *Article 28* is particularly relevant in terms of 'affordability' and resource planning in several respects:

(a) the explicit reference to the child's right to education with "a view to achieving this right progressively and on the basis of equal opportunity" (para. 1). We need to note once again the importance of setting intermediate targets and of appropriately sequenced financial and other resource planning to ensure the achievement of key goals in education; and the potentially powerful concept of "equal opportunity" as support for greater equity in the allocation of public resources for education. The latter point reinforces the non-

discrimination principle of Article 2 and invites careful assessment of the patterns of resource allocation in the field of education;
(b) the very significant requirement to make "primary education *compulsory, available and free to all*" (para. 1.a, emphasis added). This is surely one key provision in the CRC that international and national children's rights organizations and others should seek to implement, as a high priority;
(c) a somewhat less demanding standard at the secondary level but a nevertheless challenging requirement to make different forms of secondary education "available and *accessible to every child*" and to "take appropriate measures such as the *introduction of free education and offering financial assistance in case of need*" (para. 1.b, emphasis added);
(d) the legal language at the level of higher education changes further, as might be expected, to make higher education "accessible to all *on the basis of capacity* by every appropriate means" (para. 1.c, emphasis added);
(e) the reference to "the reduction of drop-out rates" (para. 1.e) is also an important provision in terms of increasing both the equity and the cost-effectiveness of educational systems.

It is perhaps also relevant to note the one provision of *Article 29* that clearly legitimizes the establishment of private educational institutions (para. 2). It can be anticipated that a major issue in educational reform and educational finance in many countries in the coming years will be the appropriate balance between public and private education and the many questions of equity, quality and efficiency that need to be the subject of careful analysis in this complex area. Special attention will be needed to monitor the impact on school enrolment and performance resulting from increasing tendencies in some countries to impose school fees, even for primary education.

■ 6. Summary and Conclusions

Before we shift to the more detailed analyses in the following chapters, it may be useful to summarize a number of the key points made in this introductory chapter:
(a) the starting point for a constructive interpretation of the reference to "available resources" in Article 4 of the CRC must be a broad definition of resources — human, economic and organizational — that explicitly recognizes their availability at all levels of society, from the family to the international level (Table 1.1);
(b) there are far more "available resources", even in 'resource-poor' societies, relevant for realizing children's rights than are typically recognized; among the most important of these less 'visible' resources are the time, knowledge, organizational and other skills of families and communities for the healthy development and protection of children;
(c) who controls resources and how they are distributed in society is a key question which needs to be addressed by child rights analysts and advocates;

ılitics as well as the economics of children's rights is a critical area of ıry and action;

lack of control of resources by women, when combined with very limited esource availability, is likely to be especially detrimental for children's rights;

(e) both governmental and non-governmental programmes to benefit children can be much less costly, in terms of economic resources, if there is greater recognition of the State's and the civil society's ability and obligation to *respect* and *protect* relevant individual and group rights, as well as societies' many initiatives to benefit children, particularly at the community level;

(f) at all levels of society, governmental and private, the mobilization of *human resources* and *organizational resources*, including political and leadership skills and creativity, may be an especially effective strategy for achieving children's rights, often with a more modest investment of economic resources than typically associated with the direct provision of services for children;

(g) for reasons of equity, non-discrimination, and sometimes sheer child survival, care must be taken not to shift more of the burdens of resource mobilization to those in society least able to contribute more than they already do;

(h) an approach of the sort described in this chapter strengthens participation (potentially including the enhanced participation of children), which, from a human rights and a human development perspective, should be viewed as a desirable end in itself.

It has also been argued that the rather nebulous concept of the obligations of States Parties to the CRC can be sharpened considerably in several ways. A framework has been presented (Table 1.2) that specifies, from the community to the international level, varying types of governmental obligations with regard to children's rights:

(a) to *respect*, for example, the participation rights of children;

(b) to *protect*, particularly vulnerable groups such as minority, street or working children;

(c) to *facilitate*, for example, equal and effective access to educational and vocational training opportunities; and

(d) to *fulfil*, the basic or 'minimum core' needs of high-risk children, for example of those who are victims of armed conflicts, natural disasters or the dissolution of families living in extreme poverty.

It is also clear that obligations, like resources, must be defined to include not only the realm of the public sector, but also the private, non-governmental and other sectors of the civil society. Whether or not national or international legal norms create binding obligations on these non-governmental sectors, effective implementation of the CRC, as well as the NPAs, will undoubtedly require extensive public/private-sector partnerships, at all levels of society.

More practical applications of the concept of the obligations of the States Parties to the CRC will also depend on the implementation of a process that might be described as 'social planning for achieving children's rights'. Planning, management and monitoring child rights work *by objectives* is a key element of this approach. Effective popular and community participation is

another critical component. A four-step implementation strategy for this approach has been outlined. This strategy requires a systematic approach to implementing the CRC beginning with:
(a) a rights-oriented situation analysis;
(b) the setting of goals or standards to be met within agreed time-frames;
(c) the development of plans and programmes of action, at all levels of government, including for the estimation of costs and plans for resource mobilization; and
(d) the provision of monitoring and/or enforcement mechanisms to ensure that goals are achieved and children's rights are respected and fulfilled.

Without a planning, programming and monitoring process of this sort, adapted of course to the circumstances and capacities of each country, it is difficult to see how those provisions of the CRC relating to "available resources", "highest attainable" standards, achieving rights "progressively", and the promotion of international cooperation can be successfully implemented and the implementation process adequately monitored. Achieving an approach to the CRC based on social planning and management by verifiable objectives would represent a major step forward in the human rights field. This accomplishment would also convert the Convention on the Rights of the Child from just another declaration of noble intentions to a genuinely effective tool for enhancing the well-being of children and ensuring the respect, protection and fulfilment of their now widely recognized rights.

Notes

1 United Nations Children's Fund, 1991b, p. 5.
2 See, for example, Alston and Brennan, 1991; Newell, P., 1991, p. xi; Permanent Council of the Organization of American States, 1992, pp. 305-318; United Nations Children's Fund, 1991a; United Nations Children's Fund, 1990c, p. 4; Cury et al., 1992; Xuan Xung, 1991.
3 Grude Flekkφy, 1991, pp. 214-218.
4 United Nations Children's Fund, 1991a, p. 3.
5 Grude Flekkφy, 1991, pp. 218-219.
6 Alston, 1991, pp. 216-257.
7 Alston and Quinn, 1987, especially pp. 172-181.
8 *Human Development Reports* have been produced yearly since 1990 (published by Oxford University Press).
9 Alston, 1991, p. 231.
10 Alston, 1990, p. 367.
11 Alston, forthcoming; see especially 'Article 4: Measures of Implementation'.
12 Ibid., Sec. 4.34.
13 Ibid., Sec. 4.31. For a discussion of satisfying core entitlements, see also Robertson, 1994.
14 Moseley and Chen, 1984, pp. 25-45.
15 Cornia, Jolly and Stewart, 1987, pp. 35-47.
16 Engle, 1992.
17 United Nations Development Programme, 1991, p. 4. See also Myers, 1992, pp. 421-422.
18 World Bank, 1991, p. 1.
19 Ibid., p. 9.
20 United Nations Development Programme, 1992, p. 1.
21 Ibid.

22 Himes, Landers and Leslie, 1992.
23 Engle, 1992, p. 42.
24 Weiner, 1991.
25 Alston, forthcoming, Secs. 4.3 and 4.4.
26 Robertson, 1990, pp. 185-216.
27 Ibid.
28 Eide, Oshaug and Eide, 1991.
29 Rizzini et al., 1992, pp. 34-35.
30 Some of these issues have also been examined in a series of *Innocenti Occasional Papers* on 'Fiscal Policy and the Poor', published by UNICEF, International Child Development Centre, Florence.
31 Shue, 1980, pp. 35-64.
32 Eide, Oshaug and Eide, 1991, pp. 432-433 and *passim*.
33 Ibid., p. 462.
34 Bose, 1992.
35 Jolly and van der Hoeven, 1991, p. 1803.
36 United Nations Development Programme, 1991, p. 10 and pp. 77-84.
37 Ibid., p. 77.
38 Jolly and van der Hoeven, 1991.
39 A programme of the UNICEF International Child Development Centre, Florence, focuses on issues of decentralization, participation and local governance, including an assessment of the process of decentralizing National Programmes of Action for children. See Castillo and Akehurst, 1994.
40 United Nations Children's Fund, 1995.
41 United Nations Development Programme, 1991, p. 8.
42 United Nations Development Programme, 1992, pp. 41-45.
43 Alston, 1990, p. 379.
44 Sengupta, 1992.
45 Goonesekere, 1992; Donaldson, 1992, pp. 2-11; Rizzini et al., 1992, pp. 50-55.
46 For example: freedom of expression and the "freedom to seek, receive and impart information and ideas of all kinds", *Article 13*; the right to have their views "given due weight in accordance with the age and maturity of the child", *Article 12*; or freedom of association, *Article 15*.
47 Hart, 1992.
48 Alston, forthcoming, Sec. 4.29.
49 Ibid.
50 Ibid.
51 Ibid., Sec. 4.32.
52 Ibid.
53 Myers, 1992, p. 99-152; Landers and Leonard, 1992.
54 See, for example, new directions in financing health and nutrition programmes in Thailand: Kiranandana and Tontisirin, 1992.
55 *Article 17* also includes a reference (para. b) to international cooperation in the production, exchange and dissemination of information and material of social and cultural benefit to children. *Article 23*, dealing with disabled children, contains a specific reference (para. 4) to the international exchange of information in this area. Several other articles dealing with particular groups of children in difficult circumstances or at risk due to international movements of people call for, or at least imply, the need for international cooperation. Of particular relevance in terms of resource requirements is *Article 22* concerning refugee children. *Article 4* and *Article 45*, of course, provide blanket references to international cooperation covering the entire Convention so there is no legal justification for limiting such cooperation to any specific areas or articles.
56 *Article 24* (para. 4) and *Article 28* (para. 3).

Resources and child rights: an economic perspective

David Parker

1. What Price Human Rights?

There is a tendency in human rights circles to assume that 'rights are rights' and as such should not be the subject of lengthy debates among economists and planners about resource allocation, costs and financing. This viewpoint stems partly from the general association of human rights, especially in the industrialized West, with civil and political rights, including the individual's right to personal security: freedom from government interference in matters of property, family and household, language, religion and culture. Especially when it comes to gross abuses by the State itself, such as summary executions, torture, state-instigated terror and the complete absence of due process in criminal proceedings, international human rights law allows no State to claim exemptions or to justify delayed compliance due to resource constraints.

In the areas of economic, social and cultural rights, however, sometimes transposed into 'survival and development rights' in the context of the Convention on the Rights of the Child (CRC), human rights law explicitly recognizes the constraints imposed by available resources and the need for the achievement of these kinds of rights over time. In addition to the specific reference in Article 4 of the CRC to the obligation of States Parties "to undertake such measures [regarding economic, social and cultural rights] to the maximum extent of their available resources", other provisions, for example, refer to "the highest attainable standard of health" (Article 24) and to "the right of the child to education, and with a view to achieving this right progressively ..." (Article 28).

Human rights activists and promoters of children's rights may counter, with considerable justification, that many of the problems of violations or neglect of economic, social and cultural rights have more to do with power relationships in society, or a lack of 'political will', than with resource constraints. The Introduction to this book draws attention to the key question of 'who controls the available resources' — from the national and international levels to individual households. The former Chief of UNICEF's Nutrition Section refers in Chapter Five to a complex array of social, political and ideological factors that affect the availability and control of resources at different levels of society. He notes specifically that "the basic causes of child malnutrition are social and political and ought to be addressed by governments, a responsibility that could require substantial structural changes".

From the programmatic perspective of UNICEF and its partners, there is surely little to be gained from abstract debates about the balance among economic, political, ideological and cultural constraints on progress towards implementing the CRC. All these factors clearly play a role, and even very rough weights that one might try to assign to them will obviously vary from context to context, within countries as well as across significant time periods. One thing, however, is certain: whatever the underlying historical causes, 'resource-poor' societies face particularly harsh challenges and trade-offs as they seek to attain social and economic progress as well as advances in human rights. UNICEF and other international development agencies share a special responsibility, set out in several provisions of the CRC as well as in other international human rights treaties, to respond to compelling resource constraints where needed. This responsibility is especially clear in critical areas such as health and education, where the CRC requires that "particular account shall be taken of the needs of developing countries" (Articles 24.4 and 28.3).

The analysis that follows runs two risks: human rights activists may find it overly technical, perhaps even unseemly, in its application of concepts such as 'stocks' and 'flows' and 'efficiency' to the field of human rights. Economists, on the other hand, may wish the analysis were even more thorough and perhaps more empirical. There is, however, a growing conviction, certainly shared by most of the concerned agencies of the United Nations, that much more work needs to be done in developing concepts, planning and monitoring tools and indicators to help achieve and measure progress on *both* the development and human rights fronts. In the process, considerable patience and willingness to dialogue across these lines of social policy action will be needed.

This chapter first examines the use of human, economic and organizational resources in producing social outputs, in terms of the two main forms that resources take —'stocks' and 'flows'. Based on this framework, several key measures are identified for increasing the availability of resources for the implementation of child rights, including changes in technologies and processes, and the expanded use of 'non-traditional' resources for children. The changing economic roles of different actors in the fulfilment of child rights are then considered, in relation to the *financing* of actions, the *provision* of services, and the *management* of social sectors. The chapter closes with an assessment of different arrangements among these actors that can best promote child rights concerns.

■ 2. A Framework for Resource Analysis

Part of the debate over the issue of 'economic' versus 'political/social' constraints inhibiting progress on human rights can be addressed more constructively if it is made explicit that references to 'available resources' in international human rights treaties should not be restricted to 'economic resources' alone — that is, to only financial inputs and material objects which can be purchased or donated in economic transactions. Human and organizational resources need to be brought into the debate much more consciously than is often the case by either the development or the human rights communities. *Human* resources, for example, include people's capacities and skills, which in turn include, among many others, leadership, managerial and political skills. In practical terms, these are the sorts of skills needed to help confront the more cultural, political or ideological barriers to progress in many areas of both development and human rights to which 'structuralist' observers would call our attention. *Organizational* resources, similarly, include the entire array of structural and functional relationships in society, including power relationships, which influence the ways in which resources are generated and allocated in any society.

It is worth repeating here, therefore, the threefold classification of 'resources', which is reasonably conventional in the relevant literature and which we have attempted to use consistently throughout this book:

- *human resources* — 'people': the capacities, actions, time and energy of individuals and communities;
- *economic resources* — 'things': both financial inputs, which can be budgeted for, and materials, which are purchased. They also include material inputs donated in kind, such as food and building supplies;
- *organizational resources* — the 'enabling environment': formal and informal arrangements between people and the procedures by which actions are structured in society. They include the amounts and distribution of power and political commitment, which permit the effective use of human and economic resources.[1]

It is also important to reiterate another point developed in the previous chapter: the adoption of the principle of children's rights gives rise to *obligations*, including claims on human, economic and organizational resources, *at all levels of society*, and not just on the central government on which attention is usually focused in terms of the formal obligations of 'States Parties' to international conventions. Other critical obligations, involving varying degrees of legal enforceability to be sure, nevertheless must be considered: subnational governments at the state or provincial, municipal and district levels; the private commercial and informal sectors; non-governmental organizations (NGOs); communities; and households. Improved ways also need to be developed to emphasize and specify the obligations and accountability of the international community concerned with human rights, including those of children. Among other important consequences, a more encompassing definition of obligations and claims on resources draws attention to the potential for more active partnerships in favour of children's rights, including public/private-sector cooperation, central/local-level governmental joint action, and international cooperation not just with central governments but also with local public- or private-sector initiatives.

In this perspective, a range of economic decisions are made concerning actions for children. In a context of resource scarcity, the first concern is that an action is *affordable*: Are resources adequate, from the possible different sources, at the level of scale (coverage or output) desired? Can the actions and approaches be financed with available resources? The issue of *equity* arises, especially from a human rights perspective, out of concern that the benefits, and the costs, of actions are distributed fairly among the population. Parallel to this is the concern that the action is *efficient* — that costs are as low as possible, and realistic in the programme context. The longer-term concern is with the *sustainability* of the actions: Can efforts be maintained into the future with the resources expected to be available?

□ 2.1. 'STOCKS' AND 'FLOWS'

The concept of resources may be further developed by classifying the different types of resources into the two main forms of *stocks* and *flows*. 'Stocks', also referred to as 'assets' or 'endowments', are the accumulated pools of value that society has at its disposal, to conserve or to use for different purposes. They provide the basis for present and future economic activity, establishing the range of possibilities open to society. 'Flows' are the actual expenditure or use of those resources, either through direct consumption or application (for instance, eating a meal or installing a hand-pump) or through transactions or exchanges in the market-place.

Thus, for example, human resource 'stocks' include the training, motivation and commitment that are vested in people, both as individuals and communities. These stocks are converted into 'flows' in people's efforts, as actions are undertaken in daily life and in the production of goods and services. Considering economic resources, 'stocks' are easily understood as the base of natural resources, physical goods and technologies that represent a society's productive capacity; these are consumed or exploited as 'flows' in the course of economic activity. Finally, organizational resource 'stocks' include structure and power in the political, administrative, community and household spheres. Organizational 'flows' are seen in the planning, mobilization and management of actions. A fuller illustration of these dimensions of resources is presented in Table 2.1.

Table 2.1 - **Rights-related resources: stocks and flows**

Type	Stocks	Flows
Human Resources	Skills, professionalism Motivation, will-power Aspirations, 'vision' Knowledge, experience Desire, commitment Energy	Skilled, manual and intellectual work or labour Struggle, threat, negotiation, dialogue Exchange of information and experience
Economic Resources	Land, natural resources Physical infrastructure (roads, electricity, water) Equipment, tools Assets, savings Technology, information	Budget, expenditures Credit Supplies Interest Profit
Organizational Resources	Administrative structures, norms, procedures Laws and regulations Professional organization Political power, leadership, control Political organization Local organizations and committees Service organizations Family, clans	Decisions Participation Mobilization Management Regulation Monitoring Training

The categorization above attempts to indicate the relationships among the different resources present in society. Conceptually it is of course problematic to classify resources into one or another 'type'. The framework is not intended to be exhaustive, but rather to suggest a useful way of viewing resource issues, one that is related to other economic theories used to address rights questions.[2]

From these examples, it is seen that, of the two forms of resources, 'flows' of production (income) and consumption (expenditure) are by far the most apparent and commonly considered. 'Stocks' usually remain in the background and are considered only when there is awareness that they are inadequate for a purpose (as in the case of insufficient budgets) or about to be depleted (clean water, for instance). Yet, from the perspective of child rights, society's 'stocks' are crucial: sufficient endowments must remain available to invest in and support actions to meet the needs of future generations.[3] Such an intergenerational perspective underlines the importance of long-term investment, building of human capacity, conservation of natural resources and empowerment of organizations and communities to enable actions in the future — as an *obligation*, not merely as an optional use of present efforts.

Some types of stocks can be maintained indefinitely under proper conditions — for example, savings in a context of stable financial institutions. Others, such as human skills and motivation, degrade or depreciate over time and must be replenished to remain fresh. The level of 'flows' as resources are used must be closely monitored. Within the family, for example, a parent (usually the mother) may have sufficient time to spend some extra hours caring for children in the community. If the same parent must also participate in the activities of the local cooperative and carry out extension functions for the health centre, in addition to fetching water, cooking and other household tasks, she may quickly lose her ability to perform any of these functions well, as her 'stock' of energy and motivation declines. Similarly, although households may have sufficient cash to afford fees for schooling, health care or water, expecting them to pay for all of these services may soon exhaust their incomes.

A key step in ensuring the optimum use of resources is thus to establish the process by which society's stocks and flows are combined for the achievement and enforcement of the rights of children, through concrete actions in the sectors of health, education and early child development, for example, as well as in the wider economy.[4] The processes required for the implementation of child rights are complex, first, because of the challenge to define basic needs across different country settings — and, beyond these needs, the satisfaction of other conditions for the quality of children's lives.[5] Procedures used to allocate resources at the governmental, organizational and household levels must also be redefined, in order to respond to and fulfil society's minimum needs effectively, a task for which existing procedures are not well suited.[6] A central requirement in this effort is to expand the planning and allocation functions to encompass human and organizational resources, in addition to conventional economic resources.

In this process, it is important to note that 'production' is not merely additive or linear among these three types of resources. It is clearly not the case, for example, that given amounts of skills, buildings and decisions yield a definable social improvement. Rather, it is seen that human resources (such as motivation and creativity) and organizational resources (the processes and procedures by which human and economic resources are harnessed) have a 'multiplier effect' on the yield or performance of a given set of economic resources. In other words, they determine the 'quality' or productivity of economic resources. It is thus often the case that the differences seen in results achieved by two individuals, institutions or countries — which have begun with the same endowment of economic resources and with common objectives — can be explained by the types and amounts of human and organizational resources available.[7]

□ 2.2. VALUE AND COSTS

The 'value' of a resource is expressed in terms of its *cost*. Ideally, cost is defined in terms of 'opportunity cost'; namely, the worth of the contribution of a resource if it is used in the most productive way possible. In practice, however, the value of resources is expressed in terms of prices, which often do not fully reflect a resource's real potential value.

Markets, which determine prices and arrange transactions, are best suited for dealing with economic resources. Yet in many cases — as is frequently seen in the social sectors — the prices of economic resources differ widely from 'opportunity-cost' value. For example, the high price of many drugs is often related more to monopoly production, advertising and a lack of information available to consumers than it is to therapeutic efficacy. Another example is seen in the persistent disagreements, social as well as technical, over how to account for and value a country's natural resources.

The markets for human and organizational resources are generally far more informal and less well developed. In these categories, there may even be difficulties in defining the resources themselves. For example, some people may not consider 'motivation' (identified as a human resource) or 'norms' (an organizational resource) to be distinct from other human and organizational characteristics. Many human and organizational resources are usually not quantitatively 'valued'. Instead, they are often merely described, in a combination of qualitative and quantitative ways. As a result, most calculations of costs, which naturally focus on economic resources, tend to understate the actual total utilization of resources for a given activity.

The 'value' of human and organizational resources is enhanced, enabling them to be used more fully to their potential, through the provision of 'opportunities'. Opportunities relate to changes in the context in which action takes place, in the political, technical or social setting of an activity. Thus, opportunities might include legal provision for the creation of a local cooperative, or the development of a technique to use locally made flour in a rehydration solution for diarrhoea.

■ 3. Increasing the Resources Available for Children

While decisions about the allocation of resources are, in principle, taken by and for society as a whole, economic decisions are in practice made by specific actors: central government; subnational governments, at the state or provincial, municipal and district levels; the private sector; NGOs; communities; households; and the international community. Each of these actors holds distinct values and perspectives, which are likely to be different from those held at other levels, and also different from those of an 'ideal' society-wide decision process. The central issue for child rights is to understand how these individual decisions can best contribute collectively to the achievement of a country's or society's objectives.

The result of such decisions should be to ensure that adequate resources are available for use, in the most productive way, for implementing child rights. There are several lines of action towards this objective: increasing the total quantity of economic resources, in a context of resource scarcity; increasing the use of 'non-traditional' resources, human and organizational, in activities; and, at the same time, ensuring that existing resources are used to their maximum extent. Actions are required, for example, to improve targeting of resources on vulnerable groups; to improve the cost-efficiency of programmes; to make aid procedures more flexible and appropriate; and to improve the information base on resource requirements and use. Each of these approaches is likely to require reassessment and restructuring of budgets on the part of governments, communities and households.

□ 3.1. RESTRUCTURING BUDGETS FOR HUMAN DEVELOPMENT PRIORITIES

The central reflection of a society's values lies in the overall pattern of its allocation of resources: Are resources being directed where they are most required, in terms of their prioritization towards specific needs and in favour of specific populations? At the governmental level, addressing this question of 'allocative efficiency' first relates to the choice among sectors and target groups. For example, are adequate resources going for education, health and other basic services in comparison with, say, road-building or defence? A number of initiatives are under way to seek the restructuring of government budgets in the context of child rights, through the reduction or elimination of debt burdens and a shift in allocations in favour of human priority concerns. Secondly, within a given sector, are resources being used for the actions that best reflect society's needs and resources? Within the education sector, at a given level of funding, the balance between basic and primary schooling, on the one hand, and tertiary education, on the other, must be assessed. In health, primary services, including preventive and promotive actions, must have an appropriate role vis-à-vis higher-level curative care. In the nutrition sector, community-based approaches and a focus on alleviating micronutrient deficiencies are needed rather than untargeted feeding and subsidy programmes.

The deterioration of economic conditions during the 1980s led to increased poverty in parts of the developing world. The declines were particularly severe in Africa, owing largely to falls in the prices of primary commodities, and in Latin America as a result of mounting debt. However, conditions worsened in other regions as well, including in South Asia where large populations remained in poverty and the numbers of malnourished grew. There was thus an increasingly prevalent view that development strategies should shift towards greater emphasis on poverty reduction and human development, often requiring significant policy changes. A central focus of this effort has been on the social dimension of poverty reduction, or 'human development priorities', particularly on low-cost actions in primary health care, basic education, rural and peri-urban water and sanitation, and nutrition support. To achieve substantial progress in reducing the worst manifestations of poverty by the year 2000 and beyond, additional efforts and resources are needed in most countries, as outlined in the National Programmes of Action (NPAs), described in Chapter Three, and other documents.

Available data indicate that most countries are currently spending less than 5 per cent of gross domestic product (GDP), and in the range of 10-15 per cent of government expenditures, on human development priorities. These spending patterns are predictably varied, in relation to countries' economic, social and political structures and objectives. But experience suggests that, in the case of similar countries, those that, in a sustainable fashion, have given comparatively high priority to human development in public expenditures, particularly in the social sectors, have achieved greater economic and social progress. For external assistance, it appears that donors spend on average about 10 per cent of official development assistance (ODA) on human development priorities. However, in both of these cases, and particularly for aid, incomplete reporting and lack of comparable data hamper an exact assessment of human development performance.

A range of efforts are needed to mobilize resources for basic social services, including increases in the total amount of government revenues and expenditures; restructuring of budgets both among and within sectors; decentralization of government action; debt reduction; and innovative approaches for mobilizing private resources. Many such steps are outlined in the NPAs of different countries.

In this context, several initiatives are under way to promote the allocation, by governments as well as donors, of increased budget resources for human priority concerns. One such approach, known as 20/20, proposes targets for expenditures for social priorities as a means to signal a firm commitment to social development, and to protect priority programmes against disproportionate spending cuts. It suggests that a minimum of 20 per cent of developing-country government budgets, supported by a comparable level of aid (20 per cent of aid budgets at the global level), properly targeted, can contribute substantially to meeting the short-term basic social needs of children and other vulnerable groups. This effort would thus address the worst aspects of poverty and pave the way for planning the achievement of longer-term human development objectives.[8] Other related spending targets for social priorities may also be usefully applied, including targets in relation to total national income or GDP (which recognizes the increasing importance of the private sector), since no single target is capable of reflecting all of the economic elements relevant to human development priorities. But together, these targets offer basic benchmarks for government and donor spending, translating into increased allocation of resources on a set of specific interventions which are already on the human development agendas of most developing countries and donors.

Similar considerations apply at the household and community levels, where spending patterns frequently do not address critical needs, including those of children. Instead, they often focus on less productive consumption, as a result of social and cultural habit. Social expenditures on ceremonies and social events can be many times greater than those devoted to children, severely depleting household resources and incurring substantial debt. Consumption of alcohol and tobacco is frequently very costly, while the local production of alcohol can absorb large stocks of grain that might be used for food. Well-documented patterns of food consumption, in which adults are given preference over children, men over women and boys over girls, perpetuate undernutrition of children, especially of girls. Similarly, education and related expenditures may be focused on a few children in a household, while other children, particularly girls, are kept at home for chores. In all of these instances, better prioritization of household resources can yield significant economic resources for child development, at relatively little opportunity cost.

□ 3.2. MOBILIZING NON-TRADITIONAL RESOURCES

A specific focus of efforts to increase social outputs, in relation to the implementation of child rights and other goals, is to restructure production so as to use 'non-traditional' human and organizational resources, in addition to economic resources, in generating results. This has the great potential to make actions for children more affordable and sustainable, in the absence of sufficient economic resources to achieve all of society's objectives. It can also lead to greater equity, since those without adequate economic resources are usually precisely those who are most vulnerable.

In the case of the Expanded Programme on Immunization (EPI), the strategy of mobilization of groups throughout society was refined and implemented in efforts to achieve universal immunization by 1990. In different countries, all segments of the society, including central and local government, religious leaders, NGOs, civil servants and community leaders, were mobilized and involved in immunization activities. Reviews of this experience have attributed much of its success to this process, which was used to support both intensified expansion of facility-based services (as in Turkey, Mauritania and Burkina Faso) and Immunization Days and other 'campaign' approaches at the national, district and municipal levels. The latter campaigns in particular — as seen in the examples of Colombia, Nigeria and many other countries — involved major communication efforts to inform the population about the importance of immunization, and logistical arrangements to establish vaccination points, encourage participation and provide vaccinations on a mass basis.

Analyses of the cost of campaigns, including part or all of the estimated value of non-health-sector contributions, have shown results of about $15 per fully immunized child, approximately the same as for routine EPI strategies.[9] As such, important questions are still raised about the ongoing sustainability of the EPI effort, and the ability to meet its resource requirements in the future. However, the experience has also shown how the economic resources provided by the health system and donors can be used to mobilize large quantities of additional resources — contributions of time, media coverage, food and supplies, from other government sectors (notably teachers), businesses, religious and social groups and communities — in immunizing children. Beyond these direct results, the participation of these groups has been seen, in many countries, as a springboard to their wider involvement in actions for children, including the promotion of child rights.

Information and education provided to the public has been found to have especially significant multiplier effects and long-term benefits. With regard to immunization, the mobilization process created or activated channels of communication about the value of immunization and other health actions, which often were able to reach the population more effectively than the routine health services could. Hygiene education has long been noted as one of the most crucial interventions for sanitation, both for direct health benefits and for an improved living environment. Concerning nutrition, recent research has identified the significant social gains to be attributed to the better dissemination of information about improved nutrition practices.[10]

The inputs of community volunteers are particularly effective in activities of short duration. Problems of continuity often arise when volunteers are relied upon for ongoing efforts. There are numerous examples in history of volunteer-based actions, from post-war rehabilitation programmes to systematized efforts such as the Korean *Saemaul Undong* of the early 1970s, in which the volunteers' contributions are phased out or become institutionalized as new employment opportunities develop for the use of their time. This situation has also been seen in the primary health care systems of many countries. Typically, community volunteers are recruited for 'informal' work, as the key agents for extension and first-line referral, and have been given a modest amount of training. Payments usually consist of only a stipend or nominal wage, or contributions from the community. As a result, these workers tend to have a high rate of attrition and are lost to the system (although their skills are not lost to society). In other cases, volunteers organize and seek to become integrated into the formal health or education system, a move that has tended to be resisted by professional cadres as well as by governments themselves in the budgetary process.[11]

For a shift to take place from conventional 'economic' inputs to the increased use of human and organizational resources, a longer time period and fresh organizational arrangements are usually necessary. Thus, for example, if child care by mothers is identified as a substitution for public-sector day-care provision, organizational resources in the form of a village committee structure and means of compensating the mothers must be established. This process requires that planning take place with a sufficiently long time-frame because of the periods needed for such resources to be developed and organized. Within the public sector, training needed to raise the level of basic skills may take 5-10 years to implement, whereas even retraining and reallocation of personnel requires a substantial period of time. It is important not to underestimate the similar requirements for introducing sustainable changes at the community and household levels.

An example of new organizational arrangements in the non-governmental sector is seen in the case of the *Sarvodaya Shramadana* Movement, a village-based development programme in Sri Lanka. The Movement supports a number of different activities across the country, including income generation, community health and nutrition services through a pre-school programme, and relief and rehabilitation, all based on the efforts of semi-volunteer *gramadana* workers.[12] Following evaluations of the Movement's ability to manage its growing programme and retain the workers who were at its core, several changes were made.[13] A first focus was on staff development, to increase professionalism and maintain the motivation of trained workers, for whom market wages could not be afforded. Second, field-level supervision was increased as a means for improved planning, monitoring and evaluation, through greater decentralization of responsibility. A third measure was to introduce improved systems for administration and finance, to ensure that programme quality and accountability were maintained. In these ways, the Movement has been able to retain its basic voluntary character, while increasing the range and coverage of its activities. Successful NGO programmes in other countries, including the Bangladesh Rural Advancement Committee (BRAC) in Bangladesh, have undertaken similar organizational changes as their activities have matured and expanded.

□ 3.3. IMPROVING EFFICIENCY OF TECHNOLOGIES AND PROCESSES

Once programme objectives have been agreed upon, there is a need to establish that resources are being used as productively as possible: that the maximum level of output is being achieved with a given set of inputs; or that minimum inputs are being used to achieve a given result, and are realistic in the context of alternative uses of those resources in the society.

A wide variety of technical and social factors influence the ways in which resources are used and combined for different aims. At the margin, one type of resource can often be substituted for another — for example, using bicycles instead of cars, or local building materials instead of imported cement. But the extent of such substitution varies considerably, and its long-term scope is usually limited. Economic resources are clearly the most 'fungible': flows of money and budgets can be used to purchase other economic resources (for example, supplies), human resources (for example, labour) and organizational resources (for example, a supply distribution system). Yet, in the short run, budget structures and earmarking of allocations for specific purposes may be difficult to change. And even in the longer term of, say, a five-year planning cycle, exchanging resources requires adequate markets (which are often not in place) and the availability of the resources for which exchange is sought. Thus, shifting the locus of primary health services from hospital out-patient departments to local clinics requires major changes in staffing, public knowledge and expectations, supervision and regulation (to name but a few areas); and for each of these changes, considerable lead time and planning are needed.

Still, many options exist in society for doing more with the same, or with fewer, resources in order to improve cost-efficiency. A number of examples can be given of actions that have been taken in different countries:

- *Non-professional or paraprofessional workers can be utilized instead of professional workers*; for example, community health workers trained to treat common problems and dispense a limited number of drugs, and community teachers who provide non-formal education. The use of volunteer workers raises numerous challenges to management and political processes, as discussed above. Examples of how village-level health workers have been effectively incorporated into national systems are seen in Indonesia and Thailand;[14]

- *Lower-cost buildings can be utilized to serve the necessary functions of more substantial but expensive facilities*; in many countries, for example, considerable savings have been achieved by building schools with locally available materials, which has meant that the schools can be constructed and maintained with local labour;
- *Facilities can be used more intensively and for multiple purposes*; for instance, school buildings used for multiple shifts during the day and for community meetings in the evening;
- *Less costly supplies can be used*; for example, generic rather than branded drugs in health facilities, locally produced teaching materials rather than imported textbooks, and locally produced hand-pumps.

Such choices of technology are particularly crucial when the alternative is no services at all, but they apply equally when choices must be made between expanding coverage and increasing quality or input intensity.

A basic problem in technological choice is often not that more expensive approaches are selected deliberately, but that those who are carrying out an action in a certain way are doing so because that is the only one they know, or it is the standard approach. More efficient methods, made possible by the development of new technologies and the identification of new ways of organizing activities, often exist — as in the case of low-cost hand-pumps for water supply, which in turn enable the management of operation and maintenance at the community level. It is thus important to improve the general understanding of programme costs, and then to communicate information on lower-cost technologies and approaches so that they can be applied in other settings.

3.4. FOCUSING ON CRITICAL INPUTS

To improve efficiency and reduce wastage, specific attention must be given to those inputs that are in shortest supply in relation to requirements and that constrain the level of output — regardless of the availability of other resources. It is often easy to observe the examples of inefficiency and waste that occur when existing resources cannot be used to their full capacity, and may even go idle. For example, teachers try to lead classes without books or paper; health workers cannot provide adequate care because they lack dressings and drugs, which patients must obtain if they can; and, at the household level, children experience micronutrient deficiencies even when there is a sufficient overall quantity of food. Eliminating such bottlenecks and making 'critical' resources available then becomes a major focus of action, and these resources gain a value with respect to the output that can far exceed their normal 'price'. This situation is familiar in the case of economic resources: the provision of foreign exchange for essential drugs or textbooks is often the crucial need of a health or education programme.[15]

The problem of scarcity applies equally to human and organizational resources —although it is of course less easy to quantify. When, for example, the organizational resources of political leadership and commitment are absent, it may be most productive to concentrate on strengthening these in order to mobilize other resources in society. As noted above, concentration on mobilizing political and social support, supplementing the ongoing attention to logistical and other technical elements, formed a key strategy in the effort for universal immunization during the late 1980s. An expanded version of the same priority is now a cornerstone of the implementation of the child rights agenda. Both for the ratification of the CRC itself and for the actions needed for its implementation and enforcement, political leadership and commitment are recognized as critical resources.

Similarly, at the operational level, as has been described, a combination of adequate remuneration and other actions to improve motivation and morale may be needed before health workers can function effectively, even when other inputs such as buildings, drugs and supplies are present. An important function of external agencies in this context is to help provide critical inputs so that the overall system can function more efficiently, to its potential capacity.

□ 3.5. TARGETING FOR INCREASED EQUITY

Economic, human and organizational resources are unequally distributed within society; and, above all, children do not have control over resources in relation to their needs. Thus, a major concern of resource analysis is to examine the extent to which there is equal access to resources and to the benefits of social actions by different population groups, and to take actions to improve this access, for instance, with respect to urban-rural differences, gender disparities, and differentials between income groups or social classes.

Many of the actions indicated previously are likely to increase equity. In particular, because the poor have the greatest needs, any action to increase resources and adopt more efficient technologies is likely to lead to more equitable distribution of benefits to those presently not receiving them. In addition, however, specific strategies may be needed to improve the focusing of actions on those most in need. For example, untargeted consumer subsidies that benefit urban-dwellers in general, including those better-off, might achieve their intended results more quickly by being translated into targeted subsidies. Similarly, mandating (and enforcing) basic minimum standards for education, health care and access to water supply may be needed before increased social-sector budget allocations can be expected to impact on the poor.

■ 4. The Organization of Resources for Children

It has been seen that the key approaches needed to increase and strengthen the actions taken for children for fulfilment of the CRC involve changes in the allocation of human and organizational resources in society, to complement

and support the flow of economic inputs. These implementation functions have to do principally with:
(a) *financing* — who should pay for services and other actions for children, and through what means;
(b) *provision* — the decision about who should deliver services and take other actions influencing children's well-being; and
(c) *management* — establishing and monitoring the 'rules of the game' for the different sectors and actions affecting children, through regulation, information and control processes.

The changes usually considered, and those raised especially during the past decade, have tended to focus on the distinction between 'public' and 'private' actions. However, we may usefully examine these functions in terms of the respective roles of each of the levels and actors involved in implementing child rights: government at different levels; NGOs and the private sector; communities and households; and the international community. Their roles

***Table 2.2* - Resource-related functions in implementing the Convention on the Rights of the Child**

Actor	Implementation roles		
	Financing	Provision	Management
Central Government	Public financing ('free' services) Social security Parastatal-enterprises coverage 'Contracting-out' of public services	Direct provision of services Information and education	Political mobilization Regulation, setting prices Information systems Research, training
Subnational Government	Local free or subsidized services	Local-level provision	Local regulation and monitoring
Private Sector	Private insurance systems Employment-based health and education benefits	Private schools For-profit (modern) health care Traditional sector health services	Professional norms Operational administration
NGOs	Donations Subsidies of total cost Fund-raising	NGO-operated facilities (e.g., schools and clinics)	Operational administration and reporting
Communities	Social insurance Local exemption from fees to ensure access	Community-based health workers Community teachers in non-formal education Local maintenance of hand-pumps	Community management committees Community-based information systems
Households	Taxes (indirect financing) Market prices User charges Time cost of travel and waiting	Home-based treatment Preventive health and nutrition practices Intra-household food distribution	Information and support for children's education and living conditions Participation in local management processes
Donors	Financial and technical support	Emergency relief services	Reporting systems Advocacy Training

may be briefly reviewed in the light of the criteria of efficiency, equity, affordability and sustainability. It is then possible to identify trends that are occurring in the distribution of responsibility for implementing child rights.

Table 2.2 provides a basic framework for the examination of implementation roles, with illustrations of the different ways in which the three major implementation functions can be carried out.

□ 4.1. FINANCING OF SERVICES

While services and other actions for children are obviously financed at all levels of society, in most if not all countries, the role of government has generally been pivotal. It is commonly accepted that government should fund services that meet certain basic criteria: the services are considered 'essential' to the functioning of the society; and they have a strong 'public good' quality (that is, conveying benefits to the society as a whole beyond those enjoyed by the individual recipients alone). Most basic education, preventive and public health services, basic coverage of water supply and sanitation and related services discussed in the context of child rights fall within these parameters. In many countries, including developing countries during the past several decades, such support has taken the form of 'free' services to the population as a whole. Social security networks and parastatal enterprises provide additional, large segments of insurance coverage. Government financing, at either central or subnational levels, may also include other arrangements such as contracting out to private providers for services delivered under social insurance. Crucial support to services of a public nature is, in many countries, provided by NGOs and external donors.

The organized private sector forms a second major source of financing of children's services, especially in health, either through insurance systems or benefits provided by employers. Employer-based financing — of health, child care and, in some cases, education — has historically been a key element of labour benefits, and it is now a focus of health system reform efforts in many countries. Albeit slowly, an increasing number of developing countries are following the pattern set in industrialized and better-off countries of promoting private insurance systems and employer coverage to pay for services not funded by government. In some countries, the services needing to be paid for under this heading can be quite basic, while in others a broad range of benefits are covered.

Individuals and households pay a major, though widely varying, share of the costs of services in the form of formal and informal charges and non-monetary costs to utilize services (in addition to their indirect financing through taxes). A major focus of attention in recent years has been the trend towards charging users a substantial share of the cost of formerly often 'free' education and health services. Although additional financing is often required in the wake of economic pressures and adjustment policies of governments, user charges have frequently been found to be regressive from an equity viewpoint, and inefficient administratively. It can be argued that, as an initial step, minimum standards of fairness require that the burden of costs to users be increased only when the activities are operating at an efficient level. In the absence of adequate financing by central and subnational governments or other parties, however, efficiency may not be possible to achieve. In such cases, one viable approach has been found to be community-organized financing, linked to decentralization of accountability and management to the local level.

Public financing of key services has certain clear economic advantages, which are now being reflected in reassessments of policy by a number of governments and organizations. From an efficiency perspective, a single payer is potentially able to achieve economies in administration and often in negotiation over payment levels. From an equity viewpoint, only government is able to ensure that certain basic rights are met, through direct provision as well as cross-subsidization of the poor and underserved by the wealthier and better-served. Affordability and sustainability of basic services for the poor are only possible in the long run if governments firmly commit themselves to providing the financial base for them, limiting, at the same time, their support for services of a less critical nature. The principle of government responsibility for financing a minimum set of services is currently receiving increased visibility. In education, longstanding public policies for basic education are being strengthened in the movement for 'Education for All', as discussed in Chapter Six. In health, the World Bank and other organizations have recently reaffirmed the importance of public financing of a basic package of preventive, promotive and basic curative services[16] (see Chapter Four).

□ 4.2. PROVISION OF SERVICES

The diverse ways in which basic needs are provided for has been indicated in Table 2.2. In general, however, government at the central or state/local level has historically maintained responsibility for education, health and other social services. In most countries, it is only the failure of government to provide services that has led other levels and actors, apart from communities and households, to take on increased roles. The central role of government has often been based on sound principles of efficiency, under which defined technical standards and acceptable levels of costs can only be maintained on a large scale through a common provider operating under established norms.

The decline of economic resources of government and a growing economic role of the non-governmental sectors has led to a worldwide reassessment of this traditional allocation of functions.[17] The natural monopoly towards which the social services once tended has weakened with the availability of increased human and organizational resources outside of government. Private actors have become increasingly important in the social sectors — for example, in the provision of equipment (such as medical equipment, drilling rigs) and supplies (such as pharmaceuticals, textbooks, bricks and cement), and in the construction of facilities and water installations. In the water and sanitation sector, private enterprises operate alongside public facilities in most rural as well as urban areas. In health, the private sector ranges from traditional clinics and drug stores to full-scale clinics and hospitals, and from non-profit institutions that often form a part of the public-sector system to enterprises over which little or no control is exercised by government or professional bodies. In education, basic and primary schooling is still largely the province of government, but in many cities, and increasingly in rural areas, extra sessions or even separate schools are available for children, at some considerable cost, on a private basis.

Overall, then, the supply side in the social sectors is becoming increasingly diverse. The need for government provision has not necessarily declined, but it is being focused more on three types of issues:
(a) providing broadly based services (such as primary education and public health care) that cannot be efficiently provided by other actors;
(b) being the provider of last resort where populations are not otherwise affordably served; and
(c) ensuring that minimum standards are adhered to across the country.

Additional non-governmental channels for basic services have, of course, always been available at the community level, and through formal NGOs in many countries. But in recent years, especially in developing countries, governments and donors have become more active in their support for non-governmental provision of basic services. A number of problems associated with such efforts, including the difficult process of moving to large scale, and the attrition of volunteer workers, have already been discussed, and some solutions have been suggested. Some other, related issues still need to be addressed, however, including the decentralized enforcement of quality standards, and the reconciliation of often differing community and government objectives and understandings of rights-related claims.

□ 4.3. SERVICE MANAGEMENT

Both at the central level in political mobilization and regulation and at the local level in operational administration, 'management' has traditionally been the province of government — yet it has rarely been addressed as a priority concern in the social sectors. In the health sector, for example, the typical lack of clear and enforced regulations has led to deterioration in the quality of services and the proliferation of drugs and health care providers that do not contribute to improved health. It has similarly led to the deterioration of water quality and the environment, and to the depletion of water sources in many countries, as the enforcement of even weak standards was precluded by the lack of trained personnel and effective legal procedures. In all of the social sectors, information and reporting systems have been traditionally weak, reinforcing a lack of knowledge about actual needs and service availability, and a lack of accountability of providers and officials to the populations served.

With the changes in the financing and provision of services that have been described has come growing attention to the importance of the management function. Public and political attention to social concerns in the context of scarce resources has led to increased mobilization of the population and of the government to ensure that basic needs are met. As more actors participate in the provision of services, and consumers more actively seek to make better choices, the need for improved and timely information has been recognized, and monitoring and reporting systems have been established or upgraded. Likewise, professional and service standards have been raised in many cases, and training and budgets have been increased for enforcing them, although this process is frequently slow.

These efforts have been accelerated by initiatives to decentralize management responsibility and accountability, and to increase the knowledge and power of communities in the management process. While the many complexities of decentralization are well known, in the social sectors particularly the assignment of budgetary authority, and often greater control over revenues, to provincial and municipal levels is a key step in improving the responsiveness of public and private services alike to those who use them. At the community level, improved information and the power and means to make use of it has been recognized as a central element, and not just in increasing the range and effectiveness of actions for nutrition, education, health and child development, as outlined in other chapters of this book. More importantly, it represents the linkage of often abstract concepts of 'rights' to the daily lives of communities and households, a point developed more fully by Jonsson in Chapter Five.

□ 4.4. CHANGING ROLES AND RELATIONSHIPS: THREE MODELS

In conclusion, it may be useful to identify schematically three 'models' of the economic organization of services for children, characterized largely by changes that have occurred over the past three decades in most developing countries.

The first model, prevalent following independence in many former colonies and continuing through the 1970s, emphasized strong central government involvement in the financing and provision of services. Yet coverage, both financial and in terms of physical access, was usually limited, as was the quality of many of the services provided. The private and NGO sectors were not well organized, but often filled key gaps left by the public system. Similarly, the involvement of communities and households was not well organized, and not heavily promoted by government beyond the expectation that households would pay costs and meet their own needs as required. The management function was generally not well implemented by any of the actors. Government plans, regulations and information systems existed largely on paper; and where they were in place, they frequently did not function to promote accountability and system improvement. Mobilization for basic services, at either the political or social level, was often particularly lacking.

A second approach arose in many countries during the 1980s through a combination of technical improvements in the implementation of social development actions, and a decline in the economic base of governments and of many societies as a whole. The scope of the formal economy and modern culture continued to expand, increasing the expectations of, and the claims made on, public-sector programmes in health, education and other social sectors. The capacity of governments to respond to these claims did not grow commensurately, however, because of limitations of infrastructure, of political support in many cases, and of discretionary economic resources in nearly all countries. Economic adjustment programmes were instituted in nearly all countries, either at the insistence of international financial institutions or other external bodies, or internally. Under their provisions, budget deficits were to be reduced, the scope of government action was cut back, and enlarged roles were given to the private sector in fields of traditional government involvement.

As a result of these trends, responsibility for the financing of services was increasingly passed on to communities and households, at times through specific policies and at times by default. Public-sector provision of services also weakened in most countries, and although governments remained the principal provider of education and of basic health care in most countries, the private sector, including NGOs and 'non-traditional' actors, played an increasing role in service delivery. At the same time, the management function was being strengthened in many countries with improved information systems and better knowledge of population needs. Yet, in the usual absence of comprehensive policies for private-sector involvement or for decentralization of government functions, overall efficiency and equity often could not be greatly improved.

Many developing countries remain within the framework of this second, transitional model. However, in some countries and on a limited basis in many others, a third emerging organization of roles and relationships may be identified, which holds the potential for a more effective response to rights concerns. In this model, the role of government is more clearly defined and focused, to include:

(a) responsibility for mobilizing sufficient economic and political resources for satisfying minimum needs;
(b) the financing of a minimum standard of social services;
(c) provision of education, information and management support to the social sectors as a whole, with enforcement of regulations for minimum standards; and
(d) facilitation of decentralized responsibility to plan and implement social actions.

The private and NGO sectors, in turn, play an increased role in service provision, but one that is bounded by norms and standards set either at the central or local level. Communities are gaining, though often on a slow and uncertain basis, an increased voice and responsibility for articulating their

needs and mobilizing services and local resources to ensure that their needs are met. The role of the international community and aid donors is not diminished in this model, but it is also being redefined and focused for:
(a) providing critical resources required for service provision, particularly for populations in greatest need;
(b) building the 'stocks' of human and organizational resources needed for sustainable progress by countries themselves, and for the capacity of future generations to draw upon; and
(c) promoting, through dialogue and actions, development processes that expand the definition of rights and the willingness and ability of people and governments to implement them.

This 'model' is not new in a strict sense; its elements have been identified in different contexts for some time, and it reflects development programme designs that have applied in many settings. What is a more recent and still-ongoing process is the linking of these components within a coherent theory of development, based on the central concept of rights, as articulated by Dasgupta[18] and others. In such a framework, a broadened understanding of resources and their implications for the fulfilment of child rights is a necessary step in the design and implementation of actions to make these rights a reality.

Notes

1 Insofar as all resources have 'value', human and organizational resources should of course be considered 'economic' as well. The latter term is used here to refer only to financial and material resources, however, both because of the conventional interpretation that financial and material activities form the 'economic' sphere of activity, and because of the lack of a clearer terminology.
2 Perhaps most important in this regard are the concepts of 'entitlements' and 'capabilities', used by Amartya Sen and others to address problems of famine and hunger. As defined by Drèze and Sen, 1989, "entitlements [are] the set of alternative bundles of commodities over which a person can establish ... command". They thus represent an individual's rights to exchange and consume under "prevailing legal, political, and economic arrangements", based on initial endowments and what can be acquired through exchange (pp. 9-10). Entitlements are concerned primarily with "economic" resources, while "capabilities" represent the total of what people are able to "do and be" (p. 12), and as such reflect the role of human and organizational resources in social production, as discussed more fully later in this chapter.
3 This perspective corresponds closely with the principle of 'sustainable development', which, as articulated by the World Commission on Environment and Development (the Brundtland Commission), refers to development action that "meets the needs of the present without compromising the ability of future generations to meet their own needs". See World Commission on Environment and Development, 1987, p. 8.
4 In economics this is referred to as the 'production function', which specifies in mathematical terms the way in which quantities of different resources are combined to achieve an output.
5 Stewart, 1989.
6 Dasgupta, 1993. In this major work, Dasgupta examines the failure of resource-allocation theories and processes to address basic (physiological) needs and the related social and economic problem of destitution. Dasgupta proposes a revised structure of social objectives and relationships, based on a social contract under which the State serves as explicit guarantor that these basic needs are met as a right. Implications of the analysis include a central role for basic needs policies in the achievement of economic growth, and a resource allocation process that incorporates resource decisions made by governments, the private sector, communities and households. It is unfortunately beyond the scope of this paper to examine each of these issues in detail.

7 In the case of the economic resource of *information*, for example, the quality of the information used for specific purposes clearly depends on the knowledge and experience (both human resources) available to be organized and applied, and on the actual process of thinking.
8 As an approach to securing adequate resources for social development, '20/20' was introduced in 1992 (United Nations Children's Fund, 1992c), drawing on ideas contained in the United Nations Development Programme, *Human Development Report 1991*. See also Parker and Jespersen, 1992; and United Nations Development Programme et al., 1994.
9 Brenzel, 1991.
10 Behrman, 1992.
11 Put another way, as the value of such 'non-traditional' human and organizational resources is enhanced and recognized through their mobilization for a purpose, either their initial motivation declines, or there is a movement towards their becoming 'economic' resources for which a market price must be paid. Thus, community health workers seek to be paid higher wages or to join the formal service sector in government employment.
12 The *gramadana* workers, originally volunteers, have been paid increasing amounts, in the form of expense allowances and incentives, to reduce attrition. They support the efforts of village-level workers who carry out the pre-school programme and other local development actions.
13 Sarvodaya Shramadana Movement, 1988.
14 Rohde, 1993; Sepúlveda, 1994.
15 Identifying and relieving such constraints forms the basis of a number of economic planning techniques. In cost-benefit analysis, for example, the enhanced value of critical foreign exchange inputs is accounted for by assigning 'shadow prices' to goods that must be purchased internationally. In this process, a weight is given that reflects a value higher than nominal or market prices, accounting for real scarcity value.
16 World Bank, 1993.
17 World Health Organization, 1991.
18 Dasgupta, 1993.

Realizing rights through national programmes of action for children

Robert J. Ledogar

1. Introduction

Now that the Convention on the Rights of the Child (CRC) has been ratified by so many countries (170 by March 1995), the greatest challenge is that of implementation.

'Implementation', in the context of the CRC, is a rather weak word for assuring that children get what the CRC says they should get and not have happen to them, or be deprived of, what it says should not. As this is a legal instrument, one should really be talking about 'enforcement';[1] but how does a State enforce a child's right to health, education and an adequate standard of living when it does not have the resources to do so? Because of this difficulty, Article 4 of the CRC says that "in regard to economic, social and cultural rights, States Parties shall undertake such measures to the maximum extent of their available resources and, where needed, within the framework of international co-operation". This could become an escape clause for poor countries. The issue is how to avoid the escape, via this clause, of too many and too much. How to make States Parties accountable for dedicating their available resources, and the aid they receive from international sources, to the implementation of child rights "to the maximum extent"?

One way to make States Parties to the CRC accountable is for the States themselves to set time-bound objectives, with corresponding strategies, programmes, budgets and measurement mechanisms for assuring a minimum set of children's rights. It is difficult to conceive of an instrument with greater potential for this purpose than the National Programme of Action (NPA) for Children, adopted by countries as part of the commitments they made at the World Summit for Children.

2. The World Summit for Children

"We will work to promote earliest possible ratification and implementation of the Convention on the Rights of the Child", said the Heads of State in the World Declaration on the Survival, Protection and Development of Children, and indeed the speed with which ratification of the CRC has occurred is due in no small measure to the momentum generated at the highest levels by the World Summit for Children. The Plan of Action for implementing this World Declaration called on all governments to prepare NPAs to implement the commitments undertaken at the Summit, including a set of goals for the year 2000, which correspond to many of the rights in the CRC (see Table 3.1).

Article 34 of the Plan of Action spells out in some detail what these NPAs are to contain:

- Each country is encouraged to re-examine its national plans, programmes and policies to see how it might accord higher priority to programmes for children and for meeting the major goals;
- Each country is urged to re-examine its current national budget "to ensure that programmes aimed at the achievement of goals for the survival, protection and development of children will have priority when resources are allocated. Every effort should be made to ensure that such programmes are protected in times of economic austerity and structural adjustments";
- "Families, communities, local governments, NGOs, social, cultural, religious, business and other institutions, including the mass media, are encouraged to play an active role" in this process;
- "Each country should establish appropriate monitoring mechanisms for the regular and timely collection, analysis and publication of data required to monitor relevant social indicators relating to the well-being of children ..."; and
- Governments, industry and academic institutions are requested to increase their efforts in both basic and operational research in areas related to child welfare, including more effective social mobilization, better delivery of existing social services, early child development, basic education, hygiene and sanitation and "in coping with the trauma facing children who are uprooted from their families and face other particularly difficult circumstances".

NPAs are the chief instrument for assuring that the commitments made at the World Summit will be kept and followed up. And it may be argued that they are potentially powerful instruments for social policy and strategic social planning in the 1990s.

Some 85 countries have finalized NPAs to date, 30 or so have drafts in circulation and another 30 are in some state of the preparation process. Some NPAs are rather broad general statements of goals, policies and strategies, but a good number are quite detailed documents with programmes and projects and estimates of the resources necessary to achieve their goals. In countries

Table 3.1 **- Correspondence between major goals endorsed by the World Summit for Children and provisions of the Convention on the Rights of the Child**

Major WSC goals	Right	CRC reference
1. Infant and child mortality reduction	Right to life	6
	Right to health	24
2. Maternal mortality reduction	Right to health	24.2.d
		24.2.f
3. Reduction of malnutrition	Right to health	24.2.c
	Right to standard of living	27
4. Universal access to clean water and sanitation	Right to health and environmental sanitation	24.2.c, e
5. Universal access to basic education and completion of primary education	Right to education	28, 29, 32
6. Reduction of adult illiteracy	Right to education	24.2e, f
		28
7. Improved protection of children in especially difficult circumstances	Right to protection from:	
	- violence, abuse, neglect	19
	- economic exploitation	32
	- drug abuse	33
	- sexual abuse	34
	- traffic, sale, abduction	35
	- all other exploitation	36
	- torture, death penalty, life imprisonment	37
	Right to special protection if:	
	- refugee or asylum-seeker	22
	- disabled	23
	- affected by war	38
	Right to special protection and assistance if deprived of family environment	20, 21
	Right to periodic review if placed for care, protection or treatment	25
	Right to recovery and reintegration if victim of abuse or exploitation	39
	Right to be treated with dignity and worth if in conflict with the law	40

where national development planning is taken seriously, the NPA is typically incorporated into, or otherwise harmonized with, that Plan.

■ 3. The NPA: An Instrument for Implementing Child Rights

The typical NPA follows the guidelines of the Plan of Action's Article 34: it sets goals for the decade, outlines the principal strategies and programmes for achieving them, defines institutional responsibilities, examines the costs of individual programmes and ways of financing them, and establishes indicators and mechanisms for monitoring progress towards the goals.

☐ 3.1. GOALS

By setting concrete goals to be achieved by the end of the 1990s and, in many cases, intermediate goals for the middle of the decade, NPAs define, as it were, their own 'minimum obligations' towards those portions of the CRC with which they might claim an inability to comply for lack of resources. Of course, this does not close the escape hatch provided by Article 4. Most NPAs of developing countries assume that external aid will be available to achieve their goals. If that aid is not forthcoming, they may legitimately claim inability to reach the specific target. However, NPAs that contain cost estimates for achieving the goals — some 60 so far — usually indicate the resources expected to be available nationally in order to identify the amounts needed from external sources. In addition to laying an early 'claim' for child rights activities on whatever external resources do become available, the very fact of quantifying the gap makes it possible to identify how far the country could be expected to advance towards that minimum in the absence of all or part of the external support. Even where specific costing is absent or incomplete, the fact that goals are set provides advocacy groups with a point of reference for holding the authorities to their promises.

The goals of individual countries may not be exactly those endorsed by the World Summit for Children. The global goals are, in the words of the Plan of Action, "to be adapted to the specific realities of each country in terms of phasing, priorities, standards and availability of resources". The national goals identified in the NPAs vary considerably from the global targets in a number of countries. In higher-income developing countries such as Argentina, Thailand and Tunisia, the goals are often more ambitious. In the Least Developed Countries such as Mali, Niger and Rwanda, on the other hand, the goals are understandably less so. The targets for coverage of clean water supply and sanitation are less than 100 per cent in most NPAs, even in some of the better-off countries. But the global goals are useful for prodding countries that could reasonably aim higher to do so, and as a tool for stimulating competition among States to show progress when 'league tables' for each of the goals are published and disseminated.

Since weakness in human rights fulfilment so often goes hand in hand with poverty, and since Article 27 of the CRC stipulates the rights of every child to an adequate standard of living, it is of interest how often the NPAs widen the focus of their 'social goals' to encompass specific poverty reduction measures. Burkina Faso, Mauritania, Tunisia, Egypt, Costa Rica, Bolivia, Peru and Colombia are among the countries in this category. Nepal's NPA includes credit schemes and income-generating projects. Fifty per cent of proposed resources for Panama's NPA are earmarked for community development and income-generation projects in identified poor areas. Increased agricultural production is included by Cuba and Paraguay, and household food security by a number of countries including, for example, Botswana. Many NPAs specify measures to improve the status and situation of women, and poverty reduction activities are part of these, as in Bangladesh where skills development, credit schemes and other income-generating activities are part of the package.

Child rights supporters may regret that all of the 'protection rights' of the CRC are subsumed at the global level under the very vague goal of "improved protection of children in especially difficult circumstances", but individual NPAs are often more specific about their protection targets. China has set the objective of ensuring that by 1995 all provinces, regions and prefectures formulate their own legal codes in accordance with the national law for juvenile protection and the principles of the CRC. Thailand plans for coverage of family welfare services to reach 25 per cent of low-income families by 1996 and 50 per cent by the year 2000. Jordan's NPA calls for increases in the coverage of services for disabled children by specific percentages for each category of disability. Similarly, Cameroon plans to increase functional education for disabled children from the current 30 per cent to 100 per cent by the year 2000.

Colombia has set a goal of eliminating the phenomenon of children living on the streets by the year 2000, with an intermediary goal of reducing its prevalence by 40 per cent by 1994. Guatemala has set a similar goal. The Philippines plans by the end of the decade to place 70 per cent of abandoned children legally free for adoption. Swaziland intends to increase the number of foster families by 50 per cent before the end of 1995 and 100 per cent by the year 2000. Vietnam's goals in this area are that 70 per cent of orphans without foster care will be taken care of by their relatives or adoptive parents, or at special centres providing the basic facilities of family life, by 1995; and that 70 per cent of disabled children will have access to medical check-ups, treatment and physical therapy by the year 2000. Cuba's goal for the year 2000 is that 100 per cent of children with behavioural problems will receive corrective and special educational services. Nepal has a target of setting up special centres for vocational and job-oriented skill training for working children in each of the 14 Zones of the country. The Republic of Korea plans to build 3,240 new cost-free day-care facilities for under-five children of low-income families by 1995. Portugal plans to add to its criminal code new and heavier penalties for sexual exploitation and abuse of children.

Of 105 NPAs reviewed in April 1993, 47 have programmes to deal with child abuse, 26 with child neglect, 21 with exploitation, 18 with prostitution and/or trafficking. Belize will set up a child abuse/neglect hot line, whereas Australia plans special measures to protect institutionalized aboriginal children at risk of abuse. The NPA of Laos includes a programme to deal with the exploitation of children in border regions where many are sold into prostitution. Improved conditions in institutions are also included in the NPAs of at least 19 countries. Ghana and Equatorial Guinea plan specific programmes against female genital mutilation. Legislation reforms are part of many NPAs. These have to do with child labour (20 countries); child abuse, neglect and exploitation (20 countries); and disability (25 countries).

□ 3.2. STRATEGIES

NPAs might best be looked upon as exercises in strategic planning. Strategic planning is a tool of modern management, first developed in the profit-making sector but increasingly used in the social sphere, which can be of considerable importance for the implementation of child rights. Strategic planning has made it legitimate to talk of a leader's and an organization's 'vision', a force that points beyond classical planning's elaboration of how to get from here to there with the means at hand. More comfortable than classic planning with goals that are unlikely to be achieved in a business-as-usual scenario, strategic planning takes a longer-range perspective and includes the consideration of ways to obtain the means that may be missing at the start. It pays more attention to the surrounding environment and looks for ways to shift the forces that constrain the realization of the vision and limit access to resources, identifying all those forces that might have a 'stake' in the realization of its goals and ways to enlist those 'stakeholders' into the effort to achieve them. Strategic planning is a political as well as a technical instrument.[2]

The NPAs of Costa Rica and Honduras are among those that include strategies for the mobilization of resources for social programmes. Components of these strategies include reallocation of existing resources within the social sectors themselves and between sectors, an increased share of the government budget for social programmes, privatization of some government institutions, debt-relief initiatives and a more effective and improved targeting of social programmes. The longest chapter in the NPA of Bangladesh concerns a communication strategy. One of the three main objectives of this strategy is to implement the CRC and programmes protecting children in difficult circumstances. The strategy details the various agents and partners to be enlisted in the cause, how communication will be monitored and the communication strategies for each of the major sectors. Nepal's NPA strategies include mobilizing partnerships for children, decentralization, multisectoral linkages, competence in implementation and management, growth with equity and poverty alleviation, social stability and the democratization of society.

□ 3.3. ORGANIZATIONAL MECHANISMS AND RESPONSIBILITIES

NPAs bring important organizational resources to bear on the implementation of child rights. They assign responsibilities for getting the job done and establish (or confirm where they already exist) mechanisms for coordination, without which the job usually cannot get done. Djibouti's NPA includes the text of a law instituting an interministerial follow-up committee to the World Summit for Children under the presidency of the Prime Minister. Among the specific responsibilities of this committee is the implementation of the CRC. Other examples of new mechanisms are a National Council for Child Welfare directly under the Head of State in the Sudan; an NPA Standing Committee in Namibia, with representation from all the ministries involved in preparing the NPA, which meets quarterly to monitor progress and solve implementation problems; a new unit for global social policy within the Planning Ministry of Bolivia; a Child Rights Ombudsman in Belgium and Djibouti; a policy-making body for the NPA in the Dominican Republic consisting of representatives of 13 governmental institutions together with representatives of NGOs and the churches; and in Uganda, a National Council for Children, with representatives from government, local and international NGOs, religious institutions, donors and involved members of the community charged with monitoring implementation of the NPA and supporting district plans of action. In Chile, a number of organizations including the National Support Group for the Convention on the Right of the Child assumed responsibility for disseminating knowledge of the NPA.

Burkina Faso's NPA is the first plan to be drafted by the collaborative effort of all government departments, international organizations and NGOs. Equatorial Guinea's is the country's first complete effort to define a comprehensive social development strategy. In Guatemala and Uruguay, the NPA provides the occasion for strengthening the concept of a 'Social Cabinet' in which the heads of ministries in the social sector meet regularly with the head of the planning and budgeting apparatus for the purposes of coordinating strategies and monitoring systems. In India, Egypt and several other countries, NPAs provided the occasion for incorporating a special chapter on children into the country's National Development Plan.

□ 3.4. COSTS AND FINANCING

While not all NPAs have attempted to estimate the costs of achieving their goals and objectives, some 60 of them have done so, and some plan to do so at a later stage. Costing has several advantages. One, as already mentioned, is that it makes evident what the country can do even in the absence of all hoped-for foreign assistance. Another is that good cost analysis makes it possible to review how resources are currently being spent, and to make such a review public. Costing is an index of the plan's seriousness; it confronts hope and ambition with the reality of available and expected resources, introducing considerations of efficiency and equity into the revisions that become necessary.

Cost estimation is the first step towards planning how the NPA will be financed. Once total costs are estimated and annualized, it is possible to compare them with the amount of resources existing or expected to become available. The difference remaining is the resource gap. Ways of filling the gap can then be considered.

Budget reallocations to increase the proportion devoted to the social sectors is the most important of these ways. Bhutan's NPA projects increases from 8.3 to 11.2 per cent of the budget for education, and from 4.3 to 6.7 per cent for health, during the period 1991-1997. Chile has earmarked $700 million, in addition to its current annual social-sector budget of $6 billion, for financing the NPA during the period 1993-2000. Senegal plans to increase the health sector's share of its budget from its current 4.8 per cent to 9 per cent by the year

2000. Egypt plans to increase social-sector investment from 23 per cent in the 1980s to 30 per cent in the first half of the 1990s and has assigned 7.5 per cent of the government-sector budget for 1992-1997 to NPA activities. Guatemala's NPA planned to increase spending in education, health, social services and nutrition from 2.7 per cent of gross national product (GNP) and 23.6 per cent of the national budget in 1990 to 4.5 and 33.5 per cent respectively by 1996, and corresponding increases have taken place in that country's 1992 and 1993 budgets. Reductions in expenditure on armaments are specifically mentioned in the NPAs of Namibia and Zimbabwe. (Benin's NPA also discusses the role of the military, but opts for involving the army more in national development rather than reducing its size.)

Mexico has made the NPA a centre-piece of its reinvestment in the social sector after the steep decline during the period of adjustment in the 1980s. From a low of 8 per cent of gross domestic product (GDP) in 1989, social-sector investment increased to nearly 10 per cent in 1993. Social expenditure per child nearly doubled during this period, the fastest-growing sector being the one called 'children in especially difficult circumstances', comprising programmes for street children, working children, children with disabilities, abused and substance-abusing children, and children in conflict with the law.

Some NPAs discuss ways to increase domestic revenues such as increasing the tax base (Kenya), social taxes on luxury imports (Nepal), 'sin' taxes on tobacco and alcohol (Benin), a special levy on tourists (Maldives), tax benefits to private enterprise in exchange for support to public schools (Uruguay), a national lottery (Barbados), and proceeds from privatization (Venezuela, Pakistan). Algeria created a 10 per cent tax on water connections for use in water purification and waste disposal schemes aimed at reducing diarrhoea in accordance with that country's NPA. A number of countries that underwent structural adjustment in the 1980s, especially in Latin America, created special social investment funds as a means of providing safety nets for the most vulnerable. Such funds are identified as resources for partial financing of NPAs in Mexico, Bolivia and Uruguay, for example. Guatemala has established five different funds for 'social compensation': a land fund, a housing fund, a popular credit fund, a peace fund and a social investment fund, with financial backing from the World Bank.

A number of NPAs identify cost-recovery mechanisms involving various types of user charges as a way of breaching the resource gap. From a human rights perspective these can be seen as potentially exclusionary, and it is not clear in all cases that they are not. In aggregate terms, people are probably paying less for essential drugs, clean water, education, and so on, under intelligently organized and run cost-recovery schemes than they were before such schemes were organized. Some of the most vulnerable, however, can be excluded by such schemes if special measures are not taken to include them. NPAs are weakest in analysing what their cost implications might be for households and communities. With the notable exception of Uganda, few NPAs analyse in any detail what the achievement of the goals is likely to demand of households and communities. This is an area in which it would be especially beneficial for groups concerned with human rights to participate in the NPA process.

The resource gap is frequently calculated after including current levels of external aid as 'existing'. This means that the portion of the resource gap that is to be financed externally represents an increase over current aid levels. In the present economic and political climate of the industrialized nations, large increases in official development assistance (ODA) seem more and more unlikely as economic recession leaves little room for other than domestic claims on the peace dividend. A restructuring of ODA is therefore the best hope for filling the external portion of the resource gap. The percentage of ODA allocated to basic human needs (nutrition, water, sanitation, primary health care, primary education and family planning) has been the subject of intensive scrutiny since the World Summit for Children. UNDP's *Human Development Report 1992* and UNICEF's *State of the World's Children 1993* have published figures indicating that less than 10 per cent of bilateral aid is allocated to such purposes. There are, however, many problems of definition and international comparability associated with these estimates. UNICEF and UNDP have submitted to bilateral donors a framework for improved reporting on social-sector aid flows. Meetings among agencies interested in aid reporting continue. UNDP and UNICEF are urging that the percentage of aid for basic human needs be increased to 20 per cent and that developing-country governments' budget allocations to these same sectors reach a similar percentage. If ODA and national budgetary allocations were restructured to meet this 20/20 formula, the major portion of the additional financial resources needed to reach the goals of the NPAs would be guaranteed. This advocacy effort is one in which the human rights community has a real stake.

Worth noting in this connection are reports from Scandinavian countries on follow-up to the World Summit for Children indicating that the promotion of the CRC will be an important criterion in decisions concerning allocations of aid to developing countries. The Netherlands reports that 'children in especially difficult circumstances' became a special budget item in Dutch development cooperation beginning in 1993.

☐ 3.5. MONITORING

One of the most hoped-for dividends of the NPA process is the improvement in national systems and capacities for monitoring progress towards child survival, development and protection goals. Measuring progress is necessary for good strategic management of the programmes themselves, but the production of reliable and timely data, properly disaggregated to reveal regional, ethnic, gender, age and other disparities, can, if appropriately packaged and disseminated, become a powerful tool for mobilizing political and public opinion in favour of NPA objectives. In more than a dozen NPAs, studies to determine the nature and extent of the problems of children in especially difficult circumstances are among the first steps planned.

In Indonesia, the Ministry for People's Welfare, responsible for coordinating the NPA, is developing a composite Child Welfare Indicator aimed at identifying disparities among regions of the country. Thailand's Basic Minimum Needs Surveys are being expanded to be more inclusive of the NPA goals. Morocco plans to move from monitoring of individual projects towards a centralized national monitoring system which, while not superseding existing monitoring systems within ministries, will pull together and synthesize data on progress in the situation of children. In Tunisia, the monitoring mechanisms to be set up at national, regional and local levels will be supervised by multisectoral commissions involving some prominent independent figures. A cost-effective survey methodology known as Sentinel Community Surveillance is mentioned as a measurement approach in the NPAs of Rwanda and Zimbabwe. Kenya plans to link national monitoring systems with community-based approaches. Tanzania's national monitoring system will draw data from national household surveys as well as administrative sources while improving methodologies used by the latter.

There are, of course, certain rights in the CRC that will be more difficult than others to monitor. Among these are freedom from all forms of sexual exploitation, protection against abduction and trafficking, freedom from torture and deprivation of liberty and exemption from military service below the age of 15 years. Since NPAs are official documents, it is likely that the monitoring on these subjects will tend to be weakest in those countries where the problems are greatest. Nevertheless, the NPAs reviewed thus far show a willingness to tackle some of the most difficult areas of child protection and, to the degree that these areas are included in the NPA, monitoring of them is, in principle, officially sanctioned.

■ 4. Are NPAs Affordable?

In an absolute sense, considering what the nations of the world — and even the developing countries themselves — spend on armaments, there is no question that NPAs are affordable. One must ask this question, however, within the context of the political and social realities likely to prevail during the current decade. NPAs come with a wide variety of price tags. Some indeed read like shopping lists, and there is no doubt that obtaining more foreign aid is one of the motivations behind their preparation. But it is appropriate for most developing countries to include a proportion of external support in their planning and budgeting processes. The important question is: How realistic are they?

As noted earlier, some 60 NPAs contain estimates of their total costs. As might be expected, not all countries use exactly the same methods of cost estimation. For the most part, the estimates given are for costs that are additional to current levels of expenditure; but that is not clear in all cases. While these limitations must be kept in mind, some observations concerning orders of magnitude are still valid. When analysed in terms of either costs per capita or total costs as a percentage of GNP, the cost estimates of the NPAs appear quite reasonable.

The per capita weighted average of the estimated costs for these 60 NPAs is $15. This is the same per capita cost as the Organization of African Unity and UNICEF estimated, using a process independent of the NPAs themselves, as required for reaching the goals in all of Africa.

As for percentage of GNP, UNDP's *Human Development Report 1991* analysed human expenditure for 25 countries, covering 74 per cent of the developing world and found their human expenditure ratio to be slightly less than 3 per cent of GNP. That report argues that "the human expenditure ratio may need to be around 5 per cent if a country wishes to do well in human development". Thus, an additional 2 per cent of GNP is a reasonable amount to expect countries to devote to basic education, primary health care, water, sanitation, nutrition and family planning. The average annual cost of the 60 NPAs analysed is 2 per cent of their weighted average GNP.

The largest proportion of estimated costs in NPAs is for education (39 per cent), followed by health (23 per cent) and water and sanitation (17 per cent). Because nutrition is included in the health sector of many NPAs, separate nutrition programmes account for only 3 per cent of total costing, whereas the category of 'children in especially difficult circumstances' receives 7 per cent. The remaining 11 per cent is for costs of programmes that do not fit into any of the previous sectors.

■ 5. The Degree of National Commitment to NPAs

The promises of politicians classically compel little faith, but in the era of easily retrievable video and newspaper clips, politicians are becoming somewhat more careful about what they promise. Clearly the degree of national commitment among the 71 heads of state who signed the World Summit Declaration was variable from the start, and any assessment of it is further complicated by changes in regimes as the decade progresses. Many factors enter into a determination on this issue, such as the nature of the regime and the political character of the country, the degree of commitment of the current head of state and other key leaders of the country, the extent to which the country as a society was involved in the preparation of the NPA and participates in its implementation, the degree to which the NPA is integrated into national planning and budgeting processes, and so on.

Where NPA preparation and/or implementation has been a highly public and broadly participatory process involving many sectors of society, the likelihood of enduring national commitment to it is obviously strongest. The commission responsible for NPA implementation in the Dominican Republic has representation from 125 NGOs. In Tanzania, specially convened 'summits' of the legislatures, on both the mainland and in Zanzibar, were held in 1991 to approve the bases on which the NPA was drafted. Costa Rica's NPA was approved by the country's Legislative Assembly. In the Republic of Korea, a National Council on Children and Youth, composed of government and NGO representatives, has been established to monitor implementation of the NPA. In a number of Latin American countries, the Catholic Church is a specific partner in the NPA implementation and monitoring process. In Brazil, the 'Pact for Children' brings together both the legislative and executive branches of government, the National Council of Brazilian Bishops, the Governors of the 27 States and the most important organizations of civil society. The involvement of NGOs in preparation and implementation is made explicit in the NPAs of such diverse countries as Botswana, El Salvador, Malawi, Morocco and Uganda.

The personal commitment of heads of state or government is an important factor in assuring that the NPA receives the attention it deserves from the various sectors within a country. In Mexico, President Salinas de Gortari, one of the six conveners of the World Summit for Children, has participated fully in the NPA process, holding periodic meetings in the Presidential Palace to review progress towards the NPA goals. At the third such meeting, in October 1992, he received detailed reports on progress in each sector and committed his country to the preparation of programmes of action for the country's most important cities. The Office of the President or Prime Minister has assumed overall responsibility for both preparation and implementation of the NPA in a number of countries. First Ladies have been personally involved in several Latin American and Caribbean countries.

National preparations for the World Summit for Children took place in Nepal during the transition from monarchy to multi-party democracy. Government, NGOs, professional associations, popular groups and the private sector were all deeply involved. Issues such as health, education and water supply became symbolic of the Government's responsibility to the people. It is in this atmosphere that the NPA was prepared and the CRC was ratified. Such broad participation of national society has not, of course, been the case in all countries, but the potential for broadening the base of support for NPAs still exists even where the original document was mainly prepared by technocrats.

Some generalizations can be made about national commitment by categories of countries. Developing countries as a group have taken the commitment to prepare NPAs more seriously than have the Western industrialized democracies. The latter, with some notable exceptions — namely Canada and the United States, which both have specific goals for their own children by the year 2000 — have tended to submit reports on what they are currently doing for children, both domestically and in their foreign aid programmes, rather than programmes of action for achieving certain goals by the end of the decade.

It is in the area of child rights, however, that the industrialized countries have been most specific and forward-looking. Canada's NPA includes programmes for the prevention of child abuse and the support of aboriginal communities. Finland has set goals of extending day-care places to all children under school age by 1995, providing housing at reasonable prices for families with children, and establishing special measures to ensure children's rights in family break-up situations. Germany's document mentions programmes for the integration of young settlers and refugees and a draft bill "for improvement in the presently inadequate legal protection of foreign children against abuse by sex tourists". The Netherlands describes current problems and programmes to deal with the special problems of minority children, child abuse, trafficking in children, child prostitution and child pornography. Norway looks forward to new conciliation procedures in connection with divorces and improved welfare services for children from various cultural backgrounds. Spain's still-to-be-completed NPA is being preceded by special studies on child abuse, day care, family relations and the effect of mass media on children. The United Kingdom identifies reduction of drug abuse by parents and programmes for children with special educational needs among areas for further progress. The NPA of the United States, made public at the very end of the Bush administration, which refused to sign the CRC, has a very detailed set of goals which includes, for example, "reverse to less than 25.2 per 1,000 children the rising incidence of maltreatment of children younger than age 18 (baseline 25.2 per 1,000 in 1986)".

It is in the developing countries, however, that the implementation of children's rights has the farthest distance to cover. Some indicators for judging the seriousness of national commitment to the process are:

- *the degree to which the top leadership of the country is publicly identified with the process*. Mexico's President Salinas de Gortari, as already mentioned, presides personally over the periodic review of his country's NPA implementation. In the Dominican Republic, there is a 'Summit Office' ('Summit' referring to the World Summit for Children) located within the office of the Vice-President;
- *the decentralization of the process to provincial and local levels*. The governors of 24 Brazilian States committed themselves to prepare state plans of action and to implement systems to monitor the situation of the child. In a recent ceremony, these same governors presented their plans to the President for incorporation into Brazil's NPA. Other countries, especially in Latin America, are well advanced in the decentralization process. Municipalities such as the Federal District of Mexico and the cities of Khulna and Rajshahi in Bangladesh have also prepared their own action plans;
- *the involvement of NGOs and other elements of civil society in the process*. Several examples of NGO involvement have already been mentioned; and
- *the incorporation of the NPA into national development planning and its translation into the regular national budgeting process through annual or biennial action plans*. This is especially a key issue where such planning is politically and economically important, such as in Indonesia, India and China.

NPAs can survive changes in regime — and some, as in the case of Ecuador, Mali, Peru and Turkey, have already done so. In 1993, the Government of Trinidad revised the NPA it adopted in 1992 in response to a new analysis of the situation of children in the country.

The countries of Central and Eastern Europe and the former Soviet Union form another special category. Rapid political and economic transitions have tended to put commitments made at the World Summit for Children fairly low on their lists of priorities, even for countries that were represented there by their current heads of state. But the argument can be made, and is indeed being made by UNICEF at least, that it is especially necessary during the kind of transition that these countries are undergoing to make provision for the survival, development and protection of children, and the NPA could be an excellent instrument for doing so.

In all these cases, there is a need to build and maintain public pressure for the preparation, completion and implementation of NPAs. The NPA is a process rather than a document. It can start well and falter later on. It can start poorly, but take on new life as circumstances change. But such changes are not simply matters of chance. Where all sectors of society are involved in the process, as both participants and watchdogs, the process is more likely to contribute to the achievement of a minimum core of children's rights by the end of this century or soon thereafter.

Support for this process from the human rights community around the world will be very important, and in some cases crucial.

Notes

This chapter is a slightly edited version of an article that appeared in *The International Journal of Children's Rights*, Vol. 1, No. 3, 1993, pp. 377-391, under the title of 'Implementing the Convention on the Rights of the Child Through National Programmes of Action for Children', © 1993 Kluwer Academic Publishers. Used by permission of the publisher.

1 Portions of this chapter draw upon research done by Kekelwa Nyawa Dall, consultant, and data analysis carried out by Gweneth Edward-Jenkins of UNICEF. On the concept of enforcement of economic, social and cultural rights, see Himes, 1993.

2 Bryson, 1988; Bryson and Einsweiler, 1988; Ginter and Duncan, 1990; Kemp, 1992; Wilson, 1992.

Children's right to survival and healthy development

David Parker and Claudio Sepúlveda

1. Health as a Right

'Health', defined in the World Health Organization (WHO) constitution as "a state of complete physical, mental and social well-being", has over time become strongly associated with medical perspectives and interventions. There is, however, general awareness that, perhaps especially in the developing world, rights to health must be addressed through a broad range of actions for health knowledge, health promotion and services.

1.1. THE HEALTH PROVISIONS OF THE CONVENTION ON THE RIGHTS OF THE CHILD (CRC)

Article 24 of the CRC is devoted to the health rights of children. The key provisions of the article reflect a broad-based definition of health, establishing the overall goal of reducing infant and child mortality through "the enjoyment of the highest attainable standard of health" (see Appendix One). A range of specific actions are identified for health promotion and the prevention and treatment of illness, which are to be implemented both through the health care system and through related actions in nutrition, water supply and environmental protection, explicitly according to the principles of primary health care (PHC). The role of information and education is also highlighted; States Parties should ensure that "parents and children ... are informed, have access to education and are supported in the use of basic knowledge of child health ..." (para. 2.e). Knowledge about how to obtain and keep good health, therefore, is an essential part of the right, along with the right of access to health services. This provision gives concrete contents to Articles 28 and 29 on education, pointing to the synergism of health and education rights. There is, for example, a strong connection between the promotion of child health and "the development of the child's personality, talents and mental and physical abilities to their fullest potential" (Article 29.1.a). Article 24 links child health to fertility considerations in the right established for parents to family planning education and services (para. 2.f).[1] Especially in view of the resource constraints facing developing countries, international cooperation is stressed (para. 4) as an important element in the implementation of child health rights.

In the context of many of the other, broader provisions of the CRC, Article 24 aims to empower individuals — households and communities — with the means to acquire and sustain good health. Taken together, the CRC provisions establish not a right to health services, but rather to the full range of actions that can yield a healthy state. Health, moreover, is not identified with the outcome of reduced morbidity and mortality alone, but is seen as a stepping-stone in the broader process of improving children's lives and well-being.

Article 24 is supplemented by a number of additional references in the CRC that amplify particular elements, and in whose light the health sections need to be read:

- *Article 1* states that a "child" is anyone below the age of 18 years (except where the legal age of majority is lower). At the same time, the focus of most child health actions is on infants and the under-5 population. For children aged 5 to 18 years, the disease pattern is considerably reduced. There is, however, a higher risk of injury, requiring greater health protection activities. In addition, as this period coincides with major physical and psychological development, enhanced health promotion measures are also needed.
- *Article 2* establishes the universal applicability of the CRC provisions, "without discrimination of any kind, irrespective of the child's or his or her parent's ... race, colour, sex, language, religion, political or other opinion, national, ethnic or social origin, property, disability, birth or other status". This provision is important because it sets out the principle of equity among children in their access to conditions for achieving and maintaining good health — regardless, *inter alia*, of their geographic location, income or physical condition.
- *Article 6*, in which States Parties recognize "the inherent right to life" and agree to "ensure to the maximum extent possible the survival and development of the child", underscores the role of health conditions and health actions in survival.
- *Article 18* states that "[p]arents or, as the case may be, legal guardians, have the primary responsibility for the upbringing and development of the child", underscoring the fundamental role of the family in the health area. The ability of parents to carry out this role is related to their level of education and their access to information, which is another example of the interrelatedness of the different rights set out in the CRC.

- *Article 23* addresses the situation of mentally or physically disabled children. It states that "assistance ... shall be provided free of charge, whenever possible ... and shall be designed to ensure that the disabled child has effective access to and receives ... health care services ..." (para. 3). In addition, it declares that "States Parties shall promote, in the spirit of international co-operation, the exchange of appropriate information in the field of preventive health care and of medical, psychological and functional treatment of disabled children ..." (para. 4). This is significant in that it suggests special treatment for this population as compared with other children in difficult circumstances. The reference to financing highlights the principle that disabled children are a societal responsibility, assigning to the State specifically the role of provider of last resort.[2]
- *Articles 26 and 27* address more generally the responsibility of the State for ensuring health rights. Article 26 recognizes "for every child the right to benefit from social security, including social insurance ...", while Article 27 recognizes "the right of every child to a standard of living adequate for the child's physical, mental, ... and social development" (para. 1). Principal responsibility for this rests with the parents or others responsible for the child (para. 2), whereas governments "shall take appropriate measures to assist parents and others responsible for the child to implement this right and shall in case of need provide material assistance and support programmes ..." (para. 3).
- *Article 32,* on child labour, establishes "the right of the child to be protected ... from performing any work that is likely to be hazardous ... or to be harmful to the child's health or physical, mental ... or social development" (para. 1). This highlights one of the key issues of access for vulnerable groups, and the role of health as a lever for action on rights in areas such as child labour.

The CRC therefore reflects many different dimensions of an operational definition of health. In its references to the "framework of PHC" and in the comprehensive range of health issues raised, it implies a broad view of health actions, in which health is seen as a holistic, social phenomenon. The CRC thus follows the basic direction set out in the WHO constitution, which states that enjoyment of the highest attainable standard of health is a fundamental right of every person; and in the International Declaration on Primary Health Care, issued at the International Conference on Primary Health Care held in Alma Ata, former Soviet Union, in 1978 (hereinafter the Alma Ata Declaration and Conference). For example, Article 24 includes reference to drinking water and environmental sanitation (para. 2.c), which are among the factors most critical to achieving a basic standard of health. At the same time, the specific references to elements of the health service package, and the distinction made between preventive services and the listing of predominantly curative actions, are evidence of a noticeable health service orientation in the CRC.

□ 1.2. A CONCEPTUAL APPROACH TO CHILDREN'S HEALTH RIGHTS

Beginning in the 1970s, discussions about 'basic needs' and 'basic services' led to a fundamental conceptual rift between 'human rights' specialists and 'human development' practitioners. Needs and services are the two poles of the unstable exchange between human beings and the environment. As children develop, they make constantly changing demands on their physical and social environments. If their 'basic needs' are not satisfied, they will become ill or even die. This same phenomenon occurs at the societal level. Thus, organizations, cultures and societies may be transformed, or even cease to be, if their exchange with the environment is unfavourable.

In general terms, the 'human development' community considers that their most important operational task is to locate the *technologies and resources* needed to provide 'basic services' to satisfy the 'basic needs' of the entire population. For the 'human rights' community, instead, the task is to find the *legal instruments and the enforcement mechanisms* required to ensure that human development tasks are carried out. As discussed by Jonsson in the next chapter, human development specialists turn to science for inspiration, whereas human rights specialists turn to ethics and law. In fact, however, both approaches 'till the same land'.

It is significant that legal obligation occupies a prominent place in current thinking on needs satisfaction and rights fulfilment. Two decades of technical discussions and advances on needs satisfaction have not secured as much improvement in children's situations as expected. Rational and scientific arguments have failed to influence political will to the extent needed. It is hoped that ethics and law, as embodied in the CRC and progressively incorporated in *enforceable* national legislation, will be better able to support the process of ensuring that adequate human, economic and organizational resources are allocated to achieve the objectives of the CRC.

□ 1.3. HISTORICAL AND LEGAL CONTEXT

The CRC offers one of the principal validations of the long-recognized ethical obligation to avert the preventable death and illness of all human beings. In terms of *needs*, the applicability of this obligation to children is perhaps stronger than for any other group, both because of the size of the child population and because of children's heightened vulnerability to disease and death. In fact, the 'relative' needs of children are in some respects 'absolute': if their health requirements are not satisfied, their future physical and mental development will be affected. Illness, particularly during the first years of life, imposes high burdens for the future, especially for children who are poor or otherwise disadvantaged. In addition, children cannot take care of themselves, introducing a crucial obligation on the family, the community and the State to ensure that children live and develop. It is consequently seen as morally unacceptable that 35,000 children, most of them in the developing world and most of these poor, should die each day. A less dramatic, but little less substantial, case can be made with respect to preventable infant and child diseases and nutritional deficiencies, which, especially in developing countries, can lead to irreversible disabilities.

Recognition and implementation of the right to health has, however, been limited and inconsistent. National constitutions vary considerably in the extent to which health is identified as a right and in the form in which it is articulated. In general, it appears that the expression of a health right influences only partially the nature and provisions of national health systems.[3] In this perspective, countries have by and large fallen into three major groups in their basis for action in health:

- In the first of these, health services have been developed as a feature of social welfare systems, established on *utilitarian* principles. Most industrialized countries have followed this course, with a frequently large role played by the State in providing health care. Thus, Germany at the end of the last century, the United Kingdom following the Second World War, and Chile, for example, all developed widely based schemes for social protection, based on population needs and on the social and political benefits of satisfying them. Health has been seen as a factor in labour-force productivity, leading to a focus on the working-age population. Children's health needs have also been highlighted, with pre- and post-natal care, along with other provisions for children such as meals, having been widely introduced. Health rights have in most of these countries either not been specifically identified, or they have been equated with the right of access to a defined range of health services.

- A second case is that of the *'libertarian'* State, in which the government seeks to ensure a minimum standard of health and other social conditions, although the role in actually providing services may be limited. Thus, while the State has some role to play in the respect and protection of health rights, the primary responsibility for health is seen to be the individual's. This is reinforced by a perception that resources for health are used most efficiently in the hands of the provider and consumer, subject to certain minimum standards being satisfied. A combination of regulatory policies and increasing privatization and 'contracting-out' of health services and support has evolved in many such countries, including the United States. This approach may also be seen as needs-based, rather than rights-based, but with a stricter reading of the scope of needs and guided by a philosophy of limited state intervention in both the social and the economic spheres. In consequence, provisions respecting and protecting the rights of children have often been limited, either in their formulation or their enforcement.

- A third group has pursued health policy on *'equalitarian'* principles, most notably in the historically socialist countries, where health has generally been promoted as a part of overall social and economic policies. Although this has involved a response to needs, in many countries health has been promoted as a matter of social justice or rights, and health has generally been identified as one of the obligations of the State. In the former Soviet Union, in much of Central and Eastern Europe and in developing countries such as Tanzania, Mozambique, Cuba and Nicaragua, health programmes have been strong, and this momentum was often carried forward even after the collapse of the former socialist regimes. In recent years, elements of market-based systems have been introduced in many of these countries, most notably through a growing private sector in health services. At the same time, economic decline has affected the ability of the State to meet the responsibilities previously set out for it, leading to a crisis situation in the health systems of many of these countries.

The distinctions between these policy approaches have become blurred in recent years, with most countries now having adopted a combination of 'utilitarian' and 'libertarian' policies for health.[4]

In this context, there has been wide discussion over the role of health in the achievement of 'social justice'. Bryant, for example, applies Rawls' theory of justice to the health system, deriving a series of principles for distributing health resources under differing conditions of scarcity.[5] Other authors have examined justice in the health systems of industrialized countries, such as the situation of large numbers of the U.S. population being either uncovered or inadequately covered by health insurance, or living in 'medically underserved' regions, in a country that spends a substantial proportion of its gross national product (GNP) (currently some 14 per cent) on health.[6]

The linkage between justice and health rights has been subject to debate. Kriel argues that, irrespective of the existence of a 'right to health', criteria of justice can usefully be applied to health systems with respect to the distribution of health resources and their utilization in relation to the needs of different population groups having different health conditions.[7] Susser, by contrast, places the issue of distributive justice squarely in the domain of rights. He emphasizes that a health right is societal rather than individual in nature, insofar as individual contracts cannot be made to ensure good health for every person.[8]

The societal nature of a health right stems from two factors: on the one hand, the commonality of human exposure to, and utilization of, the environment; on the other, the collective and unequal action of individuals and groups on the environment. The resulting equilibrium is beyond the ability of any individual to alter (as, for example, in the case of the ozone layer). We would argue that a rights approach to health suggests a societal commitment for health, which is also identified with the principle of 'equity'. Equity in terms of health can be seen as having four dimensions:

(a) equal access to appropriate services for all members of all groups;

(b) equity in health states for all social groups as an explicit aspiration, followed by 'good faith' attempts to promote health in groups at a disadvantage;
(c) evaluative mechanisms to monitor the distribution of states of health and specific needs for health; and
(d) equitable sociopolitical arrangements that give a voice to all groups on health matters.[9]

From this perspective and from historical experience, it is at least apparent that fulfilment of health needs is distinct from achieving health as a right. The fulfilment of health rights, defined in the limited sense of 'health services' and in the absence of other economic and political rights being fulfilled, is not likely to be sufficient for the satisfaction of the population's needs and long-term aspirations.

It is also important to consider the degree to which the child's right to health is implemented, whether intentionally or not, through the segmentation, prioritization or sequencing of interventions over time. Article 24 foresees such sequencing by setting a goal of "achieving progressively the full realization" of the right to health (para. 4). Health interventions can be segmented by targeting specific geographic areas (for instance, rural rather than urban); they can emphasize one technical or organizational level over another (such as primary health care rather than sophisticated curative care); or they can aim to reach certain target groups, including age-groups, within a given population (infants rather than adolescents, for example). As a corollary, whichever priority is chosen, services need eventually to be expanded to the components initially excluded.

Some of the approaches listed above (segmentation by type, age or level, in space or over time) may be more capable than others to promote rapid and full expansion of coverage — which, in turn, may signify faster and more efficient satisfaction of the child's right to health.

□ 1.4. PRIMARY HEALTH CARE

During the 1970s, health formed a key component of 'basic needs' as developed especially by the International Labour Organisation (ILO), with later involvement of other United Nations organizations and the World Bank. Despite oil price shocks during this period, the general expectation prevailed that future economic growth would permit developing countries to increase social expenditures substantially throughout the government sector. 'Basic needs strategies' were developed, aiming at identifying minimum requirements for services in health as well as in education, water supply and other service sectors. In the health sector, reviews by WHO drew on successful experiences in a number of developing countries — some undergoing major national-level policy changes, others in which existing health systems were extended, and others still where local community development efforts were gaining strength. The concept of 'basic health services' emerged as an approach reflecting national commitment to increase service coverage through community participation, the use of paraprofessional workers and adoption of simplified techniques and technologies.[10] A Basic Services Strategy, developed by UNICEF, applied these principles specifically to the needs of children. Programmes were introduced or strengthened in many countries, both by governments and by non-governmental organizations (NGOs), to expand health services based on these principles.

A major articulation of the strategy for achieving the goal of health emerged from the Alma Ata Conference. In many respects, the Alma Ata Declaration represented a radical departure from previous practice, not merely elaborating on the health services approach but dramatically broadening the concept of health and health action. The goal of 'Health for All' established at the Alma Ata Conference represented a fundamental revolution in thinking about health, which was no longer considered a technically complex medical matter, but rather a daily concern, which individuals could, and should, face themselves. Difficult cases — the exception rather than the rule — would require a referral system, which could also train support personnel and help to monitor people's health.

PHC has been concisely defined as health knowledge plus social organization or, more fully, as "essential health care made universally accessible to individuals and families in the community by means acceptable to them, through their full participation and at a cost that the community and country can afford".[11] The latter definition implies that health performance cannot be measured by service indicators such as doctor-population ratios, but must instead be judged according to overall improvements in the health of the population.

PHC was identified at the Alma Ata Conference as having eight principal components: education concerning prevailing health problems and methods of preventing and controlling them; prevention and control of local endemic diseases; immunization against the major infectious diseases; maternal and child health care, including family planning; provision of essential drugs; promotion of proper nutrition and adequate food supply; appropriate treatment of common diseases and injuries; and safe water supply and basic sanitation.

While expressed in general terms, the aim of 'Health for All' as declared at Alma Ata contrasts with the lack of articulated goals and strategies in the earlier concept of basic health services. PHC was defined as being intersectoral in nature, with no single institutional base, rather than sectoral and built on existing health structures. It brought medical specialists and communities into a new relationship, requiring a redefinition of roles. Communities were identified as the key focus of PHC, in terms of their active involvement, their understanding and information about health, and reliance on local resources. Health workers, in turn, were to be oriented to preventive and essential health care, in the context of a close collaboration with the people, in contrast to their traditional curative and specialized orientation, and their frequent position as 'outsiders' to the community. Finally, while even under basic health services knowledge was seen to be acquired and used by people only through communication and education for health, PHC was meant to be established and promoted as a means of socio-economic development and for obtaining a better quality of life for all people.[12] In other words, it was to become a stepping stone to social development of a more general nature.

The Alma Ata Declaration did not specifically address the resource requirements for achieving these objectives, but it did highlight several important resource-related principles: that, as a basic benchmark, 5 per cent of each country's GNP should be devoted to health; that there should be equitable distribution of health resources within countries; and that health should be supported, when necessary, through international cooperation. The universality of the 'Health for All' principle was emphasized, by which the achievement of a basic standard of health was sought in all geographical areas and for all subgroups of the population. Performance was to be measured in terms of health service coverage (geographical or physical accessibility), and other factors such as appropriateness and economic and social accessibility to ensure that physically accessible services would in fact be used.

PHC has subsequently been implemented in different ways and to varying degrees in different countries. General policy guidelines were established by WHO in the form of resolutions and documents. However, consistent with the philosophical basis of PHC, no single planning tool or approach was put in place. The difficulty has been widely recognized of attempting to respond to health needs on a holistic basis in situations of limited resources and health systems that are resistant to change. In most countries, much of the challenge of fully implementing the PHC principles lies ahead.

□ 1.5. INTERNATIONAL COMMITMENTS FOR HEALTH RIGHTS

The implementation of basic health services and PHC, and the steps taken for child survival during the 1980s, may be seen to be largely based on the concept of meeting health *needs*. Meeting unfulfilled health needs has been considered an important element of the agendas for both social progress and social justice. However, the recognition of needs and taking steps to meet them are not the same as the fulfilment of rights (see Chapter Five). Rights rest further on specific *claims* to society's attention and resources by population groups, and they are based on some sort of legal acknowledgement of those claims.

A number of international human rights declarations and covenants have established rights to health. ('Declarations' express serious intent but, in contrast to 'covenants' and 'conventions', are non-binding instruments.) The first such instrument developed under United Nations auspices was the Universal Declaration on Human Rights (1948). Article 25 identified the "right to a standard of living for the health and well-being ... including medical care" (para. 1). It further established that "mothers and children are entitled to special care and assistance" (para. 2).

The main precursor of the CRC was the Declaration of the Rights of the Child (proclaimed by United Nations General Assembly resolution 1386

(XIV) of 1959). The Declaration set out the basic principles of child health rights, later elaborated and brought within a legal framework in the CRC. Principle 2 states that the child "shall be given opportunities and facilities, by law and by other means, to enable him to develop physically, mentally, morally, spiritually and socially in a healthy and normal manner ...". Principle 4 states that the child "shall be entitled to grow and develop in health; to this end, special care and protection shall be provided both to him and to his mother, including adequate pre-natal and post-natal care. The child shall have the right to adequate nutrition, housing, recreation and medical services."

The International Covenant on Economic, Social and Cultural Rights (adopted by United Nations General Assembly resolution 2200A (XXI) of 1966, and entered into force in 1976) affirmed these earlier commitments and elaborated them with respect to health. Article 12 establishes that the States Parties "recognize the right of everyone to the enjoyment of the highest attainable standard of physical and mental health. ... The steps to be taken ... to achieve the full realization of this right shall include those necessary for:
(a) the provision for the reduction of the stillbirth rate and of infant mortality and for the healthy development of the child;
(b) the improvement of all aspects of environmental and industrial hygiene;
(c) the prevention, treatment and control of epidemic, endemic, occupational and other diseases;
(d) the creation of conditions which would assure to all medical service and medical attention in the event of sickness."

These rights have been placed in a broader socio-economic context more recently by the Declaration on the Right to Development (adopted by United Nations General Assembly resolution 41/128 of 1986). The declaration provides that "States should undertake, at the national level, all necessary measures for the realization of the right to development and shall ensure, *inter alia*, equality of opportunity for all in their access to basic resources, education, health services, ... and the fair distribution of income" (Article 8). This provision reinforces the commitments made in earlier instruments, stressing in particular the role of social services within the development process.

The rights of girl children are addressed in the Convention on the Elimination of All Forms of Discrimination Against Women (adopted in 1979, and entered into force in 1981; ratified, as of 30 June 1994, by 138 countries). Articles 11(f), 12 and 14(b) specifically concern health issues.[13]

Throughout this process, it is seen that the right to health has been articulated in increasingly specific ways in international declarations, covenants and conventions. Yet all of these expressions have to some degree reflected the difficulty of distinguishing between a broad 'right to health', which faces definitional problems, and the more traditional 'right to health protection', which can be limited in scope.[14] Some of these commitments have referred only to health services, and others to health more broadly. But their combination provides a strong and consistent basis for a right to health, and they form the background against which the CRC elaborates child health rights.

■ 2. Health Needs and Priorities

Before the implementation of child health rights is considered, it may be useful to review briefly the nature and magnitude of child health needs in the developing world and to present a framework of the major factors influencing child health.[15]

□ 2.1. THE HEALTH SITUATION OF CHILDREN

Table 4.1 summarizes the major causes of death of children 5 years of age and under, indicating the numbers of children estimated to have died in 1985 and 1990 by major cause, and the percentage of deaths that each represents. These data, of course, provide only a partial picture of the health problems faced by children: cause-of-death reporting is incomplete and subject to errors of registration; different definitional standards are in use in different countries; and reporting fails to capture underlying or associated health conditions that may have led or contributed to the death. Nonetheless, the figures offer an initial view of children's health situation and its most tragic component, infant and young child death.

The facility with which death is measured, however, has created a conceptual vacuum. If a country has low child mortality, it is usually considered to have successfully addressed child health problems. Disability (congenital, hereditary and acquired), psychological and physical abuse, drug addiction, deviant behaviour and other unhealthy states are either not measured at all or are measured inaccurately. Yet their extent, trends and repercussions have perhaps reached higher and costlier levels for society than infant mortality. In addition, few data are available concerning the fostering of good health — that is, maximizing human potential in terms of physical strength and agility, intellectual outreach and emotional stability, all of which represent the true significance of "the highest attainable standard of health".

The data in Table 4.1 show that in 1990, pneumonia and other acute respiratory infections (ARI) alone were responsible for nearly 3.6 million child deaths, or over 27 per cent of the total, while diarrhoea alone accounted for 3 million deaths, over 23 per cent. Other single identified causes made up the remaining 50 per cent of child deaths. However, it should be noted that a number of these causes represent multiple diagnoses, and the table also shows the clustering of causes of deaths into major groupings. (As a result of some causes appearing in more than one cluster, the numbers no longer add up to 100 per cent.)

It is seen that ARI in all categories still accounted for the largest number of child deaths, some 4.3 million in 1990, or one third of the total. Pneumonia, basically of bacterial origin in children, accounts for 80 per cent of all ARI. It is the single-largest cause of child mortality, chiefly because mothers either do not know when to seek treatment, or because they do not complete treatment. Neonatal and perinatal deaths from different causes formed the second

Table 4.1. - **Estimated causes of death of children under 5 years, in developing countries, 1985 and 1990**

Cause of death category	1990		1985	
	No. of deaths (thousands)	Per cent	No. of deaths (thousands)	Per cent
1. Acute respiratory infections (ARI) alone (mostly pneumonia)*	3,560	27.6	3,300	24.4
2. Diarrhoea alone	3,000	23.3	3,000	22.2
3. Birth asphyxia	860	6.7	760	5.6
4. Malaria	800	6.2	750	5.6
5. Neonatal tetanus	560	4.3	800	5.9
6. ARI - measles	480	3.7	1,100	8.1
7. Congenital anomalies	450	3.5	400	3.0
8. Birth trauma	430	3.3	380	2.8
9. Prematurity	430	3.3	380	2.8
10. Neonatal sepsis and meningitis	300	2.3	180	1.3
11. Tuberculosis	300	2.3	300	2.2
12. ARI - pertussis	260	2.0	400	3.0
13. Measles alone	220	1.7	500	3.7
14. Accidents	200	1.6	200	1.5
15. Diarrhoea - measles	180	1.4	400	3.0
16. Pertussis	100	0.8	200	1.5
17. All other causes	770	6.0	450	3.3
TOTAL	12,900	100.0	13,500	100.0
ARI total (1,6,12)	4,300	33.3	4,800	35.6
Neonatal and perinatal, total (3,5,7,8,9,10*)	3,830	29.7	3,700	27.4
Diarrhoea total (2,15)	3,180	24.7	3,400	25.2
Vaccine-preventable, total (5,6,11,12,13,15,16)	2,100	16.3	3,700	27.4
Measles total (6,13,15)	880	6.8	2,000	14.8
Pertussis total (12,16)	360	2.8	600	4.4

Source: World Health Organization, 1993b, p. 107.
* including 800,000 deaths from neonatal pneumonia

largest grouping, accounting for 3.8 million deaths, or 30 per cent of the total. These were followed by diarrhoea-related deaths (3.2 million, or one fourth of the total), and vaccine-preventable deaths, which accounted for 2.1 million deaths, or 16 per cent of the total. Measles was responsible for nearly two thirds of these latter deaths.

The absolute number of child deaths each year was estimated to have declined by some 600,000, or by over 4 per cent, between 1985 and 1990. In this period, a shift was also seen in the relative importance of different causes of child death, with the number of vaccine-preventable deaths declining most dramatically, from 3.7 million to 2.1 million per year. Within this total, the number of measles deaths decreased by over one half. Consequently, the increasing role of pneumonia and other respiratory infections in child deaths is partly the result of an apparent decline of certain other causes, including diarrhoea-related diseases. Vaccine-preventable diseases are no longer the greatest cause of death, leaving other causes that are more difficult to prevent or treat.[16]

Whereas in industrialized countries children's life expectancy increases dramatically after the first month of life, poor children in developing countries face an opposite scenario. Because of ignorance, overall poverty and the unhealthy environmental conditions surrounding them, they fail to be protected from infections and parasites (as well as from accidents). Secondly, this exposure is exacerbated by malnutrition and lack of vaccination and of proper care, leaving them all the more vulnerable to mostly preventable diseases. This prevalence is aggravated by the simultaneous presence of other serious causes of ill-health such as low birth weight and malnutrition, which jeopardize children's immune systems, leaving them at the mercy of infection and bacterial transmission. A main cause of low birth weight is poor health of the mother, which in turn may often be traced to births that are too many or too close, or which occur to women who are too young or too old. This point underscores the view that women's health should be stressed not only as a response to women's right to health, but also as a response to children's right to health. The intergenerational context of rights fulfilment is important both biologically and socially. It is this kind of commitment to long-term sustainability that will eventually help transform the fulfilment of needs into the realization of rights.

A situation of particular significance arises in the case of AIDS. Globally, AIDS is not among the major causes of child death, and it affects only a small proportion of the child population. In some countries where the disease is prevalent in the population as a whole, the rates for children are also elevated; it appears that the correspondence between child and adult prevalence rates is increasing over time, posing growing problems for the future. AIDS is an issue of rights because there is no known treatment, and hence the best means for implementation of the right to life and to health is not clear. Because of the high cost of care, children with AIDS are frequently discriminated against, in society at large as well as in their own communities. In nearly all instances, the disease is passed to the child from the mother, raising the issue of the responsibility of the family for the child's health. The growing number of 'AIDS orphans' prompts a further concern about the proper role of the community and State.[17]

The girl child faces some specific health risks, as an element of the wider neglect of women's health throughout the developing world, including infanticide at birth, and reduced nursing and feeding which lead to malnutrition, in all social classes; limited access to health knowledge; and in many countries, immediate and longer-term consequences of female genital mutilation.[18]

As noted above, causes of mortality represent only part of the health picture. Many of the diseases commonly experienced by children may not be fatal. However, they may lead to diverse types of disabilities, mental as well as physical, seriously reducing the quality of the child's life for his or her lifetime.[19]

□ 2.2. A FRAMEWORK FOR ASSESSMENT AND ANALYSIS

Child health needs can be understood more fully with reference to the principal factors responsible for the achievement of child health outcomes — in positive terms, for a state of good health. Table 4.2 is organized according to three principal levels of factors: those directly or 'immediately' affecting health conditions and how they are responded to; those with a more indirect or 'underlying' impact, but on which actions can be taken in the medium term; and those at a broader or 'basic' level, which require sustained, longer-term efforts. At each of these levels, factors may be identified within the domain of the individual and household; the wider political, social, economic and physical environment, extending from the community to the society as a whole; and the health services delivery system. Following the example of similar approaches used in other contexts, the framework implies causality, in that the 'immediate' factors are seen to be the outcome of those at the 'underlying' level, while these are in turn the result of 'basic' conditions. However, the framework does not attempt to identify specific causal linkages between the factors, but rather is intended to highlight the major influences on the health and well-being of children.[20] As such, it represents one tool in identifying main sources of relevant resources to be mobilized for the fulfilment of the health needs and rights of children.

2.2.1. Immediate factors

'Immediate' factors are most visible at, and are usually addressed at, the local level — that of households and communities, up to the first level of contact with the health system. Their fundamental importance lies in the fact that

Table 4.2 **- Factors in the achievement of child health outcomes**

Factors	Individual behavior and understanding	Social, economic and physical environment	Health sector	Principal locus or responsibility
'Immediate'	Health practices (esp. hygiene)	Nutrition Water and sanitation Communicable disease prevalence	Actual provision and use of health services	Individual, household and community
'Underlying'	Knowledge Perceptions Motivation	Income Food security Social organization and infrastructure	Availability of health services	Community and local level
'Basic'	Values and norms Traditions and beliefs Modern media-led information	Epidemiological patterns and disease conditions Political structure and processes Distribution of resources	Health policies and structures	National
		Total resources in society International environment		National and international

health is experienced at the personal and household levels, and its improvement so largely depends on the behaviour of individuals, families and communities, supported by other levels of society. Interventions to ameliorate or respond to these factors are frequently sectoral or 'technical' in nature, implemented in vertical or separate structures. As a result, preventive measures often tend to be neglected.

Health practices within the household are perhaps the single most important determinants of children's health. Small children are often exposed to cold temperatures, to contaminated food and water substituting for breastfeeding, and to incorrect or inappropriate home health care. Practices relevant to health include the attention given to personal hygiene, household sanitation, the handling of food and the general conditions and safety of the living environment, and thus collectively represent a major part of the care given to children by their families. These practices are often outcomes of the health and education of the mother and other household members, and of their knowledge about basic hygiene and child-rearing practices.

Baseline health profiles (including genetic factors) are also significant because health status and outcomes are increasingly recognized as 'sensitive to initial conditions'. If the original or baseline health conditions faced by a child are mostly negative, progress will be blocked. Improvements in the fulfilment of a child's health right will thus depend on the underlying mix of such factors as type of household and social organization, prevailing health-related beliefs and practices, and access to health services delivery systems as well as the epidemiological profile and the prevalent health status of the population.

Nutrition is closely linked to health outcomes, and is in many ways inseparable from them. Recent research has demonstrated the interactions between malnutrition and infectious disease, most notably the relationship between malnutrition and infant mortality, acting especially through the incidence and severity of diarrhoea. Yet even in the absence of specific diseases, nutrition plays a central ongoing role in the child's physical and mental development.[21]

Water and sanitation are critical to the achievement of good health in many respects. Most diarrhoea-related illnesses are water-borne and can be prevented or lessened with improvement in water quality and sanitary conditions. It remains common throughout the developing world for people to collect their water from public wells or open natural sources filled with impurities from bathing, washing and sewerage. Water quantity and availability may play an even more significant role in their contribution to general hygiene, which may help to counteract infectious disease from other origins. Because water is often scarce and is costly to obtain in terms of the time of women and others responsible for its procurement, households typically economize in its use. Problems of poor water and sanitation are thus clustered with those of disease prevalence and poor living conditions. Remedies such as oral rehydration therapy (ORT) for diarrhoea are only palliative if they are not accompanied by improvements in water and sanitation, health education and changes in health practices.

Demand, provision and use of health services play an important, if frequently minor, role in the improvement of health. It is recognized by most professionals that health outcomes are affected to only a very limited degree by the use of health care services, although this recognition is not reflected in resource allocations in most countries. The most visible function of health services, and the purpose for which they are most valued and utilized, is curative care. However, in only the most acute cases is health improvement a medical issue, or is it susceptible to medical intervention. Similarly, although the health sector has an important role to play in promoting healthy practices and screening the population, health services can only reinforce preventive and promotive actions. In those cases, it is important that services of appropriate quality be used. The decision to provide health services in a given location, and the decisions of households to make use of the services, are influenced by a number of factors discussed below. These decisions, in turn, have significant implications for costs and resource requirements.

2.2.2. Underlying factors

The underlying factors represent features of the local environment in which people live and work, at the level of the community and household, extending to local administrative areas such as districts.

Knowledge about the causes of health problems, remedies and the means to maintain good health represents perhaps the most critical element of health as a right, and the lack of knowledge forms a major denial of this right. Traditionally, health knowledge has been closely guarded by the medical profession and health workers, and what information is given to households and communities tends to be limited and technocratic. Efforts to articulate health knowledge in ways that can be readily understood, and to disseminate it throughout the population, have formed a key component of most successful community health programmes. At the societal level, the influence of mothers' education on the health of children and other household members is widely documented, as is its effect on age at marriage, knowledge and use of contraception, and other factors in fertility reduction.

Perceptions play an important role in the interpretation and application of knowledge about health and health needs. Caregivers must perceive that certain health problems need to be treated or prevented; and they must be psychologically aware that actions within their households, or health services that are available, can in fact respond to the needs of their children and other family members. Among the poor, health is often not perceived as a priority in comparison with the other necessities of life. A frequent failing of 'health education' efforts is that they impart objective knowledge, but they fail to find practical ways to introduce this knowledge into people's day-to-day behaviour.[22]

The *motivation* to take action to improve health is a third key element in individual decision-making about health. Mothers and other caregivers must not only have adequate knowledge about what actions to take, and the perception that their actions can make a difference; they need also to be motivated to maintain and improve health, whether by a voice of authority or, more sustainably, through a heightened sense of individual responsibility. Motivation is affected by beliefs and values, as well as being strongly influenced by economic incentives related to the perceived costs and benefits of taking health actions.

The role of the above factors has been widely seen in the drive for universal immunization. As James P. Grant, the late Executive Director of UNICEF, observed, "One critical lesson of over a decade of experience is that making vaccines available isn't enough; people need to be educated, motivated and mobilized to seek out immunization."[23]

Within households and communities, *assets and income* form a major determinant of the ability to maintain children's health. At the societal level, similarly, the availability of financial and other resources plays a large role in determining the scope for allocating resources for health improvements. A minimum level of income or other resources (such as a small plot of land) is essential for food security. Beyond this, however, some level of monetary or in-kind income is required for access to health services. Families incur out-of-pocket expenses in the form of fees — whether direct, as in the case of private service or cost sharing, or hidden — and they must frequently also purchase medicines and health supplies. In addition, the costs of travel and waiting time can be substantial, in terms both of cash and of the opportunities foregone to carry out other tasks or to earn income.

Food security at the household and community level represents the degree to which nutritional resources are organized and used to meet nutritional needs, as an important input to health. It is in part a matter of food availability, but more importantly the combination of food distribution and feeding practices that determine whether nutrition requirements are met.

Social organization and infrastructure represent the broad set of physical and organizational resources that a community or area has at its disposal for improving health and carrying out other development actions. Social organization takes many forms, including local government bodies and processes; community organizations; users' groups or management bodies in water supply, education and health; women's associations; and family, religious and other informal groupings. By social 'infrastructure' is meant the more fixed resources (such as schools, community buildings and common areas, community water points and roads) that support communities and enable them to achieve development objectives.

Availability of health services determines the potential utilization of those services by the population, as a special instance of social organization and infrastructure. Availability and access have a physical or geographical dimension, and efforts are often required to identify underserved areas and to reach them through the development of new facilities, the use of outreach services, and improved transportation. Availability and access obviously have important cost dimensions as well; beyond physical distance and costs, social and cultural factors affect the accessibility of services. The social composition of populations is heterogeneous, within countries but even within villages and other local settings. Health services, like any other goods, also are subject to political control in their distribution. Often social groups that are not part of the élite or even main group (along ethnic, familial or other grounds) are discouraged from receiving care, or do not feel comfortable in seeking it. Frequently these groups are also those who are poor and who are subject to the greatest health risks.

A crucial dimension of service availability is the requirement that services be of adequate quality to produce health improvements. This means, for example, that supplies, including pharmaceuticals, are available; that health workers are properly trained, provide services appropriately and give sufficient time to users; that equipment and facilities are maintained; that mothers are made aware of the correct timing of services such as immunization; and that clinics are open at convenient times. (There is of course an important perceptual dimension to quality, and a major function of health communications is to bridge this gap so that perceptions are in line with reality; in other words, so that communities and caregivers correctly understand when services are technically effective and when they are not.)

As with the 'immediate' factors, the above dimensions tend to converge as part of the fabric of household and community life. Consequently, direct action on any one factor usually affects others in a mutually reinforcing way. Thus, for example, efforts to improve food security normally involve the strengthening of social organizations, as well as relevant knowledge and perceptions about food and nutrition. Steps to strengthen knowledge, services and other factors for achieving health improvements must frequently be of a medium-term nature as they involve the building of capacity, including a knowledge base, and acting through local groups and institutions.

2.2.3. Basic factors

'Basic' factors are less specific to localities or population groups, operating at the level of a society, nation or international community. They are diffuse, as part of the basic structure and character of a society, and so action on them must usually be effected over the longer term. However, steps must always be taken at this fundamental level in order to achieve sustainable improvements.

Values and norms embody the strength of children's claim on society's resources, and the responsibilities of households and communities in relation to the State. For example, for the female child to be accepted, to have as much food and access to education as boys, mothers need to gain self-esteem and realize that they have rights to equal opportunities and to respect. Negative attitudes towards the girl child are a major issue in many countries and communities; they often lead to a lower value being placed on her life, neglect during her upbringing, and her inferior status in society as a whole.

Traditions and beliefs are less specific, affecting values about health and medical systems, the understanding of the causes of ill-health and the actions required to maintain health. Different sets of traditions and beliefs operate in any given society. The difficulty of direct actions to 'change' beliefs is well recognized; the need, at minimum, is to identify those understandings and patterns (for instance, concerning the explanation of disease) that are supportive of a rights approach to health, so that they can be reinforced.

Modern media-led information is identified as a further factor in view of its strong influence on people's understanding of health problems and how to address them. In many cases, messages conveyed through radio, television, newspapers and videos work against the achievement of sustainable health improvements through households' and communities' own efforts, promoting instead overly 'medical', curative and commodity-based solutions to health problems. Because of the effect of modern media on perceptions, efforts have been made in many countries to use these media for mobilizing action towards health improvements.

Epidemiological patterns and disease conditions represent the 'objective' determinants of health needs and risk factors. For children, they concern particularly the broader patterns of morbidity and mortality which are manifested in actual prevalence at the local level. The prevalence of communicable diseases establishes the basic set of health risks faced by children in a given locality. As shown earlier, communicable diseases are responsible for by far the largest share of child deaths in developing countries, and recent research indicates that these diseases are relatively more prevalent in countries with higher infant mortality and shorter average life expectancy.

Political structures and processes affect the distribution of power in society and the channels through which it is exercised. These processes in turn establish the ways in which human, financial and organizational resources are allocated, and will have a major effect on the fulfilment of children's rights to health.

In the health sector, *health policies and structures* may be seen as the reflection of broader beliefs and values, knowledge about health, and political interests and processes. As has been described, national policies for health are influenced by the degree to which health is seen as a right. Countries that have achieved major improvements in infant mortality, such as Costa Rica, Sri Lanka and China, have in most cases adopted national health policies emphasizing a reliance on PHC in combination with investments in education, nutrition, sanitation and potable water.

Finally, at a level even more basic lie factors reflecting the overall makeup of society and the international climate. They are included, partly for the sake of completeness, to emphasize that particular values, structures, policies and allocation patterns are not solely the outcome of conditions and actions within the country itself. The *total resources in society* represent the endowment of factors that a country has to work with in achieving health improvements; and they set the potential scope of what can be accomplished. The *international environment* in turn reflects the relationships between a country and others, and, in the case of developing countries, establishes the lines of communication for mobilization and the provision of resources at the international level.

Taken together, this framework indicates the wide range of influences on health, and the complexity of their interrelationships. It also suggests a number of specific points for action, which are addressed more fully in the analysis that follows.

■ 3. Goals and Priority Setting in Health

□ 3.1. FROM RIGHTS TO GOALS AND TARGETS

Substantial and sustainable health improvements can only be achieved through action on each of the above sets of factors. In the context of an agreed-upon right to child health, concrete steps are required to establish priority aims and to translate these into specific efforts and strategies. A key step in this process is to identify the goals or aims of society for children's health, which reflect the obligations that society has taken upon itself to fulfil. These goals can be put in terms such as 'moral minima' or 'minimum core obligations' (as mentioned in Chapter One). However described, they need to have sufficient credibility and acceptance to provide both motivation and guidance for health action, within and outside of the formal political process.

As previously discussed, the Alma Ata Conference represented a major international consensus on the requirement for accessible and affordable health care, based at the community level with support from the health system, for all population groups. While justified at one level on the basis of health needs, PHC took on many attributes of a 'right' in view of the position it was accorded as an element of social and economic development. Yet, because of the very diffuseness of the concept of 'health' that it embodied, the major goal of PHC — 'Health for All' by the year 2000 — lacked clear measures for determining to what degree it was being achieved. Monitoring systems subsequently established for 'Health for All' have incorporated a wide range of measures related to health and development more broadly.[24]

In the late 1970s, the principle of 'selective' PHC was put forward, through which it was proposed to use cost-effectiveness and impact criteria to identify priority interventions and target groups.[25] The PHC strategy was adapted for child health in the early 1980s under the rubric of 'Child Survival and Development', with the support of UNICEF, the United States Agency for International Development (USAID) and other donors. Growth monitoring, ORT for diarrhoea, breastfeeding and immunization were specifically given priority as low-cost, high-impact interventions which could, and should, receive concerted support.[26]

Beginning in about 1985, immunization was highlighted as a particular area for action, and a major drive for universal childhood immunization was initiated. In 1986, the World Health Assembly adopted the target of immunizing 80 per cent of the world's children by 1990. The achievement of this objective has been widely documented[27] and has been an important element in the broader pursuit of 'Health for All'.[28]

The World Summit for Children, held in September 1990, identified a series of goals for children in the 1990s and established indicative targets for the year 2000. The largest number of these goals are directly related to health (see Appendix Two). The "major" goals of reducing infant, young child and maternal mortality are health-focused, while the sets of "supporting/sectoral" goals for women's and children's health encompass a wide range of child and maternal health concerns — including reproductive health and family planning, poliomyelitis, neonatal tetanus, measles and other vaccine-preventable diseases, diarrhoeal disease and respiratory infections. In addition, a number of other goals adopted at the Summit have health implications:

- the major *nutrition* goal of reducing severe and moderate malnutrition among under-5 children depends importantly on reductions in the incidence of diarrhoea and infections;
- the provision of *micronutrients* requires in most countries a functioning health system for delivery;
- empowerment of all women to *breastfeed* depends on changes in delivery practices and in attitudes and practices of health providers;
- the institutionalization of regular *growth monitoring* must in most countries be carried out through the basic health service system;
- improvement of access to *water and sanitation* involves the health system in providing information and education along with efforts to promote change in practices for obtaining water and disposing of waste in households and communities;
- similarly, the elimination of *guinea-worm disease* requires changed practices for obtaining and storing water, with the involvement of local workers trained in basic health;
- health improvements are also important for the achievement of *education* goals related to school performance at the primary level, and increased acquisition by individuals and families of "knowledge and skills for better living" includes health components.

The Summit goals were formulated in consultation with many international agencies and institutions, in the health field most notably with WHO. These goals, and subsequent intermediate targets for achievement by 1995, have been endorsed and adopted by the World Health Assembly, the United Nations Population Fund (UNFPA), the United Nations Development Programme (UNDP), the UNICEF Executive Board and other international bodies. At the regional level, they have been adopted by the Organization of African Unity and other similar groups and by governments in numerous meetings and international forums. Substantial international political resources have been mobilized around the Summit goals for children for the 1990s.

□ 3.2. FROM GOALS TO HEALTH STRATEGIES

Goals agreed upon at the political level must, of course, be translated into action, including in terms of resource mobilization. Policy makers need to determine population groups to be covered, the health outcomes that are aimed for and the time-frames within which this is to be done. In other words, they establish priorities and determine the sequencing of actions, in the context of competing, urgent demands for additional resources. The planning process, in turn, determines broad strategies to follow, the mix of specific interventions and actions that will be pursued, who will do what, and how resources are to be mobilized.

The organization of actions around the child's right to health depends on a range of factors at the national level: the relative and absolute importance of the diseases affecting children, especially up to 5 years of age (the epidemiological profile of the population); the risk factors surrounding the lower-income groups; the nature and extent of existing infrastructure and ongoing interventions; and the relative and absolute costs of different possible interventions and their correlation with the availability of funds. Clearly, each country must adopt an appropriate approach for achieving its goals, as reflected in National Programmes of Action (NPAs) (see Chapter Three).

The concept of 'packages' has been used for a number of years to specify the set of services available to designated population groups. Health 'packages' are specific to:

- different geographic regions and countries, according to the incidence of diseases and their means of transmission;
- different levels (primary, secondary and tertiary) of the health system, according to the types and severity of health problems; and
- the socio-economic situations of different countries and populations, with a view to the resources that can be made available in aggregate.

Some illustrative packages for children's and mothers' health are described in later sections.

To use available resources more effectively to meet children's and families' needs — which is the core of Article 4 — the health packages adopted in each country must be based on planning techniques, such as cost/effectiveness criteria, already used by other sectors. In the water and sanitation area, for instance, national governments and donors have begun to opt for simpler, low-cost techniques, moving away from conventional 'high-tech' methods, which require large capital investments and skilled manpower both to build the infrastructure and to maintain it. However, the simpler the technology, the more heavily it relies on local organization for its management and maintenance, a factor that has proved to be crucial and not easy to attain.

In this process, an important management ingredient is monitoring, which is essential to identify groups and sectors of communities that have poor access to health care. One example of effective monitoring is a survey methodology developed to identify 'missed opportunities' for immunization; that is, where services have not been made available to the population, or where available services have been inadequately utilized. This approach has often made it possible to develop programme strategies, technical approaches and training to ensure that advantage is taken of all immunization opportunities.[29] Similar methods can be applied in other health programmes to determine where services are not reaching those in need of them.

A decade of difficult coexistence between PHC and hospital-based health care (with a few fortunate exceptions such as Thailand, Sri Lanka, Costa Rica, Zimbabwe and China, among others) has underscored the challenge of guaranteeing equal access to all levels of health care for all populations. The expansion of tertiary health care has frequently diverted essential resources from PHC. According to a major World Bank study,

> ... it is common for 50 to 80 percent of public sector health resources, in money and trained personnel, to be used in hospitals. The remaining resources are used for preventive care, infectious and parasitic disease control programs, nonhospital maternal and child health programs, and other services. ... Reviews of the health sector in many countries suggest that these large recurrent expenditures on hospitals involve a great waste of resources because of the inappropriate allocation of funds within the health sector and the technical and managerial inefficiency within hospitals.[30]

Emphasis on tertiary care has furthered the bias towards:
(a) *urban populations*, which have continued to be attended in overly expensive and sophisticated facilities (with great inefficiencies and loss for the system as a whole) at the expense of rural areas, which for the most part continue to be underserved at low-quality facilities;
(b) *adult and elderly populations*, who account for an average of 80 per cent of hospital admissions in many countries;[31] and
(c) *upper-income groups*, who, according to a number of studies in Asia and Africa (Latin America was inconclusive), may use a substantially greater share of total in-patient services than would be expected from their proportion of the population.

Financial barriers or problems of distance can prevent patients from using the health care referral system altogether. The appropriate use of referral systems, on the other hand, is further limited by a common lack of confidence in lower-level facilities because of perceived low quality of care, including lack of drugs; the inadequate flow of information between the hospital and health centre/health post levels; and a lack of organizational and management links between levels of care.

It is important to realize that every consultation held at a higher technical level than is required costs more, sometimes much more, than needed. It is, for example, several times costlier to treat a headache with aspirin at a provincial hospital than at a health post. Such misuse of resources, multiplied by millions, makes health services inefficient, and at the same time insufficient as the availability of resources is reduced each time a service is delivered. Patients bypassing the PHC system generally also bear needless additional costs (for example, transportation costs or opportunity costs of foregone work).

The health system, at a minimum, should be able to respond to the basic health problems of children and their families, and should have within easy reach a referral service for life-threatening health problems which require a higher level of skill and equipment. With regard to Article 6 (recognizing every child's "right to life"), intensive care within the tertiary level is one of the most expensive categories of health services. Given a situation in which resources are scarce and not all the population has yet been reached with basic services, a choice has to be made between concentrating the resources per capita on a few and spreading them more thinly among a larger group of beneficiaries. In terms of priorities, the claims of the PHC level come first. As the system expands, the availability of secondary and tertiary care, for referral, can be increased.

Thus, the revitalization and expansion of the health sector in order to make available preventive and curative services to reduce the main causes of infant ill-health and mortality are fundamental to guaranteeing children's rights to health. These actions, in turn, entail a serious reconsideration of national budgetary allocations as well as the restructuring of the sector itself.

Market mechanisms exist for meeting certain health needs; they ensure quality by allowing choice, liberating the public sector from the burden of giving service to those who can afford to pay. Government intervention (financial, regulatory or both), often with external support, will probably still be needed for health efforts that have 'public good' characteristics or that require national action (as is the case of immunization and other preventive care, public health issues such as reducing infant mortality, and water and sanitation). In addition, an increasing amount of research suggests that households typically do not have enough information about the benefits and costs of preventive and curative health care to enable the most efficient decisions about meeting health needs. A well-functioning market should ensure quality through the demand process, so that people only consume or pay for services that meet their needs. However, markets generally do not function this way, especially in rural areas. Although alternative providers are available, and indeed there is wide evidence that more than one provider is consulted for a large proportion of disease episodes, households may not be able to discriminate clearly regarding technical quality. Thus, improving consumers' understanding and knowledge of health problems and their treatment is an important element of quality assurance.

Overall, then, the intersection of supply and demand is not likely to coincide with the best interests of children if allowed to float freely according to market forces. For example, immunization, which tends to spread its benefits beyond those immunized, is not offered by the private market in the right amounts and at prices that would make it available to all. Curative care, although mainly favouring adults in urban areas, is oversupplied, to the detriment of preventive measures that effectively diminish child mortality and morbidity.

Especially in the presence of wide income disparities, the market, if left to itself, is incapable of guaranteeing equal access to health services and health-related activities and inputs, thus not safeguarding children's right to health. In market-led systems, poor and remote areas with insufficient effective economic demand for health services are likely to become marginalized in health. Because of the lack of roads, communication facilities and other infrastructure, as well as high costs, it is virtually impossible for children in these communities to have access to the different tiers of the health system. The chief casualties are preventive and promotive activities. The resulting untimely demand leads to a greater need for sophisticated, and hence costlier, interventions, still further discouraging underserved populations from seeking health care. The final price is not just higher financial costs, but often, sadly, loss of children's lives.

Single-purpose interventions implemented in a more vertical manner may increase coverage of key health actions at a faster rate than the expansion of basic health services. However, complying with Article 24 goes beyond making single interventions available: it also has implications for the way in which such interventions are provided. A child vaccinated against poliomyelitis who has no access to diarrhoeal disease treatment is not a child whose right to health is guaranteed. An integrated strategy based firmly on primary prevention is the only way to make a significant difference in child ill-health and mortality. Otherwise, by treating each episode of ill-health as a separate autonomous case, there is a risk of simply deferring the next episode of ill-health or mortality. A rights-based approach to health requires attention both to the interrelationships and synergies among health conditions and health actions, and to the linkage between health and the broader development of children and communities.

■ 4. Organizing Health Action

As discussed in Chapter One, actions by States Parties to meet their obligations for child health can be undertaken at different levels of society: the household and community, or local level; districts and municipalities, as intermediate levels of state presence; central authorities, including the executive ('government'), parliamentary and other bodies; and international cooperation. The main actions at these levels were summarized in Table 1.2. In the first three cases, the relevant State is the national government, while in the last case the reference is to other States acting either through international bodies such as the United Nations, or as donors.[32] For each category, actions are identified under four headings: 'respect', or take care of existing activities and recognized rights; 'protect', or expand on existing recognized rights and promote the sustainability of actions; 'facilitate', or promote processes and organizational arrangements among actors; and 'fulfil', or directly provide support or services.

In health, the roles needing to be carried out are those of beneficiary, provider, financer and regulator. Each actor has specific responsibilities in the health process according to different health system models and how the financial burden of attaining and preserving health is distributed among the different actors in each approach (for example, community participation versus public-sector health service delivery versus single-programme intervention).

4.1. HOUSEHOLDS AND COMMUNITIES

As has been seen, most of the causes and potential prevention of ill-health and mortality among children under 5 years of age are found at the household level, and the majority are not dependent on the health system. Since health is a daily affair (unlike disease), only household members can provide promotive support and care (especially food), observe early symptoms and seek timely assistance. Therefore it is crucial that parents, and especially mothers and often grandmothers, have the education and the information needed to maximize children's health status. This is one example of the linkage between women's and children's rights. Another important example is the need for safe motherhood, which, seen from the child's vantage point, is the right to be born healthy and to have a living mother. In this case, the key is the availability and use of essential obstetric care, since complications often cannot be predicted.

The main underlying factor of children's health remains, however, the household's socio-economic capacity to guarantee the basic requirements for sustaining a minimum standard of health of all its members; in other words, the means through which they can satisfactorily cover their basic needs.

Community involvement clearly plays a fundamental role in helping people to be aware of their health situations, informed about preventable diseases and the maintenance of health, and knowledgeable about the benefits of available inputs towards better health. In fact, some studies have suggested that if enough time is given to communities to develop the necessary management tools, they prove interested in and capable of taking 'ownership' of health services that respond to their needs.[33]

Clearly, substantial behaviour change must be sought and major educational elements incorporated into efforts to promote meaningful community participation in health. Women's education may play an especially important role in this process, since it has been shown that poor literate mothers have children with less malnutrition relative to others in their income groups. Improved means must be found to share information and education about basic health with appropriate population groups. Such efforts include general health and hygiene education, through the school system and through other means of communication. *The Facts for Life* initiative developed by UNICEF, WHO, UNESCO, UNFPA and leading medical and children's organizations, which conveys basic child health information in a simple format, is a good example of action of this sort.

A second area of action at the household level concerns the problems of income and poverty. Although Article 24 is worded in a sectoral perspective, the underlying message is broader: the right of every child to a healthy development. This may not be ensured only by the availability of health services and preventive policies, since cases of ill-health may be only a consequence of their real cause — namely, poverty, and its associated environment that fails to prevent the child from being exposed to malnutrition, infection and other negative influences. From this perspective, the right to health can hardly be dissociated from the right to attain the basic means with which to procure the minimal conditions for a healthy life, including shelter, clothing and the ability to produce income.

Among actions to improve the economic position of households, efforts to increase the time available to women are perhaps the most important. These include, first, measures to reduce the total burden of household work, such as the reduction of time required to obtain fuelwood or water, through community efforts (for example, siting of hand-pumps close to dispersed villages) or improved technology (for instance, fuel-conserving cooking stoves). A second area is a wider distribution of labour within households, as in many cultures men may not be employed or working, but continue to leave women and children to perform most of the household chores, including child care, cooking and cleaning, going to the market, as well as work in the fields.

To make a real difference in children's health, the community must be involved in the planning and management of the health services at the local level. Also, the household and the community can provide manpower, facilities, logistics and other functions related to children's health and well-being. A variety of arrangements are possible for the management of services, particularly those in the public sector, to enable greater control by service users and local communities. These measures also have the potential to increase 'ownership' at the local level and to improve accountability for decisions made by the health services. An improved, more active and equitable relationship between health workers and the local community is important in maintaining the quality of services provided, and in paving the way for other development actions.[34]

□ 4.2. THE DISTRICT LEVEL

Government at the intermediate or district level plays a number of crucial roles in health: it adapts national policy and strategies to the local context; it finances and/or implements an important range of health services; it serves as a bridge between first-level facilities and the national system; and it represents the most important point of convergence between official institutions, NGOs, service providers, communities and local government in the health arena. The need for effective management at the district level is accentuated by recent trends of decentralization of decision-making and (sometimes) financial authority from the national level, providing increased potential to plan and support health activities in line with local needs and opportunities. In this way, the concept of 'access' can be made locally specific, rather than representing merely the application of national policies and of plans and targets derived from national averages. Decentralization can also enhance community participation through training and other support for the co-management of local services, strengthening the voice of households and communities in the attainment of improved health, while holding the health services more accountable to communities.

A 'district' is identified principally in terms of the population base: it represents a compact administrative unit, at the lowest level of the formal government structure, covering a relatively small number of people (on the order of 100,000-200,000).[35] District health services normally comprise a network of health centres backed by a district hospital. Health centres offer integrated services aimed at supporting self-care to a population ranging from 5,000 to 15,000 people, through out-patient and usually some in-patient services, and outreach activities that take place in the communities and count on and foster their participation in health promotion and care.

It is at the district level that health sector activities must be coordinated within a broad primary health framework, for example, integrating specific interventions such as immunization and the prevention and treatment of diarrhoeal disease within integrated child care, so that they will have a relevant and sustainable effect. Sustained high levels of immunization coverage and resulting significant reductions in infant and child mortality have been most frequently seen in the presence of well-functioning health centres and integrated maternal and child health services. A range of studies have concluded that countries with weak health infrastructures have not significantly improved their survival rates, despite local or temporary reductions in disease-specific mortality.[36]

The right to health is not being guaranteed if PHC is offered without a reliable referral system that allows children with complicated cases access to secondary and tertiary services. For this purpose, the district hospital has an important role to play, since it is the link between local basic health services and the rest of the health system. The hospital typically provides first-level referral care and support to 10-20 health centres, although it is estimated that only from 5 to 10 per cent of communities' total health requirements would need to be met at this level. Hospitals at the district level also undertake a range of other activities supporting PHC, such as administrative leadership, nurse training, out-patient rehabilitation and health education, as well as direct services as part of PHC including health promotion, family welfare and ambulatory care.

In a district-centred system, the health institutions thus ideally respond to needs, rather than 'provide services'; and they adopt a 'convergent' approach taking into account all actors inside and outside of government. To work effectively, such an approach requires processes for the articulation of demands from below, interaction between different sectors and institutions, and the administrative and technical capacity to respond to health needs. This ideal is of course not always met in practice, but it is one that is increasingly pursued in many health systems.

☐ 4.3. CENTRAL GOVERNMENT

The national government's functions in implementing Article 24 of the CRC include financing, providing services and mobilizing resources for PHC to ensure access and quality care to all children; addressing those issues and activities that the private sector finds itself unable to cover; and giving priority to issues related to children's health such as ameliorating the status, health and education of women. National policies should also support improvements in household food security and nutrition, water and sanitation, housing, information channels, and economic, education and population policies related to health.

Thus the government has an important role to play both through regulation and direct intervention aimed at complying with children's right to health. It also works in coordination with the private sector (that is, NGOs, community-based organizations, and others) in actions set around the common goal of attaining a minimum standard of health and well-being for all children.

The role of government in health care financing has changed radically in the past decade. Many governments, while recognizing their core responsibility to protect vulnerable populations and provide public goods, have been unable, for economic and/or political reasons, to fund services to the extent they had in the past. The decline in government-provided services is also linked to increases in privatization. In some cases, governments have become purchasers rather than providers; that is, they maintain economic responsibilities for certain segments of the population, but contract out the provision of services to the private sector. Despite changes in their financial roles, however, governments remain responsible for establishing and overseeing health policies, national goals and minimum standards, and for determining how national health priorities will be met.

Increased openness in the health care sector, as seen in many if not most countries, considerably complicates this task. Not only can it be harder to implement policies, as the role of non-governmental agencies in financing and provision of health services needs to be taken into account; but policy making itself becomes subject to a wider range of influences, mainly because individuals and population groups are more vocal.

As a result of changes in financing systems, there is now a clear need for governments to become more forceful regulatory agents. Regulation is the principal way in which governments attempt to exert influence on the private and non-governmental sectors, by controlling prices, controlling quantity and distribution, and controlling the quality of services.[37] Regulation enables governments to dictate the 'rules of the game' and to provide a strategic framework in health, emphasizing one approach or one target group over another. Precisely for this reason it is now widely seen as important for advocacy groups to target government with their messages and action, since priority on children may be achieved (among other means) through regulation.

The government can also help tap local resources and raise community awareness to improve children's health status. This mobilization would, and should, translate into a change in priorities (and a consequent reallocation of resources) at both the community and the household levels. At its best, this process is self-reinforcing, since once communities are made aware of the health needs of their children, they are likely to apply pressure and hold the public services accountable. Moreover, they will be more ready to participate, contributing resources to achieve health status. Such support by government is thus key to promoting a holistic approach that entails more than the curative aspect of health, touching upon all the elements of health promotion, including, among others, nutrition and sanitation.

A notable trend in recent years has been the emergence and the encouragement of private providers in many countries to help compensate for shortfalls in government provision of health services. Private-sector health activity is seen to be growing in all regions of the world. Taking only a few examples, by 1990, private-sector health expenditures had come to account for about 51 per cent of total health spending in Ghana, and 44 per cent of the total in sub-Saharan Africa as a whole; 78 per cent of total health spending in India, 40 per cent in China, and 57 per cent in Malaysia; 50 per cent in Mexico; 55 per cent in the United States, and 38 per cent for the established industrialized economies as a whole.[38] Yet while undoubtedly contributing to increased physical access and service options for the population, the trend towards privatization in health gives rise to a number of equity issues, as discussed in Chapter Two.

At the national level within the public sector, the commitment to Article 24 should be translated into a multisectoral strategy promoting policies favouring health on many different fronts. Such a strategy should entail involving, for example, the Ministry of Education for health education activities both inside and outside school, the Ministry of Public Works for the expansion of the water and sanitation network, the Ministry of Communications for the diffusion and advancement of health-promotion activities, the Ministry of Commerce for the regulation of the drugs market as well as some other private services related to health. The Ministries of Finance, Justice and Planning also need to be involved in policy and budgeting issues. Earlier rather than 'last-minute' interaction with finance ministries, in particular, can help prevent serious disappointments for health planners when annual budget proposals are presented.

□ 4.4. INTERNATIONAL COOPERATION

Through a combination of technical and financial support, advocacy and, in some cases, direct provision of services, the international community — multilateral agencies, bilateral donors and NGOs — make important contributions to the improvement of child health. While the significance of this contribution must not be overstated, it should nonetheless be recognized so that the best use can be made of these inputs. Experience in recent years has shown that international action can play a decisive role in encouraging policy change and shifts in the allocation of resources, through advocacy for investments in social goals coupled with strategic financial and technical support. Thus, as a result of individual meetings with heads of states and other high-ranking officials over the course of a decade, WHO, UNICEF and other international organizations were able to secure the political commitment needed to establish and realize the goal of 80 per cent immunization coverage by 1990. These organizations also assured a supply of vaccines and provided technical inputs to governments in improving management procedures and strengthening cold chains. WHO, in particular, helped to train tens of thousands of immunization staff in more than 100 developing countries.[39]

The immunization experience highlights the major, long-standing features of international cooperation in health. At a technical level, international donors and advisors have contributed to research for better understanding of the main health problems in developing countries; to the development of new and improved technologies (such as, currently, the drive for more effective and temperature-stable children's vaccines); and to raising the capacity of national health systems to meet the complex needs of child health. As financers in the health sector, donors have provided a steady flow of resources to help fill gaps in national funding and to stimulate additional government and local spending in key health areas. The concerted international support for child survival, described in this chapter, has been fuelled by a substantial increase in the overall provision of external resources for health.

At the same time, donor-supported health interventions have not always been successful in meeting health objectives. They are seen sometimes to emphasize more vertically organized programmes to address specific health problems, rather than strengthening existing health care systems, particularly at the peripheral level. To avoid this situation, comprehensive national policies and strategies designed around the needs of the population should serve as the framework for implementation of donor assistance, in the context of an active orientation to reducing disparities and building national capacity.

In the area of service provision the international community plays only a limited role, given the capabilities in nearly all developing countries to deliver preventive, promotive and curative care. The part often played in the past, especially by missions and other NGOs, in providing care has in recent years declined considerably, although it remains crucial in parts of some regions, especially Africa. The principal exception is in the case of emergencies. WHO, UNICEF, the United Nations High Commissioner for Refugees and many private international relief agencies for emergency medical aid, such as the International Red Cross and Médecins Sans Frontières (to name just two), provide humanitarian support in cases where national institutions are not functioning. They have given expert medical and public health assistance in countries affected by war or natural calamities. International health professionals are also in a unique position to monitor health-related issues, including violations of human rights (for example, torture or systematic violence against population groups).

Perhaps most significantly, international cooperation has enabled the promotion of a global movement for child health rights by consolidating technical and financial support and linking it to effective advocacy. The challenge in the coming years will be to further strengthen strategies and messages in promoting changes in attitudes and policies on the basis of the CRC, and to broaden the network of actors mobilized to advocate for child health rights.

5. Meeting Resource Needs for Health

This discussion has highlighted the need for a reassessment of roles and a redistribution of responsibility between government and communities in putting health rights into practice. In the context of limited resources, efforts are needed to identify new ways of supporting health actions without imposing undue hardships on the people, and to make better use of the resources that are currently available for health. Several issues in improving the balance between resource requirements and resource availability may be briefly surveyed, with a view to identifying action priorities and policy options.

5.1. HUMAN AND ORGANIZATIONAL RESOURCES

It is clear that the principal requirements for resources to improve children's health and maintain good health are human and organizational in nature. As has been emphasized, the health of children is chiefly the outcome of factors at the household and community levels — knowledge about health problems and how to address them; motivation, especially within the household, to take responsibility for child health and action that promotes it; and support within communities for mothers to monitor the health status of their children and to enable access to information and, when needed, health services.

Key to the support process are trained health workers who are capable of preventing most of the causes of ill-health and mortality among children. An important step in compliance with children's right to health is the prioritization and strengthening of the role of health workers by improving their skills and providing the logistic support needed for their work (such as the availability of drugs and other resources, training opportunities, communication and transportation facilities and referral systems). This strategy should permeate all policy decisions affecting health workers, from the number and levels of personnel (for example, fewer doctors and more primary health care workers) to the determination of salaries and benefits. Careful attention is needed to assigning priorities in terms of allocations for recurrent costs of primary health care programmes.

Beyond improvements in the actions of existing health workers, however, there remain needs for the use of additional human resources, and better organization of health promotion at all levels. One important way to expand resources is to make use of 'non-traditional' assets such as volunteers. In Thailand, for instance, village health volunteers facilitate early case detection and linkage with the formal health system. Estimated to cover about 65 per cent of the villagers' health needs, they are responsible for growth monitoring; distributing supplementary food; mobilizing for immunization; providing first aid, basic medication, and family planning supplies and education; and administering revolving drug funds (for which they receive a compensation), which give communities permanent on-site access to essential medical drugs at lower-than-market prices. Studies show that volunteer health workers have been able to redistribute demand away from provincial and district hospitals to village health centres, which doubled in number between 1980 and 1989. This redistribution in itself reduces wastage, since, as pointed out earlier, the same service has lower costs the further down the ladder of referral it is provided.[40]

Information and social knowledge, as critical organizational resources, are also required to make the benefits of scientific progress available to the world's poor. Impressive informational resources were, for example, at play at every step of the 'going to scale' of ORT: from *in vitro* studies in scientific laboratories; to testing in clinics, in the field and in pilot projects; to the formation of the WHO Control of Diarrhoeal Diseases Programme; to international conferences on ORT; to the formation of national CDD programmes in over 100 developing countries; to the design, production and dissemination of ORT-related publications, videos and other materials; to training courses and workshops for practitioners and middle-level workers; and finally — sometimes even using house-to-house visits as in the case of the Bangladesh Rural Advancement Committee which reached 13 million households within a decade — to sick children throughout the world.[41]

□ 5.2. ECONOMIC RESOURCES

While in many ways less critical than human and organizational resources for the realization of health rights, a minimum level of financial inputs is needed both at the household level and in the health service system for the maintenance and improvement of health. The cost requirements for improving health are in general not well known, particularly regarding ongoing expenditures to prevent disease and maintain good health in communities and households. A growing body of research in developing countries indicates the often substantial amounts of household budgets that are spent on health services, on the order of 10 per cent or more of total household spending, and frequently higher among the poor. However, there have been few attempts to quantify the cost requirements for adequate nutrition, water supply and sanitation needed to ensure a basic standard of health in its preventive and promotive dimensions.

At the level of health service provision, a number of efforts have been made to assess the unit costs of specific health actions, such as immunization, and to relate these to current budgets and expenditures.[42] However, owing to problems of linking particular inputs to health outcomes, and to a fundamental lack of data on costs in different regions and administrative settings, there has been until recently only limited understanding of the resource requirements of health services. A significant step in improving the understanding of financial requirements has been made by the World Bank, in preparation for its *World Development Report 1993: Investing in Health*.[43] The report assesses the costs and effectiveness of a wide range of health interventions and groups these into two principal 'packages' for implementation.

The package of 'public health' interventions includes:
(a) 'EPI Plus', the current standard immunization package supplemented by hepatitis B and yellow fever vaccines in selected countries, and vitamin A and iodine supplements in regions where deficiency of these micronutrient interventions is highly prevalent;
(b) school health activities to treat worm infections and micronutrient deficiencies, and to provide health education;
(c) information and education on health and nutrition, family planning, vector control and disease surveillance;
(d) activities to reduce consumption of tobacco, alcohol and other drugs; and
(e) AIDS prevention, including the prevention and control of sexually transmitted diseases.

The World Bank estimates the average cost of this package as a whole to be approximately $4.20, or about 1.2 per cent of GNP per capita in low-income countries; and $6.80 per capita, or 0.3 per cent of GNP, in middle-income countries (see Table 4.3).

The report also provides estimates for a minimum essential package of clinical services. Short-course chemotherapy for tuberculosis, management of the sick child, prenatal and delivery care, family planning, treatment of sexually transmitted diseases and limited medical care (assessment, advice, alleviation of pain, treatment of infection and minor trauma, and treatment of some more complicated conditions) is estimated to require some $7.80 per capita, or 2.2 per cent of GNP per capita, in low-income countries, and $14.70 per capita, or 0.6 per cent of income per capita, in middle-income countries.

Table 4.3 **- Proposed package of public health interventions**

Measure	Cost per capita in US dollars: Low-income countries	Middle-income countries
'EPI Plus' programme	.50	.80
School health	.30	.60
Health information and education	1.40	3.10
Tobacco and alcohol control	0.30	0.30
AIDS prevention	1.70	2.00
Total	4.20	6.80

Source: World Bank, 1993.

Within this package covering the entire population, services for the management of the sick child require about $1.60 per capita in low-income countries and $1.10 per capita in middle-income countries, while prenatal and delivery care are estimated at $3.80 and $8.80 per capita in low- and middle-income countries, respectively.

Taking these two packages together, the World Bank estimates that $12 per capita in low-income countries, and $21.50 per capita in middle-income countries, would be needed for full implementation, with the result of averting some 32 per cent of the total economic burden of disease in the low-income countries and 15 per cent of the disease burden in middle-income countries. At the global level, some $36 billion per year in low-income countries and $26 billion per year in middle-income countries, for an annual total of $62 billion, is required to implement the two packages. It is, however, judged that the majority of the total resources required is already, or could be, met through existing spending — current financing for actions within these two packages, plus the proceeds from potential restructuring in the health sector away from discretionary clinical services.

The remaining amount of some $10 billion annually is thus needed for the low-income countries (excluding China).[44] This amount is higher than the estimates of additional resource requirements for achieving health and nutrition goals developed at the World Summit for Children, which were for $6 billion per year. The two estimates are, however, roughly comparable if the requirements for population (family planning) — amounting to an additional $5 billion per year — are included in the World Summit estimates, bringing the total to approximately $11 billion per year.

New solutions must be found in each country to identify and mobilize the necessary resources for child health. The economic crisis of the 1980s and the prospects for the rest of the 1990s have clearly made governments unable to respond to all the health needs of their populations. Many governments have already taken significant steps to improve efficiency and reduce waste, for example by contracting out to the private sector services such as hospital catering, security and maintenance. As described in Chapter Two, there is also considerable scope for reallocating resources among sectors in favour of health, and reallocating within the sector in favour of 'priority' services along the lines that have been discussed above. Strengthening the tax base and making it more efficient and equitable over time is an even more fundamental need in many countries to make more resources available for the social sectors.

Sharing of the costs of services with service users, through community financing schemes or more formal cost-recovery programmes, has in recent years been promoted by many donors and governments. However, experience to date provides only limited general guidance on how charges should be set and for what services. Although there is considerable consensus about the feasibility and benefits of charging reasonable fees for different levels of services, a reliable way of exempting the very poor has yet to be found. When used properly, discriminatory pricing and sliding scales can ensure that the poor effectively receive services. (For many child health actions, particularly those of a public health nature, charges should of course normally be nominal or zero.) The issue is therefore not so much whether to transfer part of the financing responsibility from State to society, but rather how to transfer it in order to make services viable and contribute to improved health. For example, if a community is able to build or pay for a health centre at a certain time of the year, but is unable to pay a fee in cash throughout the year, one solution could be to limit their contribution to building the unit and waive the fee-for-service requirement. A variety of administrative issues are thus likely to be relevant to the implementation of cost sharing, depending on the situations of specific countries.

A major consideration in the allocation of resources is the sustainability of actions, and their associated benefits, into the future. In part this is an issue of cost-effective strategies, but it is also related to the present and expected future availability of resources. It is particularly important with respect to external assistance, in which many basic health services are financed initially by aid donors. Governments often do not make adequate provision to finance operating costs, and likewise aid-supported services at the local level often cannot be maintained on the basis of locally available inputs. As is stressed throughout this book, however, the challenge is not limited to the issue of mobilizing financial resources. The motivation of the population and the availability of leadership and other skills at the community level are essential complements to governmental allocations.

Notes

1 Access to family planning is identified as a right related to child health in Article 24, but it is an area that pertains less directly to children themselves than to their parents, particularly mothers. Family planning issues are raised at relevant points in this paper, but are not extensively discussed. For fuller examination of the rights aspects of women's reproductive health, see, for example, Cook, 1993, pp. 11, 41, 43.

2 Similarly, the 'Principles for the protection of persons with mental illness and the improvement of mental health care', adopted by General Assembly resolution 46/119 of 17 December 1991, establishes, *inter alia*, that "[e]very patient shall have the right to receive such health and social care as is appropriate to his or her health needs, and is entitled to care and treatment in accordance with the same standards as other ill persons" (Principle 8), and emphasizes that "[s]pecial care should be given within the purposes of these Principles ... to protect the rights of minors ..." (Principle 2).

3 In their comprehensive study of the right to health in the Americas, Fuenzalida-Puelma and Connor, 1989, found that a right to health and/or a duty of the State in regard to health was included in 20 constitutions in the western hemisphere. Whether and how health rights are mentioned were seen to depend on the nature of the country's legal system (common, civil or socialist law), the history of its constitutional development and specific political features.

4 For a fuller discussion of distribution principles in health, see de Jong and Rutten, 1983. In many developing countries, the movement towards 'middle-range' health systems has emerged as a consequence of economic adjustment policies, frequently entailing specific health policy changes to ensure that the needs of the poor are met (Cornia and de Jong, 1992; World Bank, 1993).

5 Bryant, 1977, identifies the basic principle, adapting from Rawls, that "whatever health services are available should be equally available to all. Departures from equality of distribution are permissible only if those worst off are made better off." Related distribution rules propose a floor of minimum

health services for all, the distribution of additional resources according to need, and involvement of the population receiving health care in decisions about the distribution and use of resources.

6 See, for example, Bayer et al., 1988, who propose standards for universal health insurance coverage, for a needs-based determination of services that should be made available, and for equitable sharing of the cost burden. These views reflect those of many observers of the U.S. scene over the past two decades. Along with the aim of containing rapidly escalating costs, concerns for equitable access to health services underlay the recent attempt to reform the U.S. health system. Mariner, 1994, assesses the implications of alternative reform models for individual rights.

7 Considering the case of health care formerly in South Africa, Kriel, 1989, observes that "equality of treatment is only just if it actually means the same thing to all. ... A segregated health service is a fundamentally unjust health service", p. 575.

8 Susser, 1993.

9 Ibid. Examining Great Britain and Cuba, the author concludes that equity alone in health services is insufficient to bring about equity in health status, and that achieving such broader equity in health conditions requires action at all levels of society.

10 Newell, 1975.

11 World Health Organization, 1978.

12 United Nations Economic and Social Commission for Asia and the Pacific and United Nations Children's Fund, 1985.

13 Cook, 1993.

14 Fuenzalida-Puelma and Connor, 1989, observe that "[a]dopting a definition of health in a legal text is problematic because of the difficulties of achieving uniformity of viewpoint. Fashioning a legally meaningful right to health is rendered more difficult by the clear disparities in individual health. ... International texts on the right to health do not show any uniformity of approach."

15 This discussion is necessarily summary in nature. For more detailed reference, the reader is referred to the sources cited.

16 At the same time, it has recently been found that some 80 per cent of pneumonia among children under 5 years is bacterial, rather than viral in nature. It is thus possible to go directly to treatment of these cases, increasing the likelihood of cure.

17 AIDS raises a number of issues in the case of adults, which are increasingly viewed as being among the most critical emerging rights questions both inside and outside of the health sector. See, for example, Parmet, 1989, and the work of many recent authors.

18 Cook, 1993.

19 For this reason, many studies now seek to reflect the 'burden of disease' in terms of 'disability-adjusted life years', a procedure followed in recent work by Jamison et al., 1993, and subsequently applied in the World Bank's 1993 *World Development Report* on health.

20 Table 4.2 draws on a variety of previous efforts to model or to interpret health-related outcomes. It is primarily based on the framework used to explain child malnutrition, developed as part of the UNICEF Nutrition Strategy and presented by Jonsson in the next chapter.

21 See Jonsson's discussion in following chapter.

22 Requirements for food, water and shelter are nearly always seen as more important priorities than 'health'. At the same time, the lack of these necessities may contribute to more than one half of morbidity and mortality in poorer communities. Responding to these felt needs is thus the first requirement for effective community health programmes. These and other issues are addressed by Arole and Arole, forthcoming, in their analysis of the Jamkhed community health project in Maharashtra, India.

23 Grant, 1994, p. 18.

24 World Health Organization, 1993b. Monitoring and evaluation exercises have been carried out on the achievement of 'Health for All' targets periodically since 1983. However, reporting tends to be incomplete, with limited systematic attention given to the processes by which health outcomes are being achieved, and it is difficult for the official assessments to measure performance comprehensively.

25 Walsh and Warren, 1986. The debate over 'selective' versus 'comprehensive' PHC strategies has continued since that time within WHO and the international public health community. Advocates have stressed the need for focus and for tools to assist in resource allocation, while critics have pointed to the interventionistic and partial nature of the selective approach; see, for example, Werner 1994.

26 To these four were later added food supplementation, female literacy and family planning. Similarly, USAID identified immunization and oral rehydration therapy as 'twin engines' of child survival, and emphasized these in their health assistance.

27 Goodfield, 1991.
28 World Health Organization, 1993b.
29 A study by WHO (Hutchins et al., 1993) reviewed 59 surveys from developing countries and 20 from industrialized countries. Missed opportunities were found in all but one survey, with nearly one third of all eligible women and children having experienced at least one missed opportunity. The reasons why immunization opportunities were missed were, in decreasing order of importance, vaccines not given simultaneously according to schedule; false contradictions to immunization registered by the health staff; negative health worker attitudes (e.g., fear of wasting vaccines); and logistical problems, including shortages and poor clinic scheduling.
30 Barnum and Kutzin, 1993, p. 1.
31 Ibid, pp. 2-20. The authors conclude that children, "... after they survive their first year of life, ... are much less likely to need hospitalization (for epidemiological reasons) during their pre-teen and teenage years than they will be in later life".
32 It should be noted that the categorization is of levels of state action, rather than of specific actors in the child rights arena. Some relevant actors, such as NGOs, the private sector and 'civil society' are thus not specifically included in the chart. The efforts of these actors are relevant in different ways at each level of society, and are discussed at appropriate points.
33 McPake et al., 1992.
34 Ibid.; Arole and Arole, forthcoming.
35 This population corresponds to the 'district' unit found in much of Africa; in other regions such as South Asia the 'district' is much larger in size, with the relevant smaller unit being identified, for example, as the *panchayati raj* in India.
36 World Bank, 1993.
37 See, for example, World Health Organization, 1993a, p. 65, and 1991.
38 World Bank, 1993, pp. 210-211.
39 United Nations Children's Fund, 1995.
40 See Sepúlveda, 1994.
41 Northrup, 1993.
42 For example, Patel, 1989.
43 World Bank, 1993.
44 Data are from the World Bank's *World Development Report 1993*, as compiled by Nigam and Parker, 1994.

Children's right to nutrition: food, care and a healthy environment

Urban Jonsson

1. Nutrition as a Human Right

1.1. NUTRITION IN UNITED NATIONS DECLARATIONS AND CONVENTIONS

The concept of 'nutrition' has changed over the years. For decades 'nutrition' was more or less synonymous with 'food' and 'alimentation'. During the last 15 years, however, 'nutrition' has been recognized as a much broader concept, in which nutritional status is seen as an outcome of several factors, including food, care, a healthy environment and access to health services. This should be kept in mind when reviewing the history of nutrition as a human right.

Nutrition is mentioned specifically in some United Nations declarations; for example, in the 1959 Declaration of the Rights of the Child (Principle 4) and in the 1969 Declaration on Social Progress and Development. In the latter, the "elimination of hunger and malnutrition and the guarantee of the right to proper nutrition" (Article 10.6) are listed as main goals. In most conventions and declarations, however, nutrition is not explicitly recognized as a human right, although it is implicit in the concepts of 'food' and 'freedom from hunger', which have been the subject of a large number of international and United Nations declarations and conventions. One instance is the famous 'Four Freedoms Address' made by United States President Franklin Delano Roosevelt in 1941, declaring "freedom from want" as one of the four basic freedoms. He identified "freedom from hunger" as a major component of "freedom from want" in his proposal at the 1943 international conference in Hot Springs, Virginia.

At about the same time, an international group of experts, under the auspices of the American Law Institute, prepared a draft report on essential human rights. The report included an article on the right to food and was presented by the Government of Panama to the 1945 San Francisco conference at which the United Nations was founded. The proposed article influenced the preparation of the Universal Declaration of Human Rights, adopted by the United Nations General Assembly in 1948, which sustains that "everyone has a right to a standard of living adequate for the health and well-being of himself and his family, including food ...". The right to food was further elaborated in the two covenants that together with the Universal Declaration of Human Rights constitute the International Bill of Human Rights:
(a) the International Covenant on Economic, Social and Cultural Rights (1966), which states that "States Parties to the present Covenant recognize the fundamental right of everyone to be free from hunger..."; and
(b) the International Covenant on Civil and Political Rights (1966), which recognizes that "[e]very human being has the inherent right to life" (Article 6.1).

In interpreting that right, the Human Rights Committee (established pursuant to the Covenant) has observed that "the protection of this right requires that States adopt positive measures". Such measures must include the elimination of malnutrition.

In her review of international laws relating to the right to food, K. Tomasevski enumerated the many contexts in which the right to food is identified: freedom from hunger; safeguarding of the right to food in armed conflicts, including food for prisoners; provision of food for refugees; disaster relief; international crimes involving deprivation of food and adequate nutrition; minimum wages; social security and social assistance; adequate nutrition for infants; consumer protection; food strategy; population policy; natural resources; fisheries; prohibition of slavery and forced labour; special categories of agricultural workers; education and vocational training in agriculture; rural organizations and associations; elimination of discrimination against women; and elimination of racial and ethnic discrimination.[1]

Over the years, several United Nations agencies have issued declarations in which the right to food has been clearly stated. The Food and Agriculture Organization (FAO) has naturally been in the front line of the fight against hunger in the world. The emphasis on food as a human right, however, has varied over the years, depending on who has led the Organization.[2] For example, although FAO was not actively involved in the early drafting stages of the Covenant on Economic, Social and Cultural Rights, the Organization began to give new emphasis to the right to food when B.R. Sen became its Director-General. The 'Freedom from Hunger Campaign' was launched worldwide in 1962, and Sen played an important role in the adoption of the Covenant's Article 11.2, which deals specifically with freedom from hunger.[3] FAO also promoted the inclusion of food as a human right in the 1974 World Food Conference Declaration and contributed to the adoption of a 'World Food Security Compact' in 1983.

The World Food Programme, established in 1961, submitted a document in connection with the preparation of the United Nations General Assembly Resolution on the Right to Development, in which it identified the right to food as "the most fundamental of all human rights, and a precondition to development". It also stated that the "right to development is seriously in jeopardy whenever the right to food cannot be fulfilled".

The United Nations World Food Council (WFC), established in 1974 after the World Food Conference, was seen by some as a realization of the 'World Food Board' proposed by Sir John Boyd Orr, the first Director-General of FAO (1945-1948) and winner of the Nobel peace prize in 1949. This was not, however, to be WFC's role: it became instead an advisory body to the United Nations General Assembly on policies. On two recent occasions, WFC has expressed a clear idea about food as a human right: in its Thirteenth Ministerial Session, Beijing, China, 1987, the ministers proclaimed that "access to food constitutes a human right which must be defended by governments, peoples and the international community"; and in its Fifteenth Ministerial Session, Cairo, Egypt, 1989, it was declared that WFC "strongly believes that access to enough food should be proclaimed by the international community as a basic human right".

□ 1.2. NUTRITION AND THE CONVENTION ON THE RIGHTS OF THE CHILD

Nutrition is explicitly mentioned three times in the Convention on the Rights of the Child (CRC) (emphasis added in each case). In Article 24, which recognizes the child's right to the highest standard of health and medical care attainable, it is mentioned twice. States Parties agree to take appropriate measures:

> To combat disease and *malnutrition*, including within the framework of primary health care, through, *inter alia*, the application of readily available technology and through the provision of adequately nutritious foods and clean drinking water ... (para 2.c);
>
> To ensure that all segments of society, in particular parents and children, are informed, have access to education and are supported in the use of basic knowledge of child health and *nutrition*, the advantages of breast-feeding, hygiene and environmental sanitation ... (para. 2.e).

In Article 27, which asserts the child's right to an adequate standard of living, nutrition is again specified:

> States Parties ... shall in case of need provide material assistance and support programmes, particularly with regard to *nutrition*, clothing and housing (para. 3).

It may seem surprising that so little is said in the CRC about nutrition, given its crucial importance for child survival and development. If one considers the earlier emphasis in human rights documents on 'food', however, the CRC is clearly a step in the right direction in its wider focus on 'nutrition'. Moreover, if a broader concept of nutrition is used, such as the one promoted by UNICEF in which food, care, a healthy environment and access to health services are equally necessary, 'nutrition' is almost everywhere in the CRC.

□ 1.3. PROGRESS IN IMPLEMENTING NUTRITION AS A HUMAN RIGHT

To be 'empowered', the poor must be involved in a process that reduces their poverty. Amartya Sen defines development or poverty reduction as a "process of expanding capabilities of people".[4] Poverty reduction is related to resources and resource transfers. Empowerment implies poverty reduction and increased control of resources, but the reverse is not necessarily true. Empowerment is much more than poverty reduction. Empowerment means not only that resources are transferred to or generated by the poor, but also that the poor have a *right* to these resources; that they are entitled to these resources and have the power to control the transfers and necessary changes to ensure these entitlements.

An assessment of the progress of nutrition as a human right must therefore recognize the difference between:

(a) the achievement of poverty-reduction targets, including nutrition-related targets; and

(b) the achievement of nutrition as a right.

The second implies the first, but the first does not necessarily imply the second.[5]

This does not mean that efforts to achieve the Goals for Children and Development in the 1990s, endorsed at the World Summit for Children held in New York in September 1990, must necessarily conflict with efforts to implement nutrition as a human right. It all depends on *how* the goals are achieved. Achieving the Summit goals must be a democratic and empowering process involving the poor as actors and emphasizing capacity-building, ownership and sustainability. In such a way, work towards achieving the goals and work towards implementing nutrition as a human right become mutually reinforcing.

Progress, if any, towards the achievement of nutrition (or even food) as a human right has been slow. As Philip Alston summarized:

> The right to food has been endorsed more often and with greater unanimity and urgency than most other human rights, while at the same time being violated more comprehensively than probably any other right.[6]

The implementation of the International Code of Marketing of Breast Milk Substitutes (1981) probably represents the most important exception to the rule, although progress was very slow at first. After 10 years, only a handful of countries had enacted the Code as national law. In 1990, however, the Innocenti Declaration on the Protection, Promotion and Support of Breastfeeding included national action to implement the Code as one of its four operational targets for 1995. These targets were endorsed by both the World Health Assembly and the UNICEF Executive Board as the basis for their joint effort, the Baby-Friendly Hospital Initiative.

As a result of the Initiative, all but three developing countries where manufacturers and distributors of breastmilk substitutes had routinely provided free supplies of infant formula to hospitals and maternity facilities adopted policies to ban this marketing practice. Nine countries incorporated in national legislation their bans on free and low-cost supply and distribution of breastmilk substitutes. More than 20 countries are currently pursuing such comprehensive legislation. The European Union is planning to issue a directive based on the Code. These positive results make it clear that rights embodied in intergovernmental policy documents need concerted advocacy efforts if they are to be realized at the programmatic level.

The United Nations Security Council in its Resolution 794 of 3 December 1992 authorized the use of "all necessary means" to establish a secure environment for humanitarian relief operations in Somalia. This was the first resolution ever to authorize the use of force in support of humanitarian goals and represented "a major advance toward a new standard which says it is impermissible to massively and systematically interfere with a people's access to food".[7]

An important example of legal efforts to achieve nutrition as a right comes from Orissa, India. A lawyer and human rights activist, Biswapriya Kanunga, petitioned the Government of India and the State of Orissa to address the problem of high infant mortality in Orissa. He referred to previous court rulings and case law, quoting in particular a 1981 Supreme Court interpretation which found that the concept of "right to life" as contained in Article 21 of the Indian Constitution "is not restricted to mere animal existence. It means something more than just physical survival."[8]

In December 1992, FAO and the World Health Organization (WHO) organized the International Conference on Nutrition. The Conference was preceded by two years of preparation at national, regional and international levels. During this preparatory phase, several agencies and international nongovernmental organizations (NGOs) promoted the human rights aspect of nutrition. The first paragraph of the Conference's Declaration recognizes that "access to nutritionally adequate and safe food is a right for each individual". The Declaration also refers to international law in paragraph 15:

> We affirm in the context of international humanitarian law that food must not be used as a tool for political pressure. Food aid must not be denied because of political affiliations, geographic location, gender, age, ethnic, tribal or religious identity.

These and several other statements about food and nutrition as human rights were debated at the Conference. Many proposals were watered down or never made it to the final Declaration. Compared with the 1974 World Food Conference, the International Conference on Nutrition will not be remembered as a milestone for promoting nutrition as a human right.

□ 1.4. SCIENCE AND ETHICS IN NUTRITION

Ethics or moral philosophy aims at the "understanding of moral concepts and justif[ies] moral principles and theories".[9] Science is descriptive, whereas ethics is normative: it deals with what ought to be, with what is right or wrong, or permissible, behaviour with respect to basic values.

Science is mostly advanced by observation and logical deduction or induction. Ethics, in contrast, is advanced by reaching consensus through dialogue, reflection, enquiry or, sometimes, confrontation. Although many laws are based on ethical consensus, ethics is not the same as law. *Unethical* behaviour can normally only be sanctioned by praise and blame, referring to one's conscience; *unlawful* behaviour can always be sanctioned by punishments determined by a judicial body.

Human rights represent ethical positions. A 'right', however, does not mean "the same in the human rights system as it does in positive international law".[10] Human rights are not necessarily enforceable, but are instead broad, general standards that must be given concrete meaning through specific national action. National legislation is required to enforce the right.

The nutrition goals agreed upon at the World Summit for Children can be defended on both scientific and ethical grounds. On the one hand, it is scientifically proved, for example, that reduction in iron deficiency anaemia increases productivity and income, or that reduced protein-energy malnutrition lowers the cost of health services. On the other hand, the Summit nutrition goals represent a "moral minimum",[11] which can be justified by ethical arguments. It is in this context that nutrition as a human right becomes both better understood and more powerful. Because nutrition goals *can* be achieved, "hunger and malnutrition are unacceptable in a world that has both the knowledge and the resources to end this human catastrophe".[12]

The CRC recognizes the child's right to nutritional well-being. This brings the issue of child malnutrition from the realm of an ethical position, stressed by many, into the area of international human rights, "from which legally enforceable rights should be constructed at the national level".[13]

In conclusion, there are both scientific and ethical reasons for eliminating child malnutrition. Interventions to achieve the goals should be designed and implemented so that they reinforce the promotion, protection and support of nutrition as a human right. It should be recognized that the achievement of the nutrition goals is a necessary condition for the implementation of this right.

■ 2. Nutrition and Science

□ 2.1. BRIEF HISTORY OF NUTRITION

Human nutrition is a relatively new scientific discipline. It became a separate discipline towards the end of the last century with the discovery of the existence and role of vitamins. Researchers found that diets deficient in vitamins explained such well-known diseases as pellagra and scurvy. The supplementation of very small amounts of different vitamins prevented these diseases. The idea that nutritional diseases are caused by deficiencies dominated nutrition research for decades.

In 1933, Cecily Williams published her discovery that a severe form of oedema in young children, prevalent in present-day Ghana, was most likely associated with a monotonous maize diet.[14] She gave the name *kwashiorkor* to the disease. With the new discoveries in protein biochemistry, scientists soon concluded that kwashiorkor was a result of *protein deficiency*. Both WHO and FAO sent missions to Africa in 1950, which reported that kwashiorkor was very common and contributed to the slow progress in the continent.[15] J. Waterlow found a similar situation in the Caribbean.[16]

Protein deficiency as the major cause of malnutrition dominated nutrition research, education and programmes for 25 years (up to 1974) and is still influencing the work in many developing countries. The concept was gradually refined by translating protein deficiency into protein-deficient diets and protein-deficient foods, and then into foods deficient in particular amino acids. In 1962, a United Nations committee concluded that a "world protein crisis" was "impending".[17]

The protein-deficiency paradigm was increasingly challenged by both researchers in human nutrition and practitioners trying to solve the problem of malnutrition. By 1970, there was ample evidence that protein-deficient foods were, in fact, *not* the major cause of protein-energy malnutrition. It had been found that most diets consumed by young children would provide adequate amounts of protein, provided that the total dietary (energy) intake was sufficient. A heated debate took place in *The Lancet* about 'the protein fiasco'.[18] At about the same time, an increasing number of social scientists became interested in the problem of malnutrition. They emphasized social, economic and political factors as major causes of malnutrition. During the years before and immediately after the World Food Conference in 1974, there was, thus, a clear paradigm shift: the problem of malnutrition came to be identified as a societal problem that manifested itself in human nutritional diseases.

Most economists and political scientists in the 19th and early 20th centuries studied aspects of the production and consumption of food, which has always been recognized as a basic necessity for human survival. Poverty was their major interest, and they saw low food consumption as a direct reflection of poverty. In the 1930s, the apparent overproduction of food in Europe and the United States was blamed for the economic crisis, and political pressure was built up to reduce food production.[19] Boyd Orr and others, however, had discovered enormous food deficits in developing countries and sustained that, in view of global needs, food production should continue to be increased. A task force was established in the Health Committee of the League of Nations; it produced a series of impressive studies on the theme 'Marry Agriculture and Health',[20] based on Boyd Orr's pioneering book *Food, Health and Income*, published in 1936.

After the Second World War, this 'Geneva Circle' (Boyd Orr, A. Mayer, F.L. McDougall and others)[21] exerted influence on President Roosevelt to address the world food problem. The President had already promoted the idea of a "World Food Plan" and had presented a proposal by the Geneva group to the 1943 international conference in Hot Springs, Virginia, at which agreement had been reached to establish FAO. When the Organization was founded in 1945, nutrition was placed first in the preamble of its constitution (adopted in 1947). Member States are urged to promote the common welfare and to take collective action to "raise the levels of nutrition and standards of living of the peoples under their respective jurisdictions".

□ 2.2. THEORY AND PRACTICE

All problems, including development problems, have a scientific and ethical aspect. Science tells what *can* be done, whereas ethics states what *should* be done. Science attempts to deal with facts and uses logic as the means of communication, whereas ethics progresses through dialogue and enquiry.

Science normally consists of theory and practice. These two aspects are dialectically interrelated. A theory normally does not mean anything without testing and use in practice; conversely, practice is 'blind' without a theory. Statements such as "A theory is the most practical thing" (Einstein) and "You find what you look for" (Kuhn) reflect this interrelationship.

The principal domain of a science influences science itself. This reciprocity has not been recognized by nutrition scholars, creating serious conceptual problems. The science of human nutrition was developed to increase the knowledge of bio-chemical metabolism of nutrients and its physiological and clinical implications. People trained in this particular science are normally called nutritionists. During the 1950s, when the problem of malnutrition in developing countries was discovered by Western observers, nutritionists saw it as their responsibility to 'solve' the problem, and non-nutritionists supported their viewpoint. It was not until the 1970s that scholars and observers began to recognize that the problem of malnutrition in society could not be adequately addressed by nutritionists, but would require the work of economists, political scientists, anthropologists, ecologists and other social scientists. Today it is obvious that there is an urgent need to develop a new science on nutrition problems in society, which is quite different from the science of human nutrition. As in all new sciences, a theory will be required.

Theories emerge from the interaction between broad 'conceptual frameworks' and practice. A 'conceptual framework' is not a quantitative model, but rather a set of logical entities and their likely causal relationships. In that sense, a conceptual framework reflects a certain paradigmatic position. The UNICEF Nutrition Strategy, discussed in the following section, promotes this kind of conceptual framework and will be used in the subsequent analysis of nutrition as a human right.

☐ 2.3. UNICEF CONCEPTUAL FRAMEWORK ON NUTRITION PROBLEMS IN SOCIETY[22]

Nutrition is defined by WHO as "a process whereby living organisms utilize food for maintenance of life, growth and normal functioning of organs and tissues and the production of energy". Nutritional well-being or 'nutritional security' therefore implies survival, growth, development and activity. The *nutritional status* of an individual describes the situation in relation to nutritional well-being. A number of anthropometric, biochemical and clinical indicators have been developed to measure nutritional status.

The nutritional status of an individual, including any of the four major forms of malnutrition (protein-energy malnutrition, iodine deficiency disorder, vitamin A deficiency and iron deficiency anaemia), is an outcome of complex biological and social processes, as summarized in the conceptual framework of Figure 5.1.

Figure 5.1: **Causes of malnutrition**

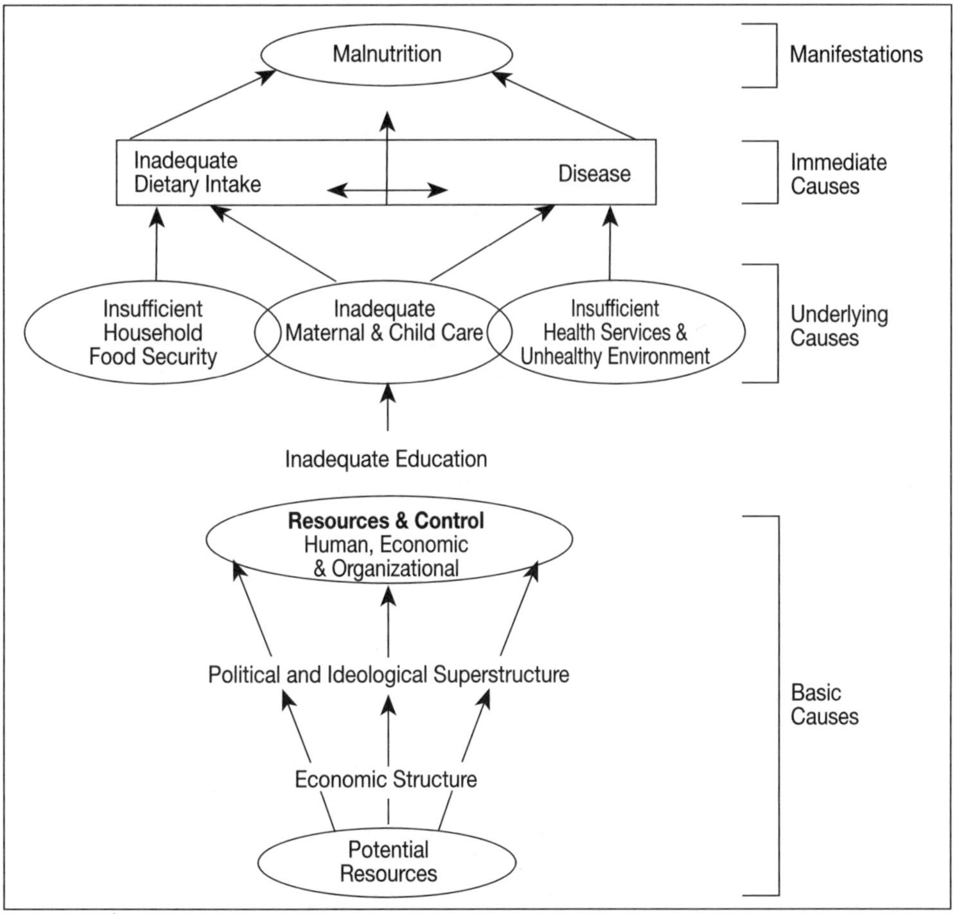

Source: United Nations Children's Fund, 1992d.

2.3.1. *Immediate Causes*

Inadequate dietary intake and disease are the immediate causes or determinants of malnutrition. The inadequacy may include total energy, protein, vitamins or minerals. Inadequate dietary intake may increase the susceptibility to and severity of infection; conversely, many diseases reduce dietary intake and utilization through loss of appetite and reduced absorption.

2.3.2. *Underlying Causes*

The numbers of possible underlying causes seem almost endless and their interrelationships complex. All, however, reflect a particular utilization of resources in the past and in the present. One way of grouping these causes is to identify a set of outcome conditions necessary for adequate nutrition or, more precisely, for adequate dietary intake and absence of disease. Three such conditions can be identified:

- adequate access to food (household food security);
- adequate care of children and women; and
- a healthy environment and adequate access to basic health services.

Each of these conditions is necessary for adequate nutrition, but not sufficient by itself. If all three are fulfilled, however, it is likely that dietary intake will be satisfactory, disease controlled and adequate nutrition secured.

Household food security is defined here as access to food, adequate in quantity and quality, to fulfil all nutritional requirements for all household members throughout the year. Household food security is an outcome of technical and social processes in society, but ultimately depends on the availability, access and use of resources. In an analysis of the household food security situation, it is important to estimate not only the degree of household food security achieved, but also the amount of resources utilized relative to the total resources controlled by the household. With such an analysis, it is then possible in a given situation to identify vulnerable groups and to establish the degree of their vulnerability by calculating the amount of household resources utilized to attain household food security.

Adequate maternal and child care has only recently been fully recognized as having an important bearing on the nutritional status of mothers and children. 'Care' refers to caregiving behaviour such as breastfeeding and adopting complementary feeding practices, ensuring personal hygiene, diagnosing illnesses, stimulating language and other cognitive capabilities, and providing emotional support. Care also refers to the support that the family or community provides to its members, and to behaviours within the household that determine how the household food supply is allocated. In addition, care includes the utilization of health services and water and sanitation systems to create a healthy micro-environment for household members.

Child care, like household food security, is the outcome of complex processes in society, but ultimately depends on the availability, access and use of resources. Important causes of inadequate child care include: poor health of the mother; lack of education and wrong beliefs of caregivers; lack of self-confidence of the mother; insufficient social support from the community, the family and the husband; the excessive workload of the mother; and the mother's lack of control over available resources.

A healthy environment and access to health services together form the third necessary condition for good nutrition. Access to water and safe excreta disposal are prerequisites for control of diarrhoea and other diseases influencing the nutritional status of children. Pre- and post-natal care, immunization (particularly against measles), oral rehydration therapy, distribution of micronutrient supplements, de-worming, family planning and health education are all important health services with great impact on nutrition. The achievement of the 'health' condition ultimately depends on resources in the same way as the achievement of the 'food' and 'care' conditions does.

2.3.3. Basic Causes

As has been discussed in the previous chapters, human, economic and organizational resources are available at different levels of society and controlled in many different ways. At the household level, men usually control more of the resources, which often constrains the achievement of the necessary conditions of 'food', 'care' and 'health'.

The use of resources depends on the way a problem is understood as well as on the perception and priorities of those who control resources. Education plays a particularly important role in determining how resources are utilized to secure 'food', 'care' and 'health' for children. It is important to recognize the interaction between nutrition and education. Better-educated parents, especially mothers, contribute to improved child nutrition; and a better-nourished child shows greater attention and learning capacity than a malnourished child.

The availability and control of human, economic and organizational resources at different levels of society are the results of historical processes in society. These processes can be seen as the basic causes of malnutrition and can be divided into four groups:

(a) *ecological/technical conditions of production*, including the environment (soil and climate, for example), the population-resource ratio, the level of technology used, and the levels of people's skills;
(b) *social conditions of production*, including such aspects as the ownership of the means of production, the division of labour, and power relationships;
(c) *political factors* (or state interventions), including policies on employment, prices, incomes, subsidies, health, education and agriculture, as well as the legal system as a whole; and
(d) *ideological factors*, including habits, beliefs, cultural preferences and all ideas that legitimize actions in society.

The development and interaction of these different factors explain the existing availability and control of resources, which in turn explain the degree of fulfilment of the three necessary conditions (food, care and health) for good child nutrition.

□ 2.4. CONSTRAINTS AND FACILITATING FACTORS

The whole area of nutrition has been marginalized by governments, universities and agencies. This is partly because nutrition is not a 'sector' but an outcome of processes in other sectors such as agriculture, health, education and social welfare. Another reason is probably political; there is recognition that the basic causes of child malnutrition are social and political and ought to be addressed by governments, a responsibility that could require substantial structural changes. A third reason is the prevailing opinion that nutrition is a 'private' problem that should be solved by parents only. The tradition of home economics has contributed to keeping the nutrition problem 'in the kitchen'.

This marginalization is most clearly seen in the Ministries of Health. With only a few exceptions, nutrition receives almost no serious attention. Nutrition work is often delegated to small 'nutrition units' with inadequately trained workers (mainly female, reflecting the general gender bias in this discipline), second-rate offices and small budgets. At the same time, senior Ministry of Health staff do not recognize that some of the major activities they undertake are important for nutrition. Diarrhoeal disease control and immunization against measles are typical examples.

Nutrition is taught as a subject in the faculties of agriculture and medicine and is normally focused on food production and on the biochemical aspects of human nutrition. Courses in applied nutrition addressing the social aspects of nutrition are exceedingly rare.

The lack of a reasonable consensus about the nature of the nutrition problem is another major constraint in the work to eliminate malnutrition. The nutrition problem is usually reduced to an agricultural problem (not enough food), to a health problem, to an educational problem, or to a demographic problem (excessive population growth). Most often, child malnutrition is seen as a food problem, and still too often primarily as a problem of insufficient protein-rich foods. Most training courses and textbooks perpetuate these incorrect ideas. Developing countries, however, have both a *food problem* and a *nutrition problem*. It is important to recognize that these two problems are related but not the same. Food is one necessary condition for good nutrition; adequate care and access to health services and a healthy environment are other necessary conditions. The fact that protein-energy malnutrition is more prevalent in the 6 months-3 years age-group than in older children (who require *more* food) suggests that factors other than household food security contribute to malnutrition among young children.

2.5. NUTRITION, RESOURCES AND ENTITLEMENTS

Amartya Sen defines a person's entitlements as "the set of alternative bundles of commodities over which a person can establish command". His basic conclusion is that hunger and malnutrition are not primarily a result of inadequate food production, but rather of the absence or breakdown of a person's entitlements.[23] In his recent book *Hunger and Public Action*, he admits that the focus on entitlements as command over *commodities* needs to be broadened to encompass basic human capabilities.

In the perspective of the UNICEF Nutrition Strategy, Sen's entitlements are almost identical with the command over commodities and services required for the fulfilment of the 'food', 'care' and 'health' conditions. Sen sustains that there is,

> ... the need to broaden our attention from the command over food to other influences, including the command over the commodities that have a substantial impact on nutrition and health. A person's capability to avoid undernourishment may depend not merely on his or her intake of food, but also on the person's access to health care, medical facilities, elementary education, drinking water, and sanitary facilities.[24]

Sen's more recent focus on human capabilities is reflected in the UNICEF Nutrition Strategy. The fulfilment of the 'food', 'care' and 'health' conditions depends on the availability and control of human, economic and organizational resources. Individual *nutritional security* can therefore be defined as the minimum necessary access to human, economic and organizational resources required to fulfil the necessary condition of 'food', 'care' and 'health'.

3. Goals and Plans

3.1. NUTRITION GOALS AND TARGETS

A *goal* is a desirable state of affairs. The virtual elimination of iodine deficiency disorders is one example of a goal. A *target* defines the date at which either the goal itself should be achieved (virtual elimination of iodine deficiency disorders by 2000) or a specific proportion of the goal should be achieved (such as reduction of protein-energy malnutrition by 20 per cent by 1995). An agreement or 'promise' to achieve a target is, of course, much more committing than an agreement to achieve a goal.

The WFC Cairo Declaration, adopted in 1989, specifies four hunger-related goals:

(a) elimination of starvation and deaths caused by famine;
(b) tangible reduction of chronic hunger;
(c) substantial reduction of malnutrition and mortality among young children; and
(d) elimination of major nutritional deficiency diseases.

Towards the end of the 1980s, WHO, UNICEF and several other United Nations agencies discussed the specification of human development goals for the 1990s, which in this case were actually targets. A number of targets directly related to nutrition were defined. These targets were endorsed in 1990 by the World Health Assembly and the UNICEF Executive Board and were adopted by the World Summit for Children in September 1990 to be achieved by the year 2000. These targets are referred to as the 'Summit goals'. Reduction of severe and moderate malnutrition among under-5 children by half is designated as a major goal (See Appendix Two). Supporting nutrition goals (Section II.B) include, in addition, the reduction of low birth weight, the reduction of iron deficiency anaemia in women, the virtual elimination of iodine and vitamin A deficiency disorders, the empowerment of women to breastfeed, the institutionalization of growth promotion and monitoring, and the dissemination of knowledge and supporting services to increase food production and to ensure household food security.

The same targets were incorporated in 'Agenda 21', which deals with environment and development, adopted by the Earth Summit in Rio de Janeiro in 1992. The 1992 International Conference on Nutrition held in Rome reaffirmed the commitment to the Summit goals for nutrition, while also specifying two additional goals to be achieved before the end of this decade:

(a) to end famine and famine-related deaths; and

(b) to end starvation and nutritional deficiency diseases in communities afflicted by natural and man-made disasters.

During 1992, the Summit goals, including the nutrition goals, were reviewed at regional meetings in Colombo, Mexico City, Tunis and Dakar. A number of mid-decade targets were agreed upon at these meetings, including the virtual elimination of iodine deficiency disorders and vitamin A deficiency and the support of the Baby-Friendly Hospital Initiative. An additional mid-decade target was endorsed by the United Nations Human Rights Conference in Vienna in May 1993, which called for universal ratification of the CRC by the end of 1995.

□ 3.2. NATIONAL PROGRAMMES OF ACTION FOR CHILDREN

In the Declaration made at the World Summit for Children, heads of states and governments agreed to prepare National Programmes of Action (NPAs) outlining strategies to achieve the Summit goals by the year 2000. A detailed review of 55 NPAs[25] carried out in 1993 reveals a number of nutrition-related trends. Almost all (47) of the NPAs have included the goal to reduce protein-energy malnutrition, about 35 have included goals to reduce micronutrient malnutrition, and less than half (24) have included the breastfeeding goals. Many countries lack reliable baseline data for protein-energy malnutrition, and only 30-40 per cent have any baseline data on micronutrient malnutrition.

In most NPAs, 'food' and 'health' are recognized as necessary conditions for nutritional security, whereas only a few (11) have recognized 'care' as an equally necessary condition. Almost all countries emphasize the importance of participation, but few bring up the need for empowerment. Only 10 countries use an explicit conceptual framework in the analysis of the causes of malnutrition.

Several NPAs make detailed references to the CRC (as has been described more fully in Chapter Three). The achievement of the Summit goals is generally seen as a priority articulation of the CRC. In Zimbabwe's NPA, for example, it is stated that the priority rights for children for the 1990s and the main strategies in the programme are in some measure being implemented in ongoing sectoral programmes. A large number of NPAs reflect an awareness of the combined economic benefits (science) and the human rights aspects (ethics) of children's problems, including malnutrition.

□ 3.3. THE INTERNATIONAL CONFERENCE ON NUTRITION: WORLD DECLARATION AND PLAN OF ACTION

The International Conference on Nutrition, held in Rome in December 1992, was attended by 1,300 participants, including over 1,000 representatives from 159 countries (140 participants of ministerial level). The issue of human rights was emphasized by Pope John II in his opening address:

> It is up to you to reaffirm in a new way each individual's fundamental inalienable right to nutrition. The Universal Declaration of Human Rights has already asserted the right to sufficient food. What we must now do is ensure that this right is applied and that everyone has access to food, food security, a healthy diet and nutrition education.

The Conference adopted a World Declaration and Plan of Action for Nutrition. In the Declaration, Governments agreed "to revise or prepare, before the end of 1994, national plans of action, including goals and measurable targets" (paragraph 21). The Plan of Action provides a technical framework for the preparation of these national plans of action. Of the nine proposed strategies, two are especially important for the implementation of nutrition as a human right:

(a) incorporating nutrition objectives into development programmes and policies; and

(b) assessing, analysing and monitoring the nutrition situation.

Structural adjustment policies, in particular, should be exposed to a 'nutrition audit' to ensure that the most vulnerable groups in society are not negatively affected by such policies. Monitoring of the nutrition situation, in particular national trends, is instrumental in the assessment of the implementation of Article 4 of the CRC.

In June 1992, six months before the start of the Rome Conference, UNICEF sponsored a meeting on nutrition and human rights at the Norwegian Institute of Human Rights in Oslo. The meeting was attended by a group of concerned individuals from several countries, disciplines and institutions, working in the fields of human rights, nutrition, food and health. The meeting agreed to establish a *World Alliance for Nutrition and Human Rights* whose aim would be to mobilize NGOs in the areas of human rights and nutrition. The Alliance,

> ... will seek to raise the level of priority for nutrition in the allocation of resources at the international, national and local levels. It will also urge governments to introduce into their domestic law such measures as are needed for ensuring adequate nutrition.[26]

It was further agreed that the Alliance would promote compliance with the prohibition of food deprivation as a method of war, and seek to develop a nutrition-based approach to human rights monitoring.

Later, at the International Conference on Nutrition itself, a meeting was arranged with the joint participation of the Steering Committee, the new Alliance and the International Peace Research Association's Food Study Group, the Food International Action Network and the Children's World Foundation. Three task forces were established: one on children's rights to food and nutrition; a second on international monitoring of the implementation of these rights; and a third on the use of food as a weapon.

A large number of NGOs participated in the Rome conference. The 'public interest' NGOs agreed to establish a *Global Food and Nutrition Alliance* to coordinate, strengthen and monitor follow-up actions. A number of subcommittees were set up. A major task for the Alliance will be to facilitate the flow of information about conference-related activities by 'public interest' NGOs and international agencies. A newsletter will be distributed and focal points in all countries of the world will be identified. From the human rights viewpoint, this Alliance might become one of the most important results of the whole International Conference on Nutrition process.

■ 4. Progress in Child Nutrition

□ 4.1. DATA ON CHILD NUTRITION

Availability of data on child malnutrition has improved significantly during the last 10 years. By April 1993, 85 developing countries had data on the prevalence of underweight, covering about 90 per cent of the under-five population. For an increasing number of countries, two or more surveys have been undertaken during the last 15 years, which makes it possible to estimate trends in protein-energy malnutrition. Important gaps, however, still need to be filled to make monitoring of the achievement of the Summit goals feasible. Less than half of all developing countries have 'current' (for 1985 or later) data on protein-energy malnutrition, and one third have no data at all. Availability of data on micronutrient malnutrition is even more unsatisfactory, although the situation is improving.

The *Second Report on the World Nutrition Situation 1992*, published by the United Nations Administrative Committee on Coordination/Subcommittee on Nutrition,[27] provides the most comprehensive compilation of data on nutritional status currently available, including trend analyses for 14 countries. A 1993 publication by UNICEF assembles all available data from nutrition surveys.[28]

□ 4.2. NUTRITIONAL DISORDERS

4.2.1. Iodine Deficiency Disorders

According to the WHO publication *Global Prevalence of Iodine Deficiency Disorders*,[29] over 1.5 billion people are vulnerable to iodine deficiency disorders because they live in areas where the food and water normally consumed contain insufficient iodine to meet optimal requirements. Over 500 million people have goitre, the enlargement of the thyroid gland indicating inadequate iodine intake. Six million women with goitre become pregnant each year. In about 30,000 of these pregnancies, fetal damage due to inadequate iodine is so severe that the fetus dies or is stillborn. In about 120,000 pregnancies, the development of the fetal nervous system is so disrupted that the child is born a cretin. According to projections, 1.2 million iodine-deficient mothers will have children whose intelligence quotient will be reduced by about 10 points; many of these children will have sight or hearing defects. Some 50 million young children deficient in iodine will have reduced learning abilities. Moreover, 150 million adults are apathetic or have reduced mental alertness because of inadequate iodine intake.

Iodine deficiency disorders were eliminated in the United States and several countries in Europe by 1950 through the widespread use of iodized salt. Progress in controlling these disorders was achieved in a number of South American and Asian countries in the 1970s and 1980s. During the last three years, almost all remaining countries suspected of having problems eradicating iodine deficiency disorders have assessed their situations and formulated plans for control.

4.2.2. Vitamin A Deficiency

Vitamin A deficiency is caused by an inadequate intake of foods rich in vitamin A (mainly foods of animal origin) or pro-vitamin A (red and yellow fruits and vegetables). Frequent and severe infections decrease vitamin A stores and increase the risk of deficiency.

According to WHO estimates, about 190 million pre-school children live in areas where they are at risk of vitamin A deficiency. The prevalence of clinical (visible by examination) signs of vitamin A deficiency is reasonably well known; a number of countries, notably in South East Asia, have already virtually eliminated clinical signs of vitamin A deficiency, including blindness. Partly because of the difficulty of measuring, the prevalence of low-serum vitamin A, indicating sub-clinical (not visible by examination) deficiency, has been estimated in relatively few countries. Lack of agreement on the extent and prevalence of marginal vitamin A deficiency remains an important constraint to tackling the problem in many countries, particularly in Africa.

4.2.3. Iron Deficiency Anaemia

Iron deficiency, the most common nutritional disorder in the world, affects over one billion people, particularly pre-school children and reproductive-aged women. It also has a serious impact on schoolchildren and working males. Iron deficiency results from consuming diets containing insufficient iron, or diets in which iron is not readily absorbed. Iron from animal foods is most readily absorbed, and animal foods can increase iron absorption from vegetable sources. Vitamin C can also increase the absorption of iron from cereals and vegetables.

Over 370 million women in developing countries (about 40 per cent) are estimated to have anaemia, which is prevalent throughout the developing world. Nearly half the total number of anemic women are in South Asia. Although current figures on anaemia prevalence indicate little global change, there is some evidence of increases in sub-Saharan Africa and South Asia.

4.2.4. Protein-energy Malnutrition

In 1990, there were 536 million children under 5 years of age in developing countries. Of these, 184 million, or 34 per cent, were underweight (below minus two standard deviations from the median weight-for-age of the NCHS standard reference population).[30] In 1975, about 167 million, or 41.6 per cent, of the total 402 million under-fives were underweight. Globally the prevalence has gone down, although the total number of affected has increased. These global figures mask strong regional differences (Figure 5.2). South Asia shows the highest prevalence of protein-energy malnutrition (58.5 per cent) and accounts for 100 million of the total 184 million underweight children. South America has a low prevalence (7.7 per cent), whereas sub-Saharan Africa is the only region where no improvement in underweight prevalence (about 30 per cent) has taken place during the last 15 years.

The trends in protein-energy malnutrition are very promising in some countries in Asia, particularly in Vietnam, Malaysia and Thailand (Figure 5.3A). In South America as well, countries such as Brazil, Colombia and Bolivia are on the 'right track' towards achieving the Summit nutrition goals. In contrast, some African countries — notably Nigeria, Togo and Zambia — actually show deteriorating trends (Figure 5.3B). A recent survey in Ethiopia revealed that the prevalence of underweight increased from about 37 per cent in 1983 to 47 per cent in 1992.[31]

■ 5. Nutrition and Resources

□ 5.1. HUMAN, ECONOMIC AND ORGANIZATIONAL RESOURCES

It has been shown that individual nutritional security requires that three necessary conditions — food, care and health — be satisfied. Resources are needed to fulfil these three conditions, which actually often compete for the same resources (income or women's time, for instance). The three major cate-

Figure 5.2: **Regional trends in protein-energy malnutrition**

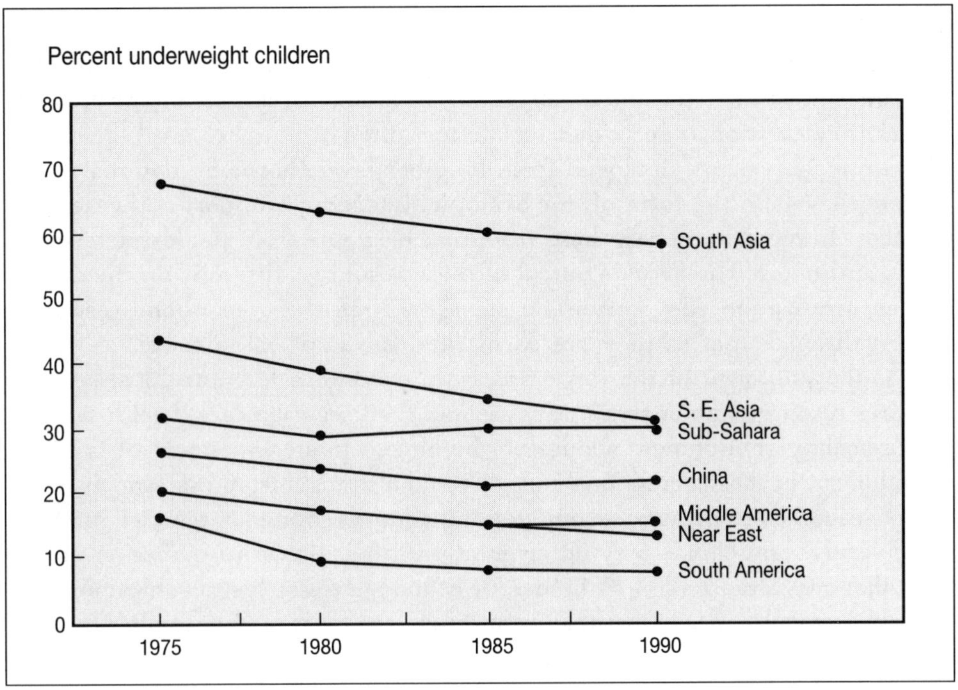

Figure 5.3: **Trends in protein-energy malnutrition, South East Asia and sub-Saharan Africa**

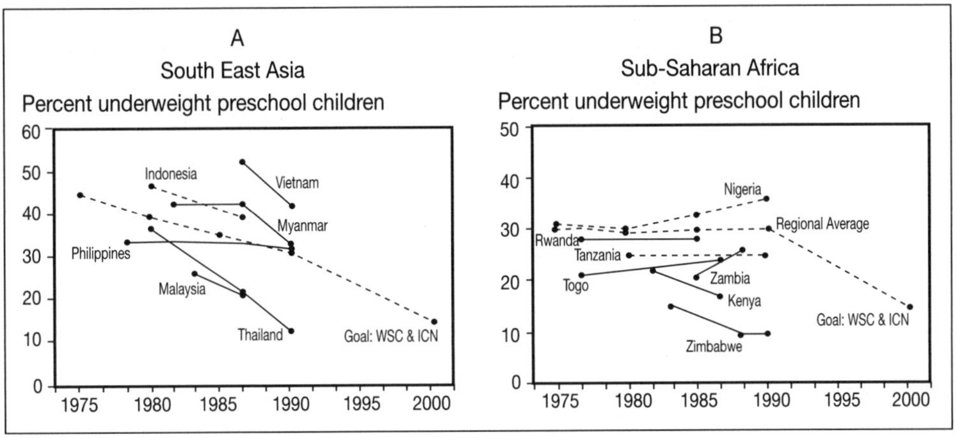

Sources: United Nations Administrative Committee on Coordination/Subcommittee on Nutrition, 1992/1993

gories of resources — human, economic and organizational resources — can also be classified as 'stocks' or 'flows', as explained in Chapter Two (see especially Table 2.1).

Before appropriate actions can be designed, the availability and control of resources must be determined. All resources are controlled, either at the level where they exist or at any other level, most often at a higher level of society. Certain resources are deployed from a higher level (normally national level) to lower levels in the form of, for example, budgetary support and extension services. In most countries, these resources originate from the lower levels as levies and taxes. The actual control of these resources depends on the degree of decentralization (devolution) in society. Often these economic resources are conditional; that is, they are earmarked for a special purpose.

As the fulfilment of the three necessary conditions for nutritional security requires resources, an analysis of household food security, care, health services and a healthy environment should not be limited to an assessment of the level of fulfilment of these conditions, but it should also include an assessment of the use of resources (type, relative amount and control). For example, two different 'food-secure' households may differ greatly in their use of resources. A household that uses almost all of its human or economic resources to achieve its food security is much more vulnerable or at much greater risk of becoming food insecure than is a household that uses a smaller portion of its resources. Four categories can be defined to assist in targeting support (Table 5.1).

As explored in Chapter One, resources are available at different levels of society. Table 1.1 provided a concise summary of the kind of resources required at different levels of society to implement the CRC, including children's right to nutrition. Therefore, only a few nutrition-specific additions will be made here.

The most important human resource at all levels of society is the ability to assess the problem of malnutrition, analyse its major causes, and design and implement resource-relevant actions. At all levels, but particularly at the national level, a reasonable *consensus* needs to be reached on the nature of the nutrition problem, including a conceptual framework. Without such a consensus, national nutrition policies and strategies are of limited use.

As far as nutrition is concerned, access to cultivable land is an important economic resource at household level. Almost all successful community-based, nutrition-oriented programmes are associated with the existence of a community organization. The multisectoral nature of the nutrition problem requires a high degree of coordination and leadership (a human resource).

Table 5.1 **- Categories of households in relation to food security**

	Food-secure household	Food-insecure household
Uses a small proportion of available resources	Best off	Not too difficult to improve
Uses a large proportion of available resources	At great risk (vulnerable)	Worst off

☐ 5.2. COSTS, BENEFITS AND EFFECTIVENESS

Resources are combined and used for a particular purpose. In Chapter Two it was seen that human and organizational resources largely determine the 'quality' of economic resources through a 'multiplier effect'. When costs are estimated, however, human and organizational resources are often not 'valued', or they are understated. Appraisals of project proposals are frequently based on estimating costs, effectiveness and, sometimes, benefits in terms of economic resources. Successful management of project implementation and monitoring, however, often depends on human and organizational resources. This dichotomy is a serious constraint in development work and needs to be addressed in a more professional way in the future.

The problem of malnutrition can be dealt with at different levels of causality — immediate, underlying or basic (see Figure 5.1). Projects and programmes aiming at the immediate causes of malnutrition are much easier to cost than those aiming at the underlying or basic causes. Attempts to undertake cost-benefit analysis of nutrition interventions are, therefore, most often limited to the first category, including supplementary feeding, supplementation and fortification of micronutrients, and basic health services.[32]

Increased availability and access to services can affect causes at any level. In most cases, however, capacity-building and empowerment are needed to address the underlying and basic causes of the nutrition problem and therefore to increase sustainability. Empowerment is more sustainable than capacity-building, which in turn is more sustainable than service delivery. The 'time-horizon' — that is, the period of time chosen (number of years) for assessing sustainability — is a value judgement, and results in very different cost-benefit ratios.

Programmes aiming at capacity-building are difficult to cost. This is partly a result of the complexity of causes. For example, for a reduction of 50 per cent in protein-energy malnutrition to be achieved in a sustainable way, a number of other goals must be fully or partly achieved: foremost among these are reduction of the incidence of diarrhoea and measles, optimal breastfeeding practices, and household food security. Empowerment-oriented interventions are even more complicated to cost. They aim at increasing the access to resources (availability and control) at different levels of society, particularly at the household and community levels.

Cost-effectiveness analysis aims at estimating the resources used to achieve a stated output (quantity and time). This technique has been frequently employed in health studies and, increasingly, in nutrition studies as well. The choice of output variable is important. The most commonly used measure in health — cost per death-averted — is not very appropriate for nutrition interventions. Improved nutrition lowers mortality, but has many other positive impacts, including decreased morbidity, improved educability and increased productivity.

There is a clear relationship between childhood protein-energy malnutrition and subsequent adult labour productivity. The cost of a given improvement in height has therefore been suggested as an output indicator. The cost per 1,000 calories delivered is another alternative.[33]

Cost per child removed or averted from a given state of malnutrition is probably the most useful measure. Most cost analyses, however, deal with unit costs; that is, the cost per beneficiary per volume of food delivered, per x number of calories per person per day, per year, and so forth. As the impact of the intervention is not included, unit cost data cannot be used in comparing different interventions. Estimating the number of beneficiaries is also difficult, in particular for integrated nutrition programmes.

Only few nutrition projects have collected data that make it possible to study cost-effectiveness, and these few studies show wide cost discrepancies which need to be explained (Table 5.2). Why does the Tamil Nadu project in India cost $33 per child removed from protein-energy malnutrition while the Iringa project in Tanzania costs $200? The basic difference between these two projects is that the Indian project was primarily a service-delivery programme with some capacity-building, whereas the Tanzanian project was a combined service-delivery, capacity-building and empowerment programme. The difference can best be understood by dividing the cost into:

(a) start-up cost (one-time cost);
(b) expansion cost; and
(c) annual operating cost per beneficiary.

In the long term, the last category is the most important. Tamil Nadu had an operating cost of about $9 per beneficiary per year. This is similar to the cost of $8 in Iringa in 1985-1986. The Tanzanian project, however, expanded rapidly to new areas much larger than Iringa at a reduced cost and sometimes with greater impact. In these new areas, the operating cost was between $2 and $4 per beneficiary per year. This reduces substantially the estimated cost per child removed from malnutrition. Moreover, besides nutrition goals, the Tanzania project contributed to the achievement of many other child goals, including health, food security, water and sanitation.

Table 5.2 - **Cost-effectiveness of interventions to reduce protein-energy malnutrition, selected countries, 1980-1986**

Country	Date	Type of intervention	Cost per child removed from protein-energy malnutrition ($)
India (Tamil Nadu)	1982	Supplementary feeding	33
Philippines	1982	Targeted food supply	331
Dominican Republic	1984-1986	Nutrition education	493
Indonesia	1983	Nutrition education	12
Morocco	1980	Nutrition education	5
Tanzania (Iringa)[1/]	1986	Integrated programme	200

Source: Horton, 1992.

[1/] Government of Tanzania, WHO and UNICEF, 1988.

The conclusion is that cost-effectiveness analysis of more-integrated nutrition programmes has most often been based on over-simplistic models of the causality of malnutrition and has not given recognition to the complexity of interactions and synergism or the long-term benefits of empowerment. The current results are therefore of limited value. Improvements in methodology are urgently needed.

A new effort to estimate cost, effectiveness and benefits in nutrition-oriented programmes is being made by the Academy of Education Development funded by the United States Agency for International Development. This work takes account of the complexities and has already provided useful estimates for Bangladesh.

Cost studies on the control of micronutrient malnutrition are much more consistent than those for control of protein-energy malnutrition. This is particularly true for supplementation and fortification programmes. As far as vitamin A deficiency and iron-deficiency anaemia are concerned, the chosen time-horizon decides the optimal mix of strategies (supplementary, fortification, dietary change and primary health care measures) and the annual cost per beneficiary. Costing programmes to combat iodine deficiency disorders is easiest because salt iodization is the preferred strategy already in the short-term. Some unit-cost data are shown in Table 5.3.

□ 5.3. SOME GLOBAL ESTIMATES

In preparation for the World Summit for Children, it was estimated that, globally, an additional $20 billion per year would be required to reach all the health, nutrition, education and water and sanitation goals. Estimates for

Table 5.3 **- Unit costs of micronutrient interventions**

	Country	Year	Estimated cost per person per year of protection ($)
Iodine			
Oil injection	Peru	1978	0.46
Oil injection	Zaire	1977	0.14
Oil injection	Indonesia	1986	0.21
Water fortification	Italy	1986	0.04
Salt	India	1987	0.04
Oil injection	Bangladesh	1983	0.25
Vitamin A			
Sugar fortification	Guatemala	1976	0.14
Capsule	Haiti	1978	0.46 - 0.68
Capsule	Indonesia/Philippines	1975	0.42
Capsule	Bangladesh	1983	0.05
Iron			
Salt fortification	India	1980	0.10
Sugar fortification	Guatemala	1980	0.84

Source: Horton, 1992.

protein-energy malnutrition ranged from $2 billion to $3 billion. The elimination of vitamin A deficiency would require an additional $20 million; the elimination of iodine deficiency disorders, $80 million; and reduction of iron deficiency anemia, about $25 million.

Detailed estimates for achieving the major goals in Africa were prepared for the International Conference on Assistance to African Children, sponsored by the Organization of African Unity and held in Dakar, Senegal, on 25-27 November, 1992.[34] The total additional cost was estimated at $8.9 million per year, of which nutrition would require $0.8 billion. A more detailed breakdown is given in Table 5.4.

■ 6. How Can Nutrition Be Implemented as a Right?

□ 6.1. TOWARDS A NEW DEVELOPMENT PARADIGM

During the last few years, development has increasingly been analysed from both a scientific and ethical perspective. In both regards, progress has been made in theory as well as in practice. It has become clear that economic growth does not necessarily lead to human development and poverty reduction. On the other hand, empirical studies have shown that direct measures for human development and poverty reduction do contribute to economic growth. This view is clearly discernible in international development thinking. Recent reports from several agencies including the United Nations Development Programme (UNDP), the World Bank, the International Fund for Agricultural Development (IFAD) and UNICEF reflect and articulate a new consensus in overall development strategies, emphasizing human development. This 'new' development paradigm is the result of two major changes in international development thinking: a changing view of the role of the poor in development and poverty eradication; and a much stronger weight applied to normative, moral or ethical arguments.

Both these changes have far-reaching implications for development cooperation. In the first, the poor are regarded as *key* actors in development and poverty eradication and not as passive beneficiaries of commodities and ser-

Table 5.4 **- Estimated additional costs of achieving the nutrition goals in Africa, 1993-2000**

	$ million/year (1993-2000)
Protein-energy malnutrition	520
Iodine deficiency	65
Vitamin A deficiency	115
Iron deficiency anaemia	121
Total	821

Source: Organization of African Unity/United Nations Children's Fund, 1992b.

vices. Local people are most capable of understanding the local situation and can judge what will or will not work. The majority of the poor know what is best for their own development, provided they have access to adequate resources, including information. This recognition is essential for 'authentic' development.

The *survival and coping strategies* of the poor need to be recognized and understood much better. The day-to-day situation for the poor is often more diversified and intricate than for the less poor. Frequent and often unpredictable changes in their physical, economic and social environment demand a constant adaptation, often involving great risks. The poorest, with the least resources, must adapt most often. Many of these coping strategies are very complex, but, given the scarce resources, probably the most efficient strategies possible. Poverty-reduction programmes should therefore support the efficient coping strategies already developed by the poor themselves, which requires understanding, patience and flexibility on the part of the 'outsider' who wants to assist.

The strengthening of existing efficient coping strategies and the development of new ones require *empowerment of the poor*. This means increased availability and control of human, economic and organizational resources by the poor; it also means enlargement of the choices available to the poor. Social injustices and gender disparities must be reduced to achieve a more equitable control of resources. Capacity-building, including education and training, is a prerequisite for empowerment.

Community participation is a means to empower as well as an important outcome of empowerment. Active participation requires communities to be involved in programme planning, implementation, monitoring and evaluation. This involvement includes assessment of problems, analysis of their causes and decisions regarding appropriate actions.

Finally, the aspects of *sustainability, replicability and costs* have received increased attention during the last few years. Thirty years of development aid efforts have resulted in numerous examples of projects that could not be sustained because resources required for sustainability were far greater than the resources controlled by communities. In many cases the community has not felt any ownership of the programme because the poor have been pushed to become passive beneficiaries instead of active participants. Participation and empowerment are needed in order to establish community ownership of a programme. Both *community ownership* and a minimum of resources are necessary conditions for *sustainability*. Local ownership is best reflected in the preparedness of community members to take risks and to contribute part of their own scarce resources to sustain and expand the programme. Cost recovery should not be a condition imposed from above, but voluntary; in which case, it is an expression of the true self-reliance of the community.

For several decades, improvements in the social conditions of the poor have been seen primarily as 'an investment in human capital', and it has been emphasized that improved health and nutrition would pay off in higher productivity, better learning capacity and reduced health sector expenditure. Many economists, in particular those working with the World Bank, have promoted such arguments. As much as these arguments are both useful and often valid, some people believe that, quite apart from these desirable outcomes, health, good nutrition and education are, first of all, *human rights*.

This position is clearly reflected in the unprecedented concurrence on the Summit goals, described earlier, and in the rapid ratification of the CRC. Governments, international agencies and NGOs have agreed to establish international and national mechanisms to monitor the progress towards the achievement of these goals.

Some aspects of a cross-cutting nature have been brought up as necessary conditions for the attainment of these goals. *Reduction of disparities*, including *gender disparities*, is the most important one. These concerns are not derived from any scientific analysis or argumentation: they are normative, as was the case, for example, in the anti-slavery campaign in the United States or in the struggle for women's voting rights in Europe. Or as the late James P. Grant stated in his speech to the World Conference on Human Rights held in Vienna on 14-25 June 1993:

> We are all ... interdependent neighbours, and it is unconscionable to believe that we can continue to live indefinitely, side by side, amidst the kind of obscene disparities in wealth, health and levels of freedom and participation that exist today.

All these changes reflect a desire and a belief in the possibility of increased *democracy* in the world. Democracy includes empowerment, participation and self-reliance. What we are witnessing today is the beginning of a *global movement* for the eradication of poverty in a world richer than ever before. The United Nations — created for peace, justice and human rights — should play a leading role in this movement.

All these aspects and implications for development in general also apply to nutrition policies, strategies and programmes. If the new thinking is to be operationalized, the distinction between the scientific and the ethical aspects of development must be clarified.

□ 6.2. NUTRITION AND PRACTICE

Section I of this chapter pointed out that the problem of malnutrition in society has a scientific and an ethical aspect, and that science normally consists of theory and practice. Theory and practice are two interacting aspects of science. The UNICEF conceptual framework for nutrition problems is an attempt to develop a theory. It also proposes an approach to practice — the 'triple-A' cycle (Figure 5.4).[35]

The conceptual framework helps to clarify what important decisions and actions need to be taken to improve the situation of women and children. The people and institutions to take these actions are implicit. More explicitly, this section examines the operation of decision-making processes: it identifies who can take action and analyses to what extent their decision-making processes may be strengthened or changed to improve their effectiveness in supporting the well-being of women and children. To facilitate the analysis, an approach is used that emphasizes the cyclical nature of decision-making. A problem is identified and assessed; its causes are analysed; and action is taken to address the problem. This 'triple-A' cycle is repeated as re-assessment and re-analysis are made after action has been taken to see what the effect of the action has been and what additional actions may be needed. The 'triple-A' process is a generic construct of any management process, whether by parents concerned about the health of their children deciding whether to take them for treatment, or by national or international executives deciding whether to allocate more funds to nutrition programmes. Decision makers are people taking action who need information not only to understand the extent of the problem they are trying to address and its causes but also to monitor and assess the results of actions taken to try to solve the problem.

Some of the problems causing malnutrition are amenable to effective actions at household and community levels. If decision-making at these levels were more supportive, more women and children would survive, and those surviving would be in better condition. Other problems can be addressed only with support from outside the community (for example, by medical services, which in turn require supplies that may need to be procured outside the country

Figure 5.4: **The triple-A cycle**

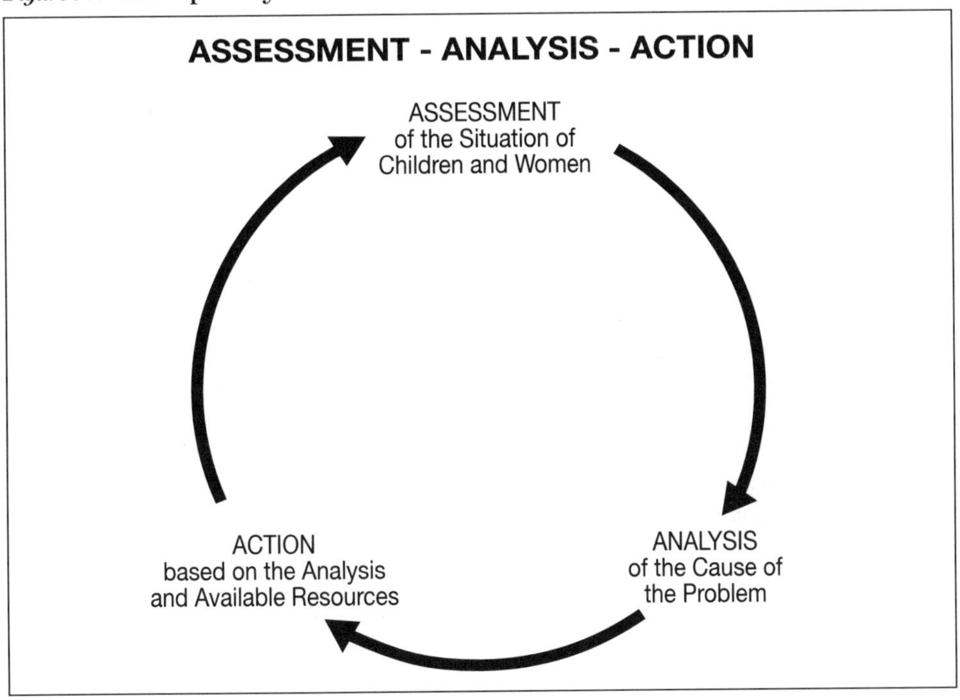

with foreign exchange). International economic and political relations affect decision-making at these levels, with implications for the strategies adopted at national level and the conditions under which households make their decisions. It is clearly important, therefore, that the critical actions and decision makers be identified and their decision-making processes understood. Processes supportive of women and children should be encouraged and those detrimental changed.

Actions to improve the nutritional situation of women and children involve the reallocation of resources in their favour. Within households, this may mean more time spent by parents with their children; greater sharing of work among adults in the household; and a larger percentage of income earmarked for goods and services of benefit to women and children. At national and international levels, planning priorities might be changed and budgets reallocated. To make decisions to reallocate resources and to justify these decisions, those controlling the resources need information.

Decision-making at all levels depends on an initial assessment, which is undertaken only when a problem is perceived and a commitment made to do something about it. Perception and commitment are dependent on the availability of information and the ability to understand the information. Analysis of the problem may be facilitated by the collaborative efforts of people most affected and knowledgeable about the situation, together with people technically trained to undertake analyses of similar problems. Although actions taken to improve the situation after this assessment and analysis may not lead to solutions of all aspects of the problems, they may contribute to creating a new situation that is more conducive to actions that may not have been feasible before.

After this cycle of assessment, analysis and action, as previously discussed, the impact of actions is re-assessed and the situation re-analysed. For this process to take place, there must be an information system in place, which must include information not only about the final result of the situation (malnutrition, for example) but also about its causes. In this way, the process will lead to more-effective, better-focused actions.[36]

'Triple-A' processes do not function in a vacuum. A number of factors are critical to their success and must be present to 'fuel' their operation:

(a) *perception and understanding* of the nature of the nutrition problem. This influences, in particular, the choice of what is assessed, how it is analysed, and what actions are regarded as feasible;

(b) *effective demand* for nutrition-related information and motivation to act. Decision makers need information for designing actions as well as for convincing others that actions are necessary and feasible (creating coalitions);

(c) *capabilities* (primarily technical) to obtain information in assessment (monitoring) and to use information in analysis and design of actions;

(d) *resources for the system*, that is, for the establishment and maintenance of the nutrition information system, including human, economic and organizational resources; and

(e) *resources for action*. When there are inadequate human, economic or organizational resources available to implement likely action, the focus of the nutrition information system must be to mobilize these resources.

From a human rights perspective, perception, understanding and effective demand for information are most important. Many problems in society can be well known scientifically for decades without being *perceived as social problems*. For example, both the consequences of and the remedies for iodine deficiency disorders have been known by scientists since the 1920s, but these disorders have only recently been recognized as a social problem. It is now becoming 'good politics' to allocate resources to eliminate iodine deficiency disorders, one of the World Summit for Children's nutrition goals.

As mentioned earlier, most Summit goals can be seen as 'moral minima' and their achievement as a necessary condition for the implementation of children's rights to nutrition. Strong advocacy can contribute to a perception that it is embarrassing if a country is not moving faster towards this achievement. Advocacy combined with an improved understanding of the problem and its solutions will create an environment that will initiate and 'fuel' triple-A processes, which will then mobilize the resources necessary for achieving the goals.

The Summit goals can be achieved in different ways. Services can be delivered and capacities built with different degrees of participation. Strategies and programmes that are implemented with no or limited participation can reduce poverty without contributing much to the implementation of rights. Empowerment implies reduction of poverty, but it is much more than that: it means power over one's own life, control of resources and choices. In that sense, empowerment means human rights. Delivery of services and building of capacities should be done in a participatory manner, one that contributes to empowerment.

6.3. NUTRITION AS A RIGHT

Individual nutritional well-being at a given point in time can be achieved through delivery of services, capacity-building and empowerment, or a combination of these strategies. Nutritional security as a part of sustainable development must involve empowerment. Nutritional security not only means that an individual has an acceptable nutritional status today, but also that his or her nutritional well-being is secured in the future. This requires a safe minimum resource base, or entitlements. The child's right to adequate nutrition therefore means that his or her entitlements must be secured. State obligations should be seen in this context of individual needs fulfilment.

Eide[37] defines state obligations at three levels. First, States must *respect* the freedom of individuals to take actions by using the resources they control. Collective or group actions must also be respected. Second, States must *protect* individual freedom of action and use of resources from other more assertive or aggressive subjects. Individuals need to be protected from powerful eco-

Table 5.5 - **Food security matrix**

GUIDING PRINCIPLES	FOOD ADEQUACY			VIABLE PROCUREMENT	SUSTAINABILITY OF SUPPLY AND ACCESS
Level of national obligations	Nutritional adequacy	Safety	Cultural acceptability		
Respect	1. *Recognize* the positive nutritional aspect of existing food patterns.	2. n.a.	3. *Recognize* the significance of food culture as part of a wider cultural identity.	4. *Recognize* customary rights to means of food procurement, consistent with basic human needs.	5. *Recognize* the positive ecological significance of existing food production systems; *recognize* the significance of informal and NGO institutions in crisis management ('buffer systems').
Protect	6. *Prevent* distortions of positive nutritional aspects of existing food patterns.	7. *Develop* national legislation on food safety; *participate* in developing international legislation on food safety ('Codex Alimentarius').	8. *Counteract*, when necessary, influences that may negatively erode positive aspects of existing food culture.	9. *Develop* national legislation and administrative mechanisms and procedures to protect and facilitate a viable food procurement for all.	10. *Develop* national legislation to counteract activities that may erode ecological balance; *protect* ecologically sound buffer systems in crisis management.
Fulfil	11. *Correct* negative aspects of existing food patterns; *guide* dietary change when necessary, consistent with the above; *incorporate* nutritional considerations in relevant development activities.	12. *Establish* a nationwide system of food control and inspection.	13. *Incorporate* positive aspects of food culture into relevant development activities (rural development, agricultural, health, educational, industrial, etc.)	14. *Formulate* and *execute* policies, plans and programmes to facilitate and assist all groups in society (with emphasis on the socio-economically most vulnerable) in obtaining viable procurement of food, consistent (not conflicting) with the realization of other basic human needs.	15. *Formulate* and *execute* policies, plans and programmes to facilitate the restoration of ecological balance; *support* and *strengthen* effective existing institutions and, as necessary, *develop* new ones for crisis management.

nomic interests, unethical trade and marketing practices. Finally, States must *fulfil* the expectations of all to enjoy their rights, either directly by providing the commodities or services needed by the individual (what Himes labelled 'fulfil' in Chapter One) or by providing opportunities (termed 'facilitate' by Himes). The three levels of national obligations with respect to food security are shown in Table 5.5.

Breastfeeding as a human right can be viewed from this perspective. States should respect the mother's final choice to breastfeed or not to breastfeed; protect the mother from misinformation about feeding in general, and from aggressive marketing of breastmilk substitutes in particular; and support the nursing mother by creating an enabling environment for breastfeeding and, more directly, through training in lactation management and establishment of baby-friendly hospitals, for example.

Three additional dimensions need to be considered in order to assess and analyse the present situation and to identify appropriate state obligations in relation to nutrition:

(a) type of nutrition problem (protein-energy malnutrition, iodine deficiency disorders, and so forth);
(b) type of obligation (respect, protect, facilitate or fulfil); and
(c) level of society (from individual to international).

Himes uses dimension (b) and (c) in identifying concrete state obligations in relation to the CRC in general (see Table 1.2). Eide uses (a) and (b) in identifying state obligations at any level of society in relation to household food security.

In the conceptual analysis of the nutrition problem, 'food', 'care' and 'health' were identified as the three necessary conditions for individual nutritional security. Availability, control and use of resources (human, economic and organizational) determine the degree of fulfilment by:

(a) direct delivery of services;
(b) capacity-building; and
(c) empowerment.

It therefore seems useful to translate state obligations into these categories. The child's right to nutritional security implies the eradication of protein-energy malnutrition. Some examples of state obligations related to protein-energy malnutrition at different levels of society are proposed in Table 5.6. This table is far from complete and only shows how a more systematic approach can be used.

The NPA process provides a useful opportunity for a human rights analysis. Many countries have already developed national legislation relevant to the CRC. The right to nutrition, however, is rarely recognized. The proposed three-dimensional instrument can be useful in moving ahead in a more pragmatic but systematic way in the necessary definition of state obligations.

In many countries, non-governmental groups have been involved in the preparation of NPAs. Many NGOs also participated in the preparation of the International Conference on Nutrition and at the actual conference in Rome.

Table 5.6 **- State obligations in relation to the child's right to protection from protein-energy malnutrition**

Level of Society	Respect	Protect	Facilitate	Fulfil
Individual/Household	*Respect* positive cultural habits in food, care and health. *Respect* individual choices, for example use of contraceptives.	*Protect* individuals/households from any type of exploitation, and deterioration of entitlements necessary for nutritional security.	*Facilitate* the transfer of knowledge and skills in relation to nutritional security (capacity-building). *Facilitate* individuals/ households in reducing poverty (empowerment) through removal of constraints to access to credit.	*Provide* direct support to individuals/ households whose entitlements have broken down or are at risk of breaking down.
Community/District	*Respect* the establishment of democratic community organizations.	*Protect* communities and areas from economic and cultural marginalization and exploitation.	*Facilitate* community/district situation assessment and analysis.	*Reduce* geographic disparities in resource allocation.
National	*Respect* the role of NGOs in poverty alleviation and nutrition.	*Protect* individuals through national legislation on the Code of Marketing of Breast Milk Substitutes, universal iodization of salt, minimum maternity leave and food safety legislation.	*Prepare* and *update* regularly NPAs for children and women. *Ensure* universal primary education. *Reduce* all gender-biased constraints.	*Provide* basic services in health, agriculture, water and sanitation. *Incorporate* nutrition goals in development plans. *Establish* a national nutrition surveillance system.
International	*Respect* different ideologies (culture, religion, habits, etc.)	*Protect* countries from the use of food as a political weapon. *Protect* civilians from unacceptable suffering in times of disaster.	*Facilitate* international exchange and transfer of information, expertise and experiences in nutrition.	*Assist* victims of natural disasters, wars and other abuses. *Monitor* the progress in nutrition.

As described earlier, there are already some strong NGO initiatives for promoting children's rights to nutrition. These NGO initiatives should be seen as the beginning of a global movement for the right to nutrition.

Other popular movements in history provide lessons that could accelerate and strengthen this movement. Some of these lessons are summarized below:

(a) Most movements are driven by normative, human rights-oriented goals. It was never primarily scientific arguments that were used in the struggle against slavery or in the fight for universal suffrage and other gender issues, for example. Usually the arguments for a change were derived from moral values, often based on a call for human rights. This normative orientation makes the work in a movement similar to, and frequently identical with, political work.

(b) Often movements are the result of protests against something that is considered basically wrong, unfair or unacceptable. In many cases, 'a common enemy' is identified, which contributes to the mobilization of both people and governments.

(c) Most movements are pluralistic. The overriding concern to attain a priority goal dwarfs most of the other aspects that previously divided individuals and groups with different political or ideological positions.

(d) Normally movements do not 'allow' anybody to be 'neutral'. All people have to take a position: 'for' or 'against'.

(e) A movement is almost always a process involving struggle, requiring a great deal of voluntary work, driven by enthusiasm, using targeted slogans and challenging existing dogma and myths.

(f) Young people, and often women, have been in the 'front line' of most successful movements. A movement deals with what could be and promises a better future for the young.

■ 7. Conclusions

The right to nutritional well-being is recognized in some United Nations declarations and conventions, but not as often as one would expect. The right to food and freedom from hunger, in contrast, has been recognized in a large number of human rights declarations and conventions. The difference is the result of past tendencies to identify malnutrition with the lack of food. This reductive concept of malnutrition has contributed to food-biased nutrition programmes and projects.

The UNICEF Nutrition Strategy promotes a broader concept of malnutrition, in which household food security, adequate care of children and women, and access to basic health services, together with a healthy environment, are identified as three necessary conditions of nutritional well-being, or individual nutritional security. 'Food', 'care' and 'health' are all recognized rights in the CRC, which makes this convention unique in promoting children's nutrition rights.

A number of nutrition-related goals were adopted and agreed upon at the World Summit for Children and the International Conference on Nutrition. These global goals represent an ethical position of what *should* be done, as well as a scientifically proved investment for economic development. Experience in many countries also shows that these goals *can* be achieved, which signifies they are 'doable' global goals. The achievement of the nutrition goals is a necessary, but not sufficient, condition for the implementation of nutrition as a right. Nutrition as a right requires people's empowerment. Service delivery and capacity-building should be used to achieve the goals. Provided that these are implemented in a participatory manner, they will contribute to empowerment. Promotion of nutrition as a right will at the same time contribute to increased resource mobilization and allocation for service-delivery and capacity-building strategies and programmes for achieving the same goals.

Participation for empowerment requires a recognition of the poor as key actors, rather than passive beneficiaries of commodities and transfers. The triple-A approach provides a generic construct for how resources are managed to address problems. The circular and iterative process of *assessment* of the problem, *analysis* of the causes of the problem, and design and implementation of *actions* to address the problem, followed by a re-assessment, improved analysis and new actions, can be strengthened and accelerated by a number of factors. Most important among these are improved perception and knowledge, creation of an effective demand for information, improved capabilities and increased resources.

Nutrition is improving in the world, but far too slowly. An increasing number of people know that the nutrition goals *can* be achieved because the world has the knowledge and the resources; and an increasing number of people think that the world *should* achieve these goals. This was clearly manifested in the rapid ratification of the Convention on the Rights of the Child and the great consensus at the World Summit for Children. More and more people are starting to ask *why* governments do not do more. In the 1990s, this will gradually create a 'global embarrassment', which will not only influence what political leaders choose to do, but also which leaders are chosen. There is both a need and an opportunity to create a global movement for children's right to nutrition. NGOs will have to play an important role in the creation of such a movement.

If a global movement to eradicate malnutrition is to be created, 'global development ethics' should be elaborated and promoted. Crocker defines development ethics as a "normative or ethical assessment of the ends and means of Third World and global development".[38] Development ethics should provide a definition of 'development'. Amartya Sen defines development as "a process of expanding capabilities of people". 'Global development ethics' should also define the responsibilities of the industrialized world and address the question of 'global justice'. An essential task for development ethics is to make development more *humane*. We have to reject all kinds of moral scepticism, moral relativism and value neutrality. We need what Crocker calls "a non-ethnocentric ethical consensus". Maybe the start could be to follow Sen's advice to identify a "cross-cultural moral minimum". The Summit Goals for Children and Development in the 1990s are exactly that. The NPA process should be used to codify gradually in national legislation concrete state obligations in relation to nutrition goals. In such a way, children's nutrition will be implemented as a human right.

Notes

1 Tomasevski, 1986.
2 Marchisio and DiBlase, 1991.
3 Traylor, 1984.
4 Sen, 1984, p. 497.
5 Kent, forthcoming in 1993.
6 Alston, P., in Eide et al., 1991.
7 Grant, 1994.
8 United Nations Children's Fund, 1993d.
9 Pojman, 1989, p. 1.
10 Eide et al., 1991, p. 425.
11 Goulet, 1988.
12 International Conference on Nutrition, 1992.
13 Eide et al., 1991, p. 427.
14 Williams, 1933, p. 423.
15 Brock and Autret, 1952.
16 Waterlow, 1955.
17 United Nations, 1968.
18 See McLaren, 1974; Bender, 1974; Miller, 1974.
19 League of Nations, 1935.
20 League of Nations, 1936.
21 A. Mayer served as the first Chairman of the FAO Executive Committee. F.L. McDougall was responsible for the proposal for a new intergovernmental organization.
22 United Nations Children's Fund, 1990e.
23 Sen, 1981.
24 Drèze and Sen, 1989.
25 Zerfas, 1993.
26 World Alliance for Nutrition and Human Rights, 1992.
27 United Nations Administrative Committee on Coordination/Subcommittee on Nutrition, 1992.
28 United Nations Children's Fund, 1993a.
29 World Health Organization et al., 1993.
30 The NCHS (United States National Center for Health Statistics) reference population consists of U.S. children who are assumed to be well-nourished and whose anthropometric measurements can be used as a standard for any ethnic group.
31 Personal communication with D. Pelletier, consultant for the evaluation.
32 Horton, 1992.
33 Pinstrup-Andersen, 1988.
34 Organization of African Unity/United Nations Children's Fund, 1992b.
35 United Nations Children's Fund, 1990e; and United Nations Children's Fund and Government of Tanzania, 1990.
36 For more details, see United Nations Children's Fund, 1993c.
37 Eide et al., 1991.
38 Crocker, 1991.

Children's right to education: reaching the unreached

Frank P. Dall

1. Introduction

It is sobering to note that more than three and a half decades after the United Nations adopted the Declaration of the Rights of the Child, which stipulated that children are "entitled to receive education, which shall be free and compulsory, at least in the elementary stages ...", more than 100 million school-age children, for a variety of preventable reasons, still have no access to any kind of basic education service. Moreover, nearly half a century after the Universal Declaration of Human Rights asserted that "everyone has a right to education", 960 million adults, two thirds of whom are women, are still illiterate, and more than one third of the world's adults have neither access to printed knowledge nor technical skills to help them adapt to their societies' rapidly changing social and economic conditions. In addition, millions of children and adults fail to complete the basic education programmes they start; and millions more enter schools, but do not learn enough to meet their basic learning needs. Growing numbers of schooled illiterates, a problem recently recognized both in Europe and the United States, are also found in many developing countries, where primary schools have ceased to function effectively over the last decade because of the rapid decline in the quality of schooling, economic hardships and political neglect.

Historically, education as a human right was one of the last human needs to receive the attention it deserves. Two reasons may account for this. First, among the list of basic human needs, health, shelter and food have always received first call on limited resources because they were assumed to be priorities for survival. Second, economists and development specialists have only recently begun to understand the positive contribution education makes to national development. The beneficial effects that education has on productivity, health, nutrition, fertility rates and child welfare in general are well supported by recent research findings. Here, perhaps, the World Bank, UNICEF and some bilateral agencies deserve credit for helping to place education on the list of international priorities.

It was not until after the Second World War that the *Universal Declaration of Human Rights* (1948) recognized education as a fundamental human right. Subsequently, the *Declaration of the Rights of the Child*, adopted by the United Nations under Resolution 1386/XIV of November 1959, established that free and compulsory basic education should be an essential building block to promote a child's "general culture and enable him ... to become a useful member of society". In a similar vein, the *International Covenant on Economic, Social and Cultural Rights* (1966) underscored that education should be "directed to the full development of the human personality and the sense of its dignity, ... shall strengthen the respect for human rights and fundamental freedoms ... [and] enable all persons to participate effectively in a free society" (Article 13.1). The United Nations Educational, Scientific and Cultural Organization (UNESCO) *Convention Against Discrimination in Education* (1960) supported the need to make education a developmental priority and a basic human right.

Other aspects of education were spelt out in subsequent UNESCO instruments, including the *Recommendation Concerning the Status of Teachers* (1966), which recognized that "advance in education depends largely on the qualifications and ability of the teaching staff" and that "teaching is to be regarded as a profession"; the *Recommendation Concerning Education for International Understanding, Co-operation and Peace and Education Relating to Human Rights and Fundamental Freedoms* (1974), which stated that education should enhance international understanding and instill a sense of civic duty; the *Revised Recommendation Concerning Technical Vocational Education* (1974), which recognized education as a lifelong process; and the *Recommendation on the Development of Adult Education* (1976), which urged that appropriate structures be set up to meet the educational needs of adults, with a special focus on women.

Unfortunately, the strong formalistic and legal emphasis of many of these provisions obscured the moral and ethical elements of the question. In fact, these recommendations largely failed to generate the response needed to meet the growing demand-supply crisis in basic education. This crisis was the outcome, on the one hand, of exploding population growth rates and, on the other, of persistent economic decline, especially among the least-developed nations of South Asia and Africa. As a result, the dream in these and other developing countries of providing every child of school age with a good and affordable education, in tune with her or his daily needs, seems to have become unattainable.

2. The Convention on the Rights of the Child: An Added Dimension

Article 28 of the 1989 United Nations *Convention on the Rights of the Child* (CRC) contains provisions frequently found in international instruments promoting the right to education. In particular, it reiterates many elements of the UNESCO Convention Against Discrimination in Education (1960),[1] including the right to compulsory and free primary education and access "to all" to secondary, vocational and higher education (see Appendix One). However, the provisions of this article inevitably involve some ambiguities regarding the specific obligations that signatories have in terms of implementing these principles. For instance, the obligation to ensure non-discriminatory policies in relation to the enjoyment of education rights has an immediate effect notwithstanding the non-availability of financial resources. The only exception in this regard, in some legal systems, relates to what may be termed affirmative action programmes.[2] But these programmes should also satisfy various criteria designed to ensure that their real purpose is to achieve equality rather than to perpetuate inequality.[3] Although the principle of non-discrimination contained in Article 2 of the CRC is applicable in terms of education, the drafters apparently believed that discrimination in schools was a sufficiently serious problem to merit stressing the principle also in the context of Article 28, including the reference to "equal opportunity".

The immediate effect of Article 2, not subject to the availability of resources, is of considerable potential importance in the field of basic education. Whatever resources are available must be allocated to ensure the enjoyment of the right to non-discriminatory education. This principle deserves emphasis, especially in countries where the shortage of resources may be used by governments as a justification for not enforcing the education provisions of the CRC, especially those relating to primary education. Moreover, the importance of this principle is shown by the fact that women and girls represent two thirds of those who currently lack access to both education and literacy. An overview of female education would show that women and girls generally have limited opportunities, face numerous obstacles, and receive an education that is of questionable quality and relevance.

Article 28 establishes — for the first time in an international instrument promoting the right to education — that school discipline should be administered "in a manner consistent with the child's human dignity" (para. 2). This innovation has ramifications that clearly go beyond the provisions of earlier instruments prohibiting cruel and degrading treatment of children in schools. Article 28 is also innovative in its call for international cooperation in matters relating to education. Overall, however, this article seems largely to reflect the spirit of the pre-existing human rights provisions that inspired the CRC.

Article 29 contains more-detailed provisions in support of the kind of education that should be made available to ethnic and other minority groups. The need to provide an education that values and develops respect for the "child's parents, his or her own cultural identity, language and values" (para. 1.c) is considered an important aspect of any education service. Article 29 also commits signatories to assist in the full development of each child's "personality, talents, and mental and physical abilities" (para. 1.a). Preparing children to live in a free society "in the spirit of understanding, peace, tolerance ... " (para. 1.d) is another important element in a world of religious, cultural and ethnic diversity. The provisions of Article 29, therefore, complement and extend the principles contained in Article 28. They also reinforce the notion that even the smallest group has a right to an education that fully respects its cultural identity and specific language needs. This is an essential added emphasis when considering the special educational needs of the numerous, and often ignored or forgotten, children of minority groups who currently lack a basic education.

□ 2.1. WHAT HAS 'JOMTIEN' CONTRIBUTED TO EDUCATION AS A CHILD RIGHT?

The World Conference on Education for All, held in Jomtien, Thailand, in March 1990, gathered most of the major actors around the same table to begin at least to ask some of the important questions. For the first time in history, over 155 governments attended a meeting whose sole purpose was to discuss the world's current crisis in education, with a special focus on basic education. Again for the first time, all the multilateral agencies, donors and a large group of non-governmental organizations (NGOs) came together to discuss key issues affecting the education of the world's children. They attended the meeting with significant motivation and political will, and the resulting joint agreement addresses the main educational issues discussed. Participants even prescribed joint actions that should be taken to satisfy clearly identified basic educational needs.

The success of this initiative can be attributed, in part, to months of careful preparation to ensure that the final agreement reflected the broadest possible local and regional discussion. Teachers, parents, pupils and educators of all sorts were asked how the issue of basic education as a child right could be meaningfully addressed within their own sociocultural contexts. Preparatory forums were convened to facilitate an exchange of the findings, experience and observations of educators and parents in Africa, Asia, Latin America, Europe and North America. A forthcoming UNESCO publication, analysing and summarizing the discussions of more than 23 panels, points to the richness, diversity and creativity of the discussions that this historical event was able to elicit.

Delegates and organizers felt that, after 30 years of failure to meet the basic educational needs of the world's populations, it was time to give the many noble declarations of intent the 'teeth' they were missing. The *World Declaration on Education For All* (Jomtien Declaration) is concise and to the point. Its 10 articles clearly reiterate the right to "Education for All"; moreover, they underscore the importance of education not only as a child right or human right (for individual growth) but also as a necessity (for national economic development). In this respect, special emphasis is given to the education of girls and women, since they constitute a largely untapped human resource for the development of nations.

The following extracts from the Jomtien Declaration illustrate this new emphasis.[4] Article 1 stresses the right of all individuals to a basic education:

> Every person — child, youth and adult — shall be able to benefit from educational opportunities designed to meet [his or her] basic learning needs. These needs comprise both essential learning tools (such as literacy, numeracy, and problem solving) and the basic learning content (such as knowledge, skills, values, and attitudes) required by human beings to be able to survive, to develop their full capacities, to live and work in dignity, to participate fully in development, to improve the quality of their lives, to make informed decisions, and to continue learning. The scope of basic learning needs and how they should be met varies with individual countries and cultures, and inevitably, changes with the passage of time (para. 1).

It also asserts that basic education is a developmental necessity:

> Basic education is more than an end in itself. It is the foundation for lifelong learning and human development on which countries may build, systematically, further levels and types of education and training (para. 4).

Article 3 emphasizes that the education of girls and women constitutes a priority. In countries where female enrolment and literacy rates are much lower than those for males,

> [t]he most urgent priority is to ensure access to, and improve the quality of, education for girls and women, and to remove every obstacle that hampers their active participation. All gender stereotyping in education should be eliminated (para. 3).

Five key elements of the expanded vision are presented in Article 2 of the Jomtien Declaration (and subsequently elaborated in Articles 3 to 7). These highlight the need to bring about with creativity and determination the following improvements in basic education:

- universalizing access and promoting equity;
- focusing on learning acquisition (as opposed to just teaching);
- broadening the means and scope of basic education (the challenge here being to develop a more appropriate content and new delivery systems);
- enhancing the environment for learning; and
- strengthening partnerships (which includes extending partnerships to those previously excluded from the teaching-learning process — that is, parents and other members of the community).

For the first time, the right to basic education is given an active dimension — the missing element in so many of the earlier attempts to define in legal terms what constitutes an education right. This dimension is described in Article 8 as a "supporting policy context" for the implementation of the principles of the Jomtien Declaration. Article 9, in turn, makes a passable effort to specify some of the necessary steps to "mobilize existing and new financial and human resources, public, private and voluntary" for this purpose. Article 10 cautions that all of the above cannot be done without "strengthening international solidarity" among donors and nations alike. Both groups need to understand how war, civil strife, peace, and the optimal conditions needed to support educational development are interrelated. The Article advises in a categorical, if rather utopian, tone that:

> All nations must also work together to resolve conflicts and strife, to end military occupations, and to settle displaced populations ... Only a stable and peaceful environment can create the conditions in which human beings, child and adult alike, may benefit from the goals of this Declaration (para. 4).

□ 2.2. A FRAMEWORK FOR ACTION

The *Framework for Action to Meet Basic Learning Needs*, which also emerged from the Jomtien initiative, is a significant and innovative tool for turning education from a utopian dream into a reality. Based on the best collective knowledge and experience of all of the participants, the Framework for Action was developed as a reference and guide for those prepared to make a commitment to implement the goal of "Education for All" by formulating coherent plans for action. The Framework provides guidelines for three levels of action:

(a) direct action within individual countries;

(b) cooperation among groups of countries sharing certain characteristics and concerns; and

(c) multilateral and bilateral cooperation in the world community.

Individual countries and groups of countries, as well as international, regional and national organizations, may use the Framework for Action to develop their own specific plans of action and programmes in line with their particular objectives, mandates and constituencies. The United States Agency for International Development and other bilateral agencies, including those of the Governments of Denmark, Sweden, the United Kingdom, the Netherlands and Italy, have collectively committed a significant proportion of their annual aid budgets to basic education, and have promised to increase this amount over the next five to seven years. The World Bank, a principal donor and actor at Jomtien, has already committed more than $2 billion to education since March 1990. Other multilateral agencies have also begun to commit resources. UNICEF, for example, has hired a team of educators to help implement the education goals by the end of the decade: five senior advisers are working at UNICEF headquarters; four more persons have been contracted to work on the implementation of plans of action in four of the six UNICEF regions; and about 50 education programme officers have been hired to work on educational issues at the country-office level. Unfortunately, most multilateral agencies still have some way to go before they reach the funding levels promised for the first half of this decade. UNICEF itself has allocated less than 10 per cent of its total resources to the implementation of education goals, versus a promised 17 per cent.

Overall, the Framework for Action calls for precise actions through a well-stated framework of goals. To make it easier for implementers to set their own specific targets in line with their national situations and budgets, participants divided the ultimate goal — meeting "the basic learning needs of all by the year 2000" — into a set of realistic intermediate goals. These subsequently formed the basis for the education section of the Goals for Children and Development in the 1990s (see Appendix Two), adopted six months later at the World Summit for Children.[5] Recommendations included: expansion of early childhood development activities; universal access to, and completion of, primary education; improvement in learning achievement by, say, 80 per cent of 14-year-olds; reduction of the adult illiteracy rate to one half its 1990 level, with emphasis on female literacy; expansion of provisions of basic education and training in other essential skills required by youth and adults; and "increased acquisition by individuals and families of the knowledge, skills and values required for better living and sound and sustainable development, made available through all education channels including the mass media, other forms of modern and traditional communication, and social action, with effectiveness assessed in terms of behavioural change".

By setting time-bound targets for the achievement of "Education for All" goals, the Framework for Action conveys a sense of urgency to meeting the educational needs of children. As societal conditions change, plans and objectives can be reviewed and updated to meet the needs of specific target groups of children. Such observable and adjustable targets provide invaluable assistance in monitoring and evaluating the progress towards reaching the goals. The Jomtien Declaration has been formulated in such a way that its effective implementation is an explicit and primary concern. Thus, countries with limited resources and low literacy and school attendance rates may now be in a better position to make hard choices and establish achievable national targets within more realistic time-frames.

The Framework for Action highlights several principles of action for the effective implementation of the goals. International donors should give priority to those countries currently least able to meet their populations' basic learning needs. At the national level, actions for implementing each child's right to a basic education should include:

- identifying whether the basic education services required are formal or non-formal. This should be done systematically, through a comprehensive education analysis or sector assessment and with the active participation of concerned groups and communities;
- adopting strategies that involve different sectors and interested groups, including private and public institutions. Basic education needs to become everyone's concern;
- evaluating the capacity of existing institutions to manage and deliver education services before creating new institutions. What already exists

may only need some adjustment or revitalization for it to provide the intended results; and

- forming new partnerships whose primary aim should be to foster a spirit of cooperation between multilateral and bilateral entities so as to help build endogenous capacities.

Since progress towards implementing the education provisions of the Jomtien Declaration will depend on national circumstances, the Framework for Action recommends that:

- a receptive policy environment be developed through advocacy and the effective mobilization of support at both the community and the national levels;
- policies for the improvement of basic education be carefully selected and the research needed to do this undertaken in a timely manner, preferably with the collaboration of a national institution;
- national capacities be strengthened to carry out the managerial, analytical and technical tasks needed to support the necessary changes in the education system;
- supportive information channels be mobilized to meet the basic learning needs of every segment of the community. For example, 'third channel'[6] options should be used to target out-of-school groups, including housebound girls and adult groups with special needs; and
- a workable plan of action be designed, which will require bringing potential partners together early in the analysis, design and planning process. The formation of a national committee for the implementation of basic education goals is proving to be an effective way of doing this in partnership with national governments, especially in Africa where the need for change is most acute.

□ 2.3. BASIC EDUCATION: A RIGHT AND A NECESSITY

Investing in basic education always has significant cultural and economic implications for both individual and national development. However, this is particularly true where existing disparities in education still closely reflect the socio-economic gap between the rich and the poor, as is the case in many parts of Asia and Africa and in such countries in Central and Latin America as Belize, Bolivia, Ecuador, El Salvador, Guatemala, Honduras and Peru. In many of the least-developed countries, a sizeable proportion of each country's wealth lies in the untapped capacities of its people. Historically, nations that have been able to sustain social and economic development have also emphasized education and training to increase their people's capacities to accumulate knowledge, communicate information and coordinate and organize themselves productively.

Accumulated experience in Africa and elsewhere in the developing world provides convincing evidence that increased investment in education, particularly at the basic or primary levels (see Table 6.1), can yield significant benefits — including improved health, lower fertility rates and higher incomes — all of which are of critical importance in the struggle for self-sufficiency and sustainable development.[7] The social returns to investments in primary education have been found to be about 27 per cent higher than the returns in most other areas of social investment.[8] The connection between the level of a mother's education and child survival is supported by a number of current studies (Figure 6.1). A clear relationship also exists between the level of female education and population growth (Figure 6.2). The United Nations Development Programme (UNDP) *Human Development Report 1991* notes that as the level of illiteracy declines, so does the average national population growth rate.

Many studies have demonstrated the effects of education on output and productivity. In the area of agricultural productivity, where subsistence farming is a key income sector supporting over 70 per cent of the world's population, studies show that farmers with only four years of education have an 8.75 per cent higher productivity rate than farmers with no education at all. Other studies show a close correlation between the kind of technologies adopted by farmers and the educational skills needed to sustain increased productivity.[9]

Although the impact of education on aggregate real output has been less well documented, a World Bank study[10] on the determinants of real gross domestic product (GDP), covering 58 countries during 1960-1985, strongly suggests that education can contribute significantly to aggregate output. An increase of one year in average years of education may lead to a 3 per cent rise in GDP.

The results of this research differ from region to region. For most groups of developing countries, the effect of education on GDP is clearly positive, and (within the range examined) the higher the initial level of education, the greater the benefits from increasing it. Sub-Saharan Africa is an exception: increasing average years of education by one year, from 3.25 in 1985 to 4.25, is expected to have a negligible effect on output. This reflects factors such as unfavourable local conditions, lack of complementary inputs, inadequate institutional capacities, and other economic obstacles that prevent people from benefiting fully from their greater skills. The results suggest that there may be thresholds in the returns to education. For example, about four years of education seem to be needed to attain functional literacy. Investments may

***Table 6.1* - Average social returns to education, in percentages, 1960-1985**

	Primary Education	Secondary Education	Higher Education
Sub-Saharan Africa	26	17	13
Asia	27	15	13
Latin America and the Caribbean	26	18	16

Source: World Bank, 1990.

Figure 6.1: **Female education and child survival, selected countries, 1989.**

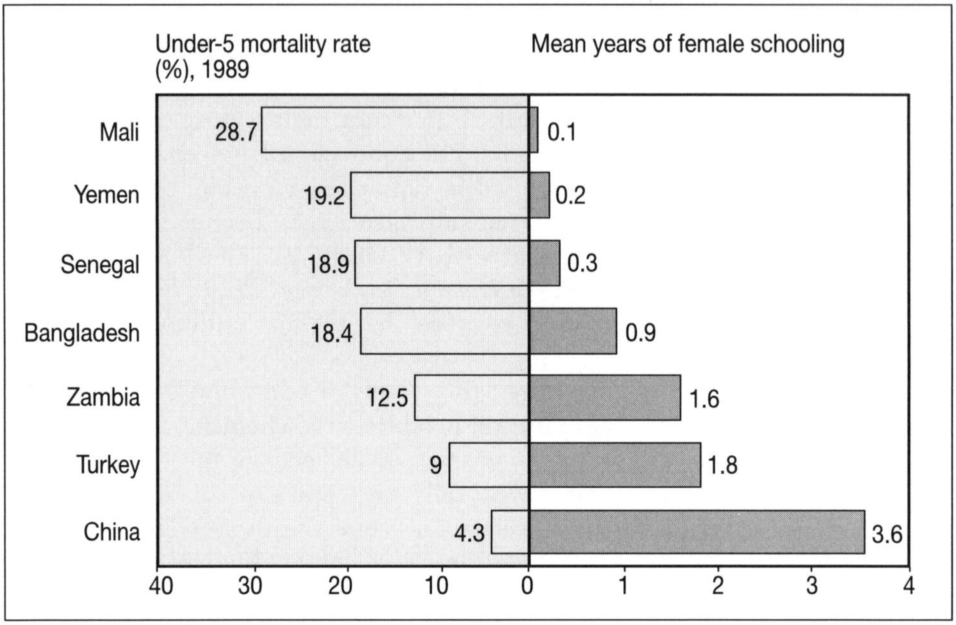

Source: United Nations Children's Fund, 1991d; and United Nations Development Programme, 1991.

Figure 6.2: **Female education and population growth, selected countries, 1990.**

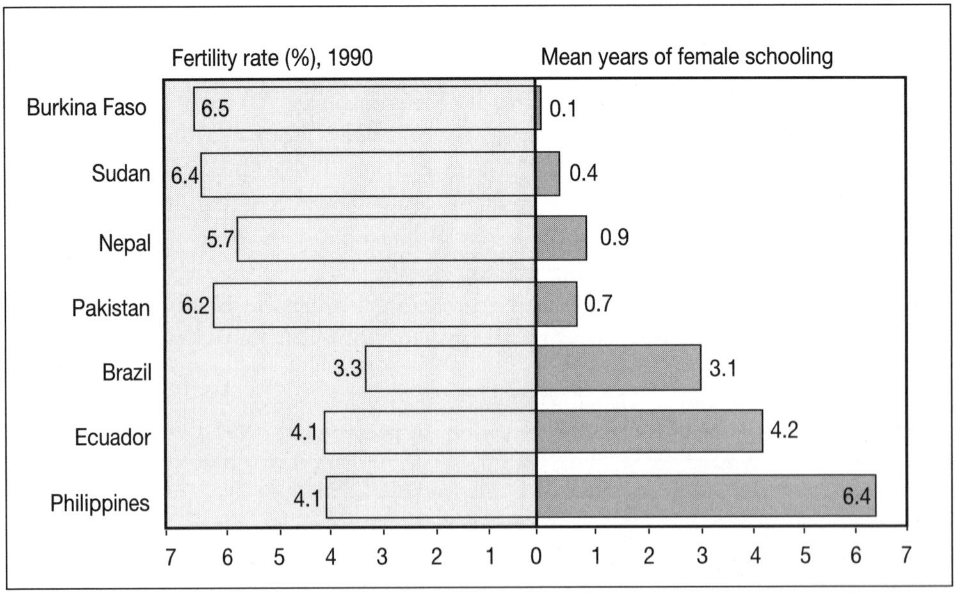

Source: United Nations Children's Fund, 1991d; and United Nations Development Programme, 1991.

yield substantial returns only when they are large enough to push the economy over such a threshold.

Education is therefore both a right and a necessity. Evidence suggests that a child who has access to good primary education has a better chance in life.[11] Basic reading, writing and conceptual skills provide important building blocks for a life of continued learning and problem solving. Basic education enables the individual to learn important life skills relating to health, family life and the environment, as well as how to work with others in harmony and how to cope with the complex challenges of a pluralistic, multicultural society.

The current worldwide resurgence of religious and racial intolerance, which is challenging and undermining the trend towards democratization in Europe, Africa, Asia and Latin America, has prompted educators and legislators to conclude that some knowledge of basic rights and democratic principles as well as tolerance and understanding of diversity are necessary if countries undergoing profound social and political transformations are to survive.[12] They argue that the formal curriculum beginning at the primary level needs to be changed to reflect and encourage an understanding of the rights and responsibilities of individuals within a democratic society, with an emphasis on the concepts of democracy, justice, equality, freedom, solidarity, peace and dignity. Furthermore, the following skills will need to be incorporated into a relevant basic education if the move towards participatory democracy is to be sustained:

- *oral and written language skills*, to be able to listen and discuss. In Africa, the right to acquire these skills in one's mother tongue needs to be stressed;
- *judgement skills*, acquired by collecting and analysing materials from different sources, to be able to detect prejudice and bias and arrive at balanced conclusions;
- *social skills*, to learn to accept differences and form non-threatening relationships; and
- *action skills*, relating, for example, to problem solving and conflict resolution, to develop leadership capabilities and harmonious group interaction.

Unfortunately, the right to a basic education — long considered a moral right and today also supported as an economic necessity — is denied to millions of children for structural and political reasons, especially in Africa and South Asia. Severe regional differences in economic and social opportunity continue to play a part in stunting child development within the first few critical years of life. Poverty is the most formidable enemy of healthy child development: it determines the quality of the environmental conditions in which many children are forced to grow up; and these conditions, in turn, influence the children's physical, intellectual and emotional growth.[13]

A Harvard University study[14] concluded that poverty may, in fact, be the single most significant factor determining children's physical and emotional development. Children who are from impoverished single-parent families and who, especially during their first three years of life, are frequently left unsupervised or in the care of disinterested neighbours or relatives, the study found, display slower psychosocial growth than children who are looked after by an attentive parent. The study also found that stressed and depressed mothers have a negative influence on the emotional growth of their children. What is not known, however, is whether the emotional stunting resulting from unfavourable socio-environmental conditions is reversible. In other words, ensuring the right to an education to children who have suffered the combined physical and emotional blights of poverty is not in itself a sufficient guarantee that, once attained, this right will, in fact, benefit the recipient.

It is not enough to verbalize the legal and social provisions of the CRC without tackling the macro issues; namely, the poverty and economic injustice that lead to the suffering of so many of the world's children. Insisting on buying a cart after the horse has bolted will not restore the owner's right to have a functioning cart. A number of educators and economists have drawn attention to the need to deal with the underlying causes of social injustice[15] before addressing issues relating to improvements in education. Education is not a social cure-all, nor can it by its sole power remedy the underlying structural causes of inequities. At best, education can highlight the social distortions that economic disparities and social deprivation generate. But this is only possible if those running the system make a conscious effort to monitor social outcomes through the school.

■ 3. Reaching the Unreached

More than ever before, development specialists and educators worldwide are realizing that the success of education systems should be measured not only by what they teach but also by whom they reach. Basic education is commonly accessed through primary schooling. Currently, for economic, geographic, ethnic and other reasons, a large proportion of school-age children fail to enter primary school. And if they do, many are unable to stay in school long enough to benefit from the exposure to learning. Providing every child with the right to five years of basic education, at a minimum, is a task that will require careful planning based on an accurate assessment of the problem. Similarly recognizing where the problem is, and then designing flexible, non-traditional ways of dealing with it, will be an imperative for governments as well as educators. It will take a special kind of determination and a sort of creativity not often displayed by Ministries of Education to reach the small groups of traditionally marginalized children and adults wishing to receive basic education services.

The accurate assessment and identification of those most at risk will be an essential first step in dealing with the problem of providing basic education services to the unreached. In some countries of Africa and South Asia, economic decline or structural adjustment pressures make it difficult to sustain public services even at their present low levels of efficiency. Basic education, unfortunately still not a high priority for many governments, is frequently the first area to suffer. For this reason, few governments maintain up-to-date data enabling them to monitor and evaluate public services by identifying and tracking individuals or groups who have been denied their basic right to education. A significant proportion of children among the growing numbers of urban poor and in isolated rural communities — especially those from marginalized indigenous groups, ethnic minorities or nomadic groups — continue to be victims of the neglect resulting from political and bureaucratic blindness. This blindness is generated by inadequate information and a lack of understanding of the special educational needs of children from different groups within each national context.

The following sections contain a discussion of children frequently belonging to disenfranchised groups that are unattached to mainstream national politics and culture. All the groups selected represent different but complementary facets of the dilemma surrounding the right to basic education. Girl children are the single largest and most educationally deprived group across every national, political and cultural border. Ethnic and indigenous minorities have generally been deprived of their full right to a relevant basic education.

□ 3.1. EDUCATING GIRLS AND WOMEN

Gender disparity in education is an injustice requiring the most urgent attention. World education indicators show that girls still have much less access than boys to education at all levels. In 1990, girls represented approximately 70 per cent of the 300 million children who did not have access to primary or secondary education. Gender disparities in enrolment are still particularly high in Africa (with the exception of Lesotho and Namibia where disparities are actually reversed in favour of girls), South Asia and the Middle East.[16] In most other regions, including the industrialized countries of the North, disparities are not as frequent or non-existent.

As far as global literacy is concerned, indicators display even higher levels of gender disparity. Recent figures suggest that adult illiteracy affects about 960 million people worldwide, of whom about 700 million are women. In 1985, few countries had male literacy rates below 20 per cent while at least 17 countries had female literacy rates below this level.

Today, in at least 29 countries, female literacy rates still remain under 30 per cent, while male literacy rates in the same countries are at least twice as high (Figure 6.3). South Asia, for example, where female literacy levels were about 49 per cent in 1985, will face an uphill challenge unless countries in the region begin to mobilize resources to remedy their female illiteracy problem. In sub-Saharan Africa, female literacy rates were 56 per cent in 1985, just under rates in the Middle East (58 percent), but far below those in South East Asia (73 per cent) and Latin America (95 per cent). A review of schooling by gender among individuals over 25 years of age indicates that, in 1980, women averaged only about one year of schooling in Africa, South Asia and the Arab countries.[17]

Despite the remarkable progress in access to basic education made during the last three decades in developing countries, gender gaps continue to be high at all levels of the education system (Figure 6.4), particularly after the first three years of primary school. The reasons for the persistent gender disparities are often complex and specific to the regional, national and local contexts.[18] However, current research in Africa and South Asia suggests three common contributing factors:

Figure 6.3: **Adult* literacy and female literacy 30 per cent or lower, in selected countries, 1991.**

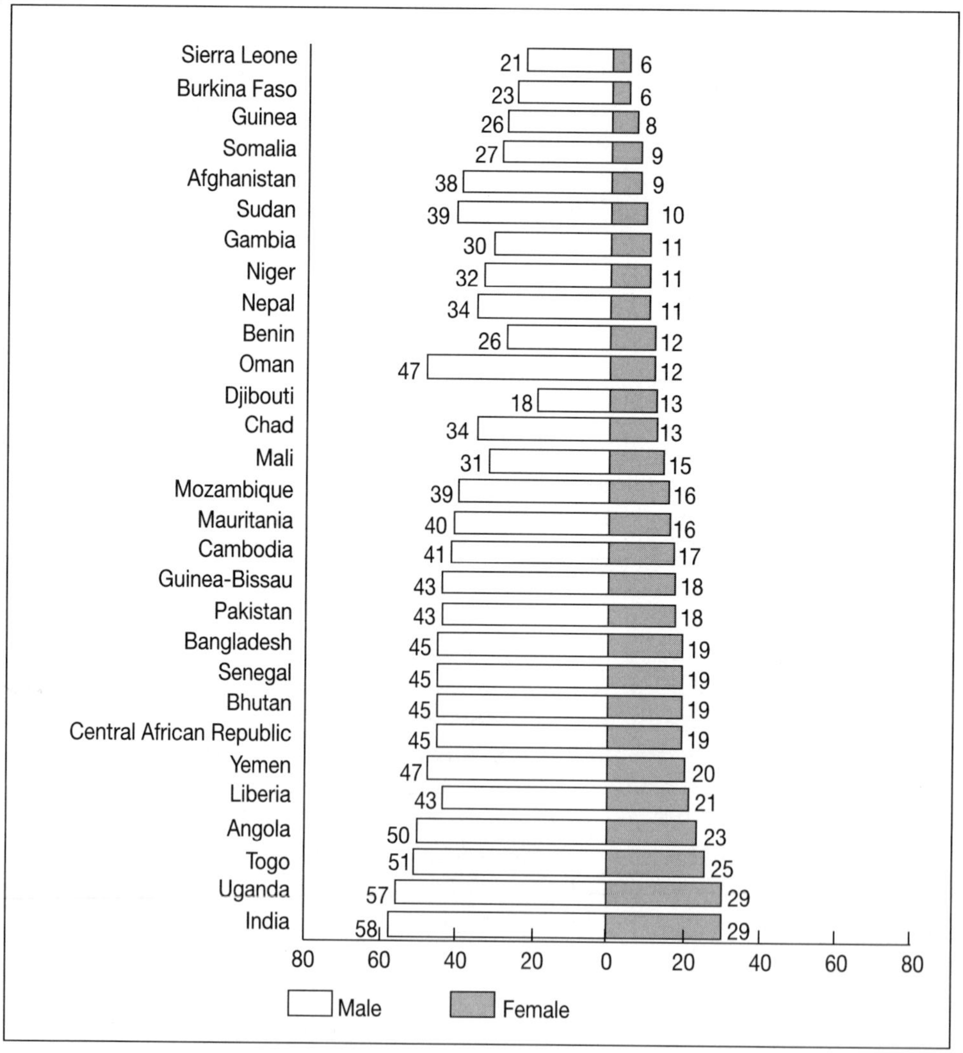

Source: United Nations Development Programme, 1991.
* 15 years of age or older

- *Persistent rural and urban poverty* plays a major role in determining whether girls have access to school. In the majority of poor households, because a daughter's labour makes an important contribution to household survival, the cost of sending her to school is too high. Cultural and economic constraints placed on girls and women — both at home and in the labour market — also prevent girls from going to school;
- *Geographical factors*, such as the distance of schools from home, also play a decisive role in whether girls go to school in many developing countries. In remote rural areas, parents will often discourage their daughters from walking long distances to local schools for fear that public exposure could result in their being molested or violated;
- *In-school factors* also contribute to making schooling a negative experience for girls in many countries: teachers are frequently male; classes are often dominated by aggressive and ill-behaved boys; the syllabus is still strongly biased towards the male child; and not much attention is paid to the girls' learning needs. The lack of schedules flexible enough to allow girls to combine schooling with household tasks and the shortage of female teachers contribute significantly to the high number of girls who drop out of school at critical stages in the primary and secondary school cycles.

To extend the right to a basic education to girls, policy makers should target this most neglected group of learners as the main beneficiaries of education programmes. In addition, girls' education cannot be separated from the broader sociopolitical context: the status of girls and women within the society as a whole is an issue that needs to be addressed.

The following is a list of already-tested strategies for helping girls gain a basic education. These strategies also concern issues of school access, retention and achievement. In particular, it will be necessary to:

Figure 6.4: **Primary school female enrolment as a percentage of male enrolment, by region, 1960 and 1986-1989**

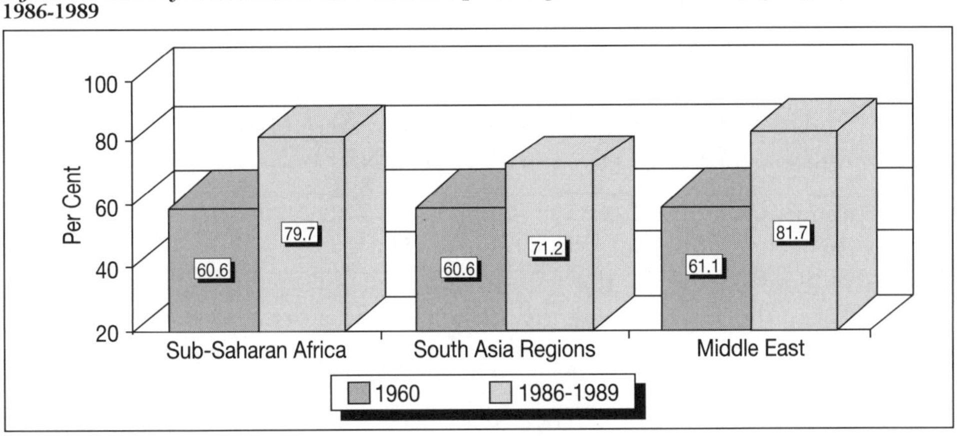

Source: United Nations Children's Fund, 1992c.

- locate schools closer to communities, make schools safer learning environments, make facilities culturally appropriate and, when necessary, establish single-sex classes;
- promote the recruitment of more female teachers and provide incentives to encourage them to teach in remote rural schools or poor urban districts. Local recruitment and placement of female teachers may also help them to remain in marginalized communities;
- reduce the real cost of basic education for parents by providing scholarships, free textbooks and uniforms, and by adopting flexible schedules to allow girls to spend part of the day working at home;
- develop gender-relevant curricula by introducing topics that are of interest to girls and coincide with their aspirations;
- increase community participation in the management and improvement of local schools, and encourage community leaders to assume responsibility for the maintenance of schools and the formulation of day-to-day policies. The decentralization of school management and decision-making would help communities to gain or regain ownership of their schools;
- mobilize local resources in support of schools. In remote areas, parents who are illiterate need to be informed of the benefits accruing from their daughters' schooling. Prepare a community-shared action plan for social mobilization, and use multi-channel approaches to spread positive messages to all members of the community about the benefits of girls' education;
- design systems to support the needs of female students, including the installation of water and sanitation facilities and the introduction of flexible schedules, gender-based monitoring and evaluation systems, and specially designed instruction; and
- support multi-channel approaches for delivering basic education to girls. Informal, non-formal and low-cost alternative formal delivery systems should be encouraged, especially for difficult-to-reach groups and out-of-school, housebound girls.

□ 3.2. EDUCATING THE CHILDREN OF MINORITY AND INDIGENOUS POPULATIONS

Ethnic minorities and indigenous populations with special educational needs – the Australian aborigines, the Inuit of Alaska and northern Canada, the Khmer of Southeast Asia, the tribes in the hills of Vietnam, the pygmies of West Africa, the bushmen of the Kalahari, the Mayas of Guatemala, the Quechuas and Aymaras in the Andes, the Gypsies of Europe, and countless similar groups elsewhere – generally represent only a small fraction of the population of these regions. Their distinctive cultures and languages have contributed to their isolation from mainstream education systems. Respect for their rights and recognition of their cultural plight constitute two of the most important educational challenges of our age. How we ultimately guarantee their right to an appropriate education, which would enable them to be self-sufficient in a world of rapid social change, will be the real test of our sincerity and determination to comply with the spirit and the letter of the CRC.

Children of minority groups have recently gained a priority position on the world's political agenda. The CRC, especially Article 2, establishes that national governments need to take an active role in protecting children from all forms of discrimination. No State Party should allow a child within its jurisdiction to lead a disadvantaged life as the price to pay for belonging to an ethnic minority. The Gypsy communities in Europe and the nomadic tribes in Africa are in many ways emblematic of the plight of minorities in general.

3.2.1. Gypsies in Europe

Recent events in Europe, particularly the increase of migration from Eastern to Western European countries (especially from Romania and former Yugoslavia), have put in evidence the deteriorating conditions of the Gypsy community as a whole. Although 'Gypsies' constitute a broad grouping of nomadic or semi-nomadic individuals from a wide variety of backgrounds, they nonetheless share a number of identifiable problems. Especially in the area of education, it would be extremely worthwhile for governments to join together to forge a transnational strategy, based on a common set of guidelines and a comprehensive analysis of Gypsy children's educational needs. As yet few efforts seem to have been made in this direction.

Education policies for Gypsy and nomadic children implemented by European governments have so far been unsuccessful. A number of indicators attest to this failure:[19]

(a) *Primary enrolment and completion levels* (Table 6.2) are, with few exceptions, far below national average. Primary enrolment rates in European Union (EU) countries averaged only about 35 per cent in 1989. Moreover, enrol-

Table 6.2 **- Gypsy primary enrolment rates, selected European countries, 1990-1991**

	Percentage
Western European Countries	
Eire (1984)	50
France	30
Greece (1986)	15
Italy	35
Spain (1987)	50
United Kingdom	40
EU (1989)	35
Central and Eastern European Countries	
Bulgaria	95
Czechoslovakia (1985)	75
Hungary	50

Source: Costarelli, 1993.

ment rates mask very low completion rates in the majority of cases. In Bulgaria, where enrolment of Gypsy children in primary school is high (95 per cent in 1990-1991), only 30 per cent actually complete their schooling. In Greece in 1986, 15 per cent of Gypsy children were enrolled in school, but only half of this group completed primary education. In former Yugoslavia in 1986, 80 per cent of Gypsy children did not complete primary school; in Hungary in 1991, the percentage was 50 per cent.

In Czechoslovakia, on the other hand, high enrolment rates and a reasonably high retention rate (50 per cent) may reflect the outcome of a successful campaign to encourage parents to send their children to pre-school. The majority of Gypsy children who attended kindergarten went on to enrol in elementary school. Kindergarten attendance has also proved to be a successful means of changing negative parental attitudes towards schooling; and it may suggest a feasible strategy for lessening the prejudice against formal education, which continues to be one of the major obstacles to servicing Gypsy children.

(b) *Transition rates* from primary to secondary school are either extremely low or non-existent. In Germany in 1985, only 1 per cent of Gypsy children attended secondary school.

(c) *Illiteracy rates* are high. Only a small proportion of Gypsy children leaving school can read or write. In 1985, 80 per cent of EU adult Gypsies were illiterate. Adult Gypsy illiteracy rates for Spain in 1987 were 80 per cent; for France in 1991, 65 per cent; for Bulgaria in 1991, 50 per cent (for adults over 30 years of age). In Greece, 80 per cent of the school-age Gypsy population was officially illiterate in 1986.

Although the causes of this situation vary, they may be broadly summarized as follows:

- the teaching methods and content are inappropriate for children coming from a predominantly oral tradition;
- nearly all national school systems teach in their national languages and ignore the Gypsy children's language and cultural backgrounds;
- teachers are neither aware of, nor adequately trained to handle, the special cultural needs of Gypsy children;
- economic and cultural pressures cause Gypsy children to drop out of school at an early age to earn a living; and
- ingrained social prejudice has contributed to labelling the Gypsy child as mentally retarded. In Czechoslovakia in 1980, 17.1 per cent of school-age Gypsies attended special schools for the mentally disabled, a percentage that reached 27.6 per cent in 1985. In Germany, 40 per cent of national Gypsy children attended special schools for the mentally disabled in 1985, whereas the non-Gypsy average was 3 per cent.

Only the removal of economic and social pressures from the Gypsy child's survival agenda will make school attendance and completion acceptable options. Children still play an important role as breadwinners in the average

Gypsy family, which is often characterized by high levels of both adult unemployment and dependence on the social security system. Because of this situation, young Gypsies may go out onto the street to beg or steal, arts learned and practised from an early age and considered by many to be legitimate means to contribute to their families' subsistence.[20]

3.2.2. Nomadic Tribes of Africa

Pastoralists or nomads represent from 12 to 16 per cent of the total population living in the arid and semi-arid regions of East and West Africa. The total nomad population in Africa is currently estimated at about 25 million, a sizeable proportion of whom are children.

In most countries, nomads are minorities (Table 6.3) whose ethnic identities, life styles, cultural values and languages differ from those of the dominant groups. The welfare of nomads is often negatively affected by increasing differentials in access to health, education and other essential services.[21] Malnutrition, sickness, illiteracy and vulnerability to external influences continue to mar their lives. The only entities capable of mobilizing sufficient resources to provide major services to these minorities, whose basic rights have persistently been denied, remain the nations where they live.

Both formal and non-formal educational interventions on behalf of nomads have been weak or non-existent. Effective education services are difficult to provide, not only because of the high level of mobility and dispersal of these communities, but also because of their special needs in terms of teaching methods, curricula and language of instruction. Stretched to provide education services to their majority groups, governments have balked at the additional cost of providing special services to groups of nomad learners.

Schools in small rural towns or villages in the pastoralist zones have mainly been filled by the children of traders and civil servants, with only a

Table 6.3 **- Total and nomad population, selected African countries, 1992**

	Total population (millions)	Nomad population (millions)	% of nomad to total population
Burkina Faso	9.0	0.5	6
Chad	5.7	1.0	20
Djibouti	0.5	0.1	15
Ethiopia	49.2	5.0	10
Kenya	24.0	3.5	15
Mali	9.2	1.0	11
Mauritania	2.0	0.3	15
Niger	7.7	1.0	13
Senegal	7.3	1.0	13
Somalia	7.5	4.5	60
Sudan	25.2	3.5	14
Tanzania	27.3	0.5	1
Uganda	18.8	0.6	3
Total	193.4	22.5	12

Source: Bonfiglioli and Watson, 1992.

small segment of school-age children from the wealthier families. A limited number of boarding schools have been set up on an experimental basis. Parents, however, have been reluctant to send their children to boarding schools because they need their labour for the maintenance of household productivity. Moreover, parents view the modern school as a culturally alienating place. 'Tent' or 'mobile' schools are among the more interesting and flexible experiments attempted in rural areas. In Mali, Mauritania and Niger, Koranic schools have been used to provide general education. Most experiences in pastoralist education have been characterized by a trial-and-error approach and lack a coherent, well-thought-out plan.[22]

Education programmes for nomads have failed primarily because decision makers have sought to use education as a tool for transforming nomad populations into sedentary ones. Teachers have generally been recruited from extra-pastoralist backgrounds, and their ideologies have clashed with the values of the pastoral societies. This has led nomad parents and children to reject what teachers teach as representing foreign values that are threatening to indigenous culture and beliefs.

A new approach is required for adapting modern education to the special needs of nomad societies. It is important that appropriate curricula be defined in line with the values and aspirations of the nomads themselves. Education should be perceived as a means for enhancing life and survival and not for changing communities. An appropriate curriculum would not only transmit reading and writing skills, but also civic awareness, management and accounting skills, basic health and nutrition concepts, and sound environmental, agricultural and animal husbandry techniques.

Various forms of tent schools — perhaps the most viable form of schooling for nomad children — should be introduced. However, the following guidelines need to be adopted to make this kind of education more responsive to the social and cultural needs of nomads:

- parents should be involved in the selection of what is to be taught;
- the programme should be flexible and, as far as possible, fit in with seasonal rhythms and changes in production cycles;
- the curriculum should provide nomad children with survival skills, including information on animal husbandry, herding and agriculture; and
- special efforts need to be made to encourage girls to attend school and complete their primary education.

Sceptical parents will have to be persuaded that schools are adequately supervised and safe, especially for their daughters. Women teachers will need to be recruited in larger numbers and deployed more efficiently to ensure an adequate level of supervision, especially in boarding schools.

Two phases are suggested for reforming basic education services to nomad groups in Africa:

(a) *Diagnosis and preparation*:
- carry out surveys to assess current school attendance, parental attitudes, achievement levels and teachers' characteristics;
- design an appropriate curriculum with parental and community involvement to include useful life-support and survival skills;
- develop adequate in-service training courses for teachers to prepare them for work with nomad communities; and
- initiate a broad programme of social mobilization among parents and nomad communities to advocate more schooling for their children. Special emphasis should be placed on the need to educate girls.

(b) *Implementation*:
- carry out intensive training of male and female teachers and prepare special teachers' manuals and teaching materials;
- set up parent-teacher associations to support special nomadic schools;
- construct schools in areas that are still unserviced;
- create special mobile primary schools (tent schools) and evaluate their effectiveness in reaching nomad children;
- provide adequate learning resources for every school and organize classes; and
- develop an adequate monitoring and evaluation system for tracking children's progress through the system.

☐ 3.3. INNOVATIVE LEARNING PROGRAMMES

A number of community-based, non-governmental initiatives have evolved in developing countries to meet the special educational needs of different population groups. Three of these programmes merit special mention: the BRAC schools in Bangladesh, 70 per cent of whose students are female; the *Escuelas Mayas* in Guatemala, which have successfully reached Mayan-speaking communities with a bilingual and culturally acceptable education; and the Tostan basic learning project in Senegal, which offers a literacy programme with a community development emphasis.

3.3.1. BRAC Schools in Bangladesh[25]

Some 68 million people in rural areas of Bangladesh live below the poverty line. Until recently, most impoverished rural children received little or no schooling. Their labour was needed for household survival. Girls, expected to marry young and join their husbands' families, often never went to school at all. To meet the needs of these children, the Bangladesh Rural Advancement Committee (BRAC) began experimental schools in 1985. The schools implement two primary school models: Non-Formal Primary Education (NFPE), which targets 8- to 10-year-olds who have never attended school or who have dropped out; and Primary Education for Older Children (PEOC), which is aimed at 11- to 14-year-olds who have never attended school.

NFPE provides three years of basic education, including literacy, numeracy and community-awareness. Games, singing and sports are part of the regular curriculum. In the PEOC programme, nearly 75 per cent of the students are unmarried girls. The NFPE curriculum is adopted, but taught in two instead of three years. In both types of schools, classes are held six days a week, 2½ - 3 hours per day, with only short vacation breaks. The setting is simple. Buildings are made of woven bamboo or mud. Children sit on mats and are given slates, pencils, textbooks, notebooks and lapboards. Teachers are furnished with a blackboard, a stool and a trunk where school materials can be kept.

Several principles have been adhered to in setting up BRAC schools. First, the community must ask for the school and provide the building, thus proving their readiness to support schooling for their children. The school building is, in turn, rented by BRAC, which ensures its maintenance. Second, parents actively participate in decisions about their children's education: they help to schedule classes at times that will not interfere with the children's household and field chores; and they also are involved in the selection of the locally recruited (and hence well-known and trusted) teachers. Third, BRAC will not start a school in a village where no one is qualified to teach.

Prospective teachers must have completed nine years of schooling and be married. Because 70 per cent of the students are girls, women are preferred as teachers. They initially receive 12 days of training at a residential training centre and then on-the-job training by BRAC field staff. After one year, they participate in a six-day refresher course. BRAC prepares teaching materials, a suggested daily lesson plan and other guidance. Once a month, teachers from about 20 neighbouring communities meet with field supervisors to discuss their classroom experiences and problems. Significantly, although parents — particularly mothers — are illiterate, they originally sought their children's education and now actively support the schools, meeting once a month to discuss their children's progress.

BRAC calculated in 1992 that the total cost per enrolled child per year was less than \$17, whereas an independent study estimated less than \$14. A third study found that the overall unit cost per pupil was roughly equal to that of state primary schools in rural areas. However, unlike state schools where teachers' salaries normally absorb 85 per cent or more of recurrent expenditures, BRAC schools allocate to this item only a small share of the total budget. This is not because of an unfavourable student-teacher ratio (class size is limited to 30 students), but rather because BRAC teachers earn considerably less than state teachers do. Reasons for this are peculiar to the Bangladesh context:

(a) most villages appear to have at least two or three women with the academic credentials needed to teach NFPE;

(b) suitable jobs for academically qualified women are scarce at the village level; and

(c) the domestic responsibilities sustained by these women make part-time BRAC work especially attractive.

Savings on salaries are transferred to the management and supervisory functions of the schools, which help to enhance their efficiency and the effectiveness of investments in other elements of the BRAC non-formal education system.

BRAC has been extremely successful: in eight years it has opened over 10,000 schools; and over 90 per cent of its pupils have continued on in the state system.

3.3.2. Escuelas Mayas in Guatemala[24]

The Convention on the Rights of the Child establishes that every child has the right "in community with other members of his or her group, to enjoy his or her own culture, to profess and practise his or her own religion, [and] to use his or her own language" (Article 30). In Guatemala, this principle forms the basis for Escuelas Mayas, which are private schools — run and financed by members of the community — that combine government-approved and Mayan curricula. Spontaneous community-based initiatives, these schools offer instruction in the regional dialect as well as in Spanish and utilize culturally sensitive teaching techniques and materials. Children of Mayan descent learn about Mayan culture, history, music, art and crafts. Teachers are recruited from local communities and trained in the history and traditions of the Mayan culture.

Although 90 per cent of Guatemalans are of Mayan descent, classes in state schools are taught in Spanish. Languages and cultural diversity are the major problems encountered in assisting Mayan children. There are 22 Mayan languages, which, in turn, include 200 dialects. Prior to the introduction of Escuelas Mayas, only 30 per cent of school-age children attended primary school. Many communities had no schools; most children worked; and parents did not encourage their children — especially their daughters — to attend schools. As a result, illiteracy rates ranged from 52 to 93 per cent.

Involving parents has been an important element in the success of the new schools. Each school is trying to develop its own curriculum in the local Mayan dialect, using whatever resources are available and affordable within the community. Parents and neighbours together plan the school hours so that children can work when needed. Most schools have high female enrolment. Girls tend to stay in school until they finish their primary education; some of them continue on to secondary school.

Parents seem happier with the Mayan schools than with the traditional state schools. Their children are now learning to read and write in their own language and are also acquiring other skills that will realistically serve them in the future and enable them to contribute to the development of their villages or neighbourhoods. The popularity of the Mayan schools extends to non-Mayan families, some of whom send their children to these schools in preference to state schools.

3.3.3. The Tostan Basic Leaning Project in Senegal[25]

One of Africa's most promising basic learning models is called *Tostan* — a Woloff word meaning 'breakthrough' or 'hatching of an egg'. Initially, a literacy project, Tostan has evolved into a programme to spread knowledge about basic services for family and community development. By participating in six modules (of two months each) over two years, women, men and young people learn how to bring about changes in their villages or neighbourhoods and how to improve family life through health measures, improved hygiene, gardening and management of the family economy. They also learn leadership skills, how to organize village projects from the initial feasibility study to project management, problem solving or avoidance, and market strategies.

Tostan teachers are called 'facilitators' as their principal role is to encourage participants in their discussions and learning activities. They are chosen by the people of their own village and given a one-month preparatory course before they begin the first module of instruction. Lessons are taught in Woloff or Pulaar, the languages of the region. Participants learn to read and write in their own language, but use the Latin rather than the Arabic alphabet so that they can go on to learn French if they so choose. Facilitators make use of theatre, stories, pictures, games and flip charts to motivate participants.

More than half of the participants are women. Although women in Senegal play an important role socially and economically, a female illiteracy rate of more than 80 per cent seriously hampers national development. Gender disparities in primary education are still apparent. Despite an increase in enrolment from 27 per cent in 1960 to 57.9 per cent in 1989-1990, only 32.4 per cent of pupils are girls. One of the goals of Tostan is to attain a 60 per cent female literacy rate in Senegal by the year 2000. Often classes are divided into discussion groups so that women feel more comfortable expressing themselves in front of male participants. The topics discussed help them to participate in village improvement activities. Thus, not only do women learn practical skills, but they also gradually gain confidence in themselves.

During the first two modules, participants begin learning to read, to write and to use numbers; they also discuss problem identification, problem-solving and planning skills. In the third module (fifth and sixth months), they learn advanced reading, writing and numeracy skills and other problem-solving methods, and are introduced to basic health techniques such as oral rehydration therapy and vaccinations. In the last three modules, they gain a greater understanding of the various aspects of community development. Emphasis is on the management of financial and material resources as well as the management of human resources, including elements of leadership and group dynamics. Participants are also taught how to carry out feasibility studies for small-scale village or community projects.

The non-formal approach and participatory learning methods of Tostan have led to high attendance and enthusiasm among participants. Behavioural changes are evident as students gain confidence during discussions and become leaders in changing community conditions. As they progress, they even travel to nearby villages, teaching their neighbours about hygiene and sanitation, oral rehydration and immunization. Subsequently, many of these villages decide to set up their own Tostan learning projects.

3.4. MEETING THE COST OF EDUCATION RIGHTS

Recent studies carried out in the United Kingdom at the Institute for Development Studies, Sussex University, have tried to estimate the cost "for all children of primary school age in developing countries to be given primary schooling" at a minimally acceptable standard by the year 2000.[26] They concluded that in those developing countries that have not reached universal primary education, the attainment of primary schooling for all (SFA) by the year 2000 would require an additional 156 million primary school places, or a 30 per cent increase in the number of schools that existed in 1990. Sub-Saharan Africa, for demographic and other reasons, will need to double its number of primary school places during the 1990s to meet the SFA goal by 2000.

Most low- and middle-income countries could fulfil every child's right to a basic education over the next 10 years by applying education and fiscal policy reforms and by giving somewhat higher budget priority to primary education. However, where existing gross enrolment rates are below 50 per cent, as is the case in some sub-Saharan countries, bridging the enrolment gap and keeping up with high population growth rates will require substantial technical and financial assistance from outside donors. Ultimately, each nation will need to establish its own education policies and programmes, setting aside the resources and trained manpower needed to achieve SFA by the end of the decade. Reliance on foreign assistance alone will not solve the problem. Countries must encourage and carry out comprehensive internal reforms in education management, administration and policy making if the ambitious goals set forth at the Jomtien Conference and the World Summit for Children are to be achieved within the foreseeable future.

It also bears repeating that universalizing school enrolment is not just a question of providing adequate facilities, but it is also likely to involve persuading parents to send their children to school. This is especially true in countries where girls are deliberately kept out of school and where economic considerations prevent children from going to school.

The additional cost of achieving SFA by 2000 is estimated to be approximately \$60 billion, which is less than the estimated \$100 billion spent on the Gulf War, for example. This figure is likely to increase to about \$140 billion by the year 2005 (assuming that unit costs and average transition rates to secondary education remain constant). If one adds the costs of improvements in the *quality* of basic education, additional expenditures will be required in many countries; but these costs can be kept down if selected education reforms are introduced in a timely manner. A significant part of the cost of SFA could be met through normal budgetary growth together with a conscious shifting of national expenditures from military and other non-essential investments to education and other social services that contribute to the improvement of the quality of life as well as to the productivity of a nation's human resources.

If all countries were willing to implement most of the cost-saving reforms suggested (such as those recommended for Africa in the following section) and increased their budget allocations to basic education by 2 per cent, only an additional $17.5 billion in external aid would be needed over the next 10 years to finance SFA. However, not all cost reforms will be possible, especially in some African countries where real public expenditures per capita continue to decline. Perhaps 36 of the poorest countries will require additional funding to encourage them to adopt the strategies and policies needed to achieve SFA by 2000.

A similar projection for Africa's schooling needs alone suggests that with a modest $6 billion to $7 billion annual investment in basic education, the majority of Africa's school-age population could gain access to primary school by the year 2000.

3.5. ACHIEVING SCHOOLING FOR ALL IN AFRICA AND OTHER REGIONS BY 2000

Fourteen years after the Lagos Plan of Action documented an impressive increase in human capital investment by most African countries — and barely four years after the 1991 milestone UNESCO/Organization of African Unity/ Economic Commission for Africa meeting for African Ministers of Education in Dakar to plan a long-term commitment to improving African education — there is no cause for complacency: the goals projected for primary, secondary and higher education in Africa are far from being reached. Economic decline, rapid population growth, migration, poor management, inappropriate fiscal policies, and other factors, have prevented many countries from satisfying the increased demand for education services, especially at the primary school level. This situation has been partly exacerbated by the tendency of some donors to favour technical, secondary and higher education over basic or primary education and by the low priority given by the countries themselves to basic education.

Thus, many African countries have ceased to be effective learning environments for the vast majority of the children living there. UNICEF and other Jomtien partners concur that education systems in Africa present the largest problems worldwide and deserve special focus during this decade.

A comprehensive strategy for tackling the need for basic education for all of Africa's children was elaborated in a paper prepared for the International Conference on Assistance to African Children held in Dakar, Senegal, in November 1992, and subsequently published in the book, *Africa's Children, Africa's Future*.[27] The paper begins by pointing out that no single packet or 'magic bullet' exists for dealing with the problem of basic education in Africa. By definition, education involves slow, long-term and highly sensitive processes that are subject to social and political controls and influenced by other systemic factors frequently beyond community or parental control. The strategy proposed is both specific and sensitive to the cultural and geographical needs of the African regions considered. It is based on the notion that the quickest and most cost-effective way to help African children obtain access to basic education is to give credibility to Africa's education systems. Because Africa's primary education infrastructure represents a one-time capital investment that cannot be easily recovered, existing primary school services will need to be revitalized. A (minimum) two-pronged strategy for making viable existing primary education services is suggested:

(a) As a first step, countries willing to reform their basic education system are encouraged to carry out a comprehensive evaluation of their educational needs by collecting and analysing local data and identifying priorities. This should help to remove the 'guess element' that has hitherto characterized the education policy planning in the majority of developing countries, and enable these countries to allocate more rationally the scarce resources available for the provision of basic education services.

(b) A second necessary step is to revitalize existing primary schools, which is considered the quickest way to give children the minimum basic education needed for survival in their fast-changing societies. Low levels of efficiency, underutilized capacity, poor teaching quality due to poorly trained and underpaid teachers, the lack of such basic learning materials as exercise books and textbooks are some of the commonly observed characteristics of many African primary schools. The major negative impact of these factors, especially in rural primary schools, has led both parents and pupils to question the relevance of schooling. Regional disparities are wide, sub-Saharan Africa being the most disadvantaged area.

A more efficient use of existing facilities and a reduction of drop-out and repetition rates would help to make schools accessible to a significant number of children, especially to girls who are still excluded from primary education in many African countries. Specific reforms for enhancing the quality and effectiveness of Africa's primary education systems are summarized in Table 6.4.

Reinvesting in Africa's primary schools will have a significant impact on both individual and national development, especially in countries where enrolment rates are still below 50 per cent. A growing awareness of the intrinsic value of education to each individual has added an important moral dimension to the case for basic education for all. The CRC, the World Conference on Education for All and the World Summit for Children have all helped to renew the emphasis on the need for African governments to establish basic education as a fundamental human right, especially for persistently marginalized groups.

□ 3.6. FINDING THE RESOURCES FOR AFRICA

If participating African governments can be persuaded at least to allocate existing levels of expenditure to their primary and secondary education budgets, and to carry out all or most of the reforms suggested — above all, providing the necessary resources to meet the increased demand for primary school education for

Table 6.4 **- Framework for the reform of Africa's primary education systems**

Cost-saving reform	Cost-shifting reform	Quality-enhancing reform	Management and supervisory reform	Community-based reform
Reduce teacher-pupil ratios over a 10-year period through the introduction of double shifts at the primary and secondary levels.	*Decrease* the recurrent unit costs of primary and secondary schools over a 10-year period by increasing private contributions.	*Increase* the annual expenditure on learning resources over a 5-year period to at least $ 5 per child at all levels.	*Restructure* and *decentralize* the administrative and management functions of the Ministry of Education to the regional and district levels.	*Enact* national legislation to enable devolution of responsibility for the maintenance of primary schools from highly centralized state controls to the community.
Increase class size over a 10-year period wherever the current level is 40 pupils or less in primary and secondary schools, and 30 or less in teacher-training and vocational schools.	*Decrease* capital costs of classroom construction at primary level over a 5-year period through increased community support.	*Increase* teachers' salaries in real terms where possible over a 10-year period.	*Develop* or *improve* a monitoring and evaluation system to permit the timely gathering of appropriate data on the performance of national education systems.	*Create* and *encourage* parent-teacher associations or other community groups in all primary and secondary schools.
Reduce primary teacher's unit costs over a 10-year period through increased use of self-study sessions, teaching assistants, parents and other community helpers.	*Freeze* higher education subsidies at current levels.	*Reduce* repetition and drop-out rates at all levels over a 10-year period while allowing promotion rates to increase concomitantly.	*Train* or *retrain* managers and administrators at both the school and ministry levels.	*Encourage* parent-community representation at all levels of the education management system in keeping with the recent moves towards more democratic and accountable government.
			Train and *empower* an effective cadre of supervisors to monitor and evaluate the implementation of the educational component of the National Plan of Action at all levels.	

all by the year 2000 — it is estimated that an additional $6 billion over the next 10 years will be required. Allowing for inflation, a further investment of about $750 million per year ($7.5 billion for 10 years) will be needed to achieve the (minimum) two-pronged SFA strategy, as outlined above. It may be assumed that governments willing to do this would also be willing to meet some of this extra cost from local resources — up to, say, 30 per cent (approximately $225 million) of this additional amount per year. It is not unreasonable to assume that increased community participation and the involvement of the private sector at the local level would be able to absorb another 20 per cent ($150 million) of the additional cost per year. This would leave about 50 per cent ($375 million per year) to be raised from other sources, including multilateral and bilateral aid contributions. An additional amount — roughly estimated to be about $250 million per year — will be necessary to promote and implement specific non-formal and other innovative basic education alternatives, including literacy projects for those countries unable to invest in formal schooling and in the attendant costly infrastructure. Here, creative, alternative stand-by delivery systems will have to be developed to fill the gap. One such alternative — second-chance learning centres for primary school drop-outs in rural areas — is discussed in the following section.

Since many governments are reluctant to spend money on the implementation of new alternatives to formal education, donors willing to promote creative innovations in basic education should assume most of these additional costs. Of the additional $250 million required yearly for non-formal education, 80 per cent could be provided by donors, and the remaining 20 per cent by government and the local community, including the private sector. These rough cost estimates and suggested sources of financing are summarized in Table 6.5.

3.6.1. Second-Chance Learning Centres for Primary School Drop-outs in Rural Areas

In most African countries, especially the nations in the sub-Saharan region, many children drop out of primary school before they complete a minimum

Table 6.5 **- Projected costs of Schooling for All and non-formal alternatives for Africa, selected countries, 1993-2003**

	Cost (in billions of US dollars)	Share (in percentages)
Schooling for All		
Government	2.25	30
Community and private sector	1.50	20
Donor aid	3.75	50
Subtotal	7.50	100
Non-formal Basic Education and Literacy Alternatives		
Government, Community and Private Sector	0.5	20
Donor aid	2.0	80
Subtotal	2.5	100
Total (over 10 years)	10.0	

Source: Dall F.P., 1992b

of four years. Many are forced out of school for economic reasons; others are unable to continue their education because there are no appropriate facilities close to their communities. Second-chance learning centres, which are mainly targeted at school drop-outs between 9 and 15 years of age who live in rural areas, represent a cost-effective, alternative method for making basic education services accessible to out-of-school children.

Modelled after the *Djamaa Centres* developed in Conakry, Guinea, second-chance learning centres are flexible and community-based. The centres are established in buildings donated by each participating community, which ensures community involvement from the initial project phase. A government or a donor can grant funds to meet the cost of refurbishing and preparing each facility.

The community is also actively involved in the education process, increasing incentive for participating in this initiative. Young men and women with secondary-level or equivalent education can be recruited from within each participating community to serve as teacher-facilitators. They are to be paid a stipend for their services to the community, and time served will be credited towards further training in the vocational area. They should initially be offered a short, but highly focused, practical training course in teaching methods. Their ongoing training will then be carried out through an in-service distance education module utilizing instructional materials specially designed for use with an 'interactive radio' learning component.

It has been proposed that four countries be identified to participate in the first demonstration phase of this project. An area-based approach will be used, and precedence will be given to rural areas with high drop-out rates and elevated gender disparities. During the first three years of implementation, no more than five centres will be established in each of the four countries. Together, these 20 centres are expected to benefit approximately 20,000 school drop-outs. The performance of each centre will be monitored and an evaluation made at the end of three years to determine whether further investment is warranted for 'going to scale'. If the evaluation is positive, separate funding will be sought from local and international sources for expansion and maintenance of already-existing centres.

The project components can be summarized as follows:

- selection and training of teacher-facilitators — 1,000 per country;
- design and production of appropriate learning materials for about 50,000 students;
- identification and preparation of basic learning facilities, about 20 in total;
- mobilization of school drop-outs using mass media. Campaigns may be carried out in four countries;
- preparation of materials, staff training and implementation of an interactive radio component (for four countries);
- monitoring and evaluation of each centre during phases one and two.

Table 6.6 - **Second-chance learning centres: estimated four-year budget for each country**

	(in thousands of US dollars)				
	1993	1994	1995	1996	Total
Preparation of 5 centres	200	200	100	0	500
Production of materials (for 20,000 learners)	400	100	50	50	600
Training 1,000 facilitators	300	100	0	0	400
Interactive radio component	500	300	100	100	1,000
Mobilization of drop-outs	100	50	25	25	200
Evaluation and monitoring	100	100	50	150	400
Total	1,600	850	325	325	3,100

The estimated budget for each national project (Table 6.6) covers four years: three for the demonstration phase of the project and a fourth to allow sufficient time to mobilize national and international resources for the 'going to scale' phase. The total cost for the implementation of these projects in four countries over a four-year period would amount to about $12.64 million. This projection is based on the assumption that stable economic conditions and comparable cost levels will continue to prevail in each participating country.

A proposal for financing of this technical package is presented in Table 6.7. The next section contains a summary of a number of cost-effective strategies to upgrade the quality of primary schools in rural areas, with emphasis on teacher training, and production and distribution of learning materials.

3.6.2. Improving the Quality of African Primary Education in Rural Areas

It has been argued (and substantiated by recent studies) that the revitalization of primary schools in Africa must begin with improvements in the quality of existing schools. This could be accomplished in a cost-effective and timely manner by:

(a) providing in-service teacher training courses to upgrade and retrain underqualified teachers; and

(b) providing assistance to help countries improve their production of appropriate low-cost learning materials so that each child would be guaranteed a packet of basic learning materials, including textbooks, and exercise books and other writing materials.

Table 6.7 - **Second-chance learning centres: proposed sources of financing**

	Percentage	(in millions of $)
Government	40	1.26
Donors	50	1.58
Community	10	0.32
Total	100	3.16

Since initiating such a strategy on a national scale would require substantial expenditures, a smaller, area-based approach may be more suitable in the first instance. A few rural school districts and a parallel group of marginalized urban school districts could be selected and carefully monitored in each country. A positive evaluation of the area-based approach could provide the experience and justification needed for 'scaling' up to the national level and be used to mobilize the additional donor support for this final phase. This kind of affordable and doable strategy should be easily applicable to countries where the political will to improve the quality of basic education exists and where donors are willing to provide the initial funds needed.

The cost of this approach in one country is estimated in Table 6.8, and proposed sources of financing are shown in Table 6.9. For four countries over four years, the total cost would be $26 million.

■ 4. A Look Ahead

Meeting the longer-term challenge to give every child the right to a basic education in a rapidly changing world is likely to require radically different thinking and solutions that are far more creative than those hitherto applied. Included in any new response to the education rights issue are the questions now beginning to be raised in connection with the ongoing, unprecedented information and technological revolution: Who has the right to which kind of education? And for what purposes? It is increasingly evident that the challenge for the future is not just how to give children those basic reading, writing and numeracy skills that so many still lack, but also how to ensure that these basic learning skills are then converted into the technical skills needed to meet the challenges of the information and technological revolution that has already begun to have a major impact on most societies. Today's moral and ethical dilemma is, therefore, not only one of guaranteeing that every child be given literacy and other basic skills, a preparation that until now has been considered sufficient for access to the labour market; the dilemma is also whether we can and should give to all children — regardless of race, creed, gender and socio-economic background — an order or range of skills needed for survival in a highly dynamic, post-industrial society.

***Table 6.8* - Improving the quality of African primary education: estimated four-year budget for each country**

	(in millions of US dollars per year)				
	1993	1994	1995	1996	Total
Upgrading of teachers (about 10,000 teachers)	2.0	1.0	0.5	0.5	4.0
Production and distribution of learning materials (for about 400,000 pupils at $5 per pupil)	1.0	0.5	0.5	0.5	2.5
Total	3.0	1.5	1.0	1.0	6.5

Ensuring that every child has the right combination of basic skills for meeting her or his immediate survival needs is not only a challenge but also a moral obligation for all educators and governments genuinely concerned with providing an education that will also address issues of equity and social justice.[28] If we continue to do nothing to reduce the widening 'technical literacy' gap encouraged by the difference in quality and content of the education being received by the rich and the poor, we may be in danger of promoting an Orwellian world of two classes, where a privileged and highly trained professional élite (concentrated heavily in the 'North') will be served by a mass of second-class workers (mainly from the 'South') permanently relegated to a life of limited opportunity for self-advancement. Will those who now belong to the so-called Third World be finally reduced to being the serving class of the rich and technically sophisticated world of 'info-managers' in the industrialized countries? Can something be done to narrow the education gap, which is dangerously close to becoming, within a generation, unbridgeable? Or is it already too late to prevent the inevitable? If education is a human right, then access to a functional level of 'technical literacy' must also play a key role in defining what constitutes an adequate educational level in our rapidly changing economies.

Making relevant basic skills and technical knowledge available to both the North and the South at an affordable cost may be a far greater and more profoundly moral challenge than limiting our goal to meeting the 'literacy needs of all', albeit a challenge we failed to meet adequately during the preceding decade. Now more than ever, however, time is not on our side. The exponential nature of the information beast's growth suggests that any tooling up to meet the new demand may need to be handled differently if we are to ensure that every child is accorded his or her right to an adequate preparation for entry into the race for new skills to meet the demands of the new information society. Unfortunately, the most pertinent point of reference — namely the Jomtien Declaration and Framework for Action — focuses on the need to make education more relevant for meeting the basic learning needs of all children, but falls short of coming to grips with the issues of technical relevance and the contribution that education should be making to the kind of world in which most of our children will be struggling to survive during the 21st century.

The right to a very different education, one that will give the learner the technical competencies needed for the new revolution, may well be as real an education priority as that accorded to literacy skills. Will planners and policy

Table 6.9 - Improving the quality of African primary education: proposed sources of financing

	Percentage	(in millions of $)
Government	40	2.60
Donors	50	3.25
Community	10	0.65
Total	100	6.50

makers, for want of vision and strong leadership, relegate developing nations to the bottom of the class again? Will the majority of developing countries, barely now entering the agricultural revolution, and those only recently entering the industrial revolution, be irreparably left behind by those about to enter the information revolution? Implicit in the answer to this question is the definition of 'basic learning needs', which, especially for individuals involved in the reform of education policy, is based on important equity and child rights issues.

'Jomtien' raised the level of international debate by challenging us to re-examine our preconceptions about what constitutes an appropriate basic education, how this should be implemented, by whom and for whom. Models for the delivery of a traditional curriculum may now need to be carefully examined and, if found wanting, changed to ensure that today's children in every part of the world have access to an appropriate basic education, one that meets the technical challenges of our age and succeeds — where traditional approaches seem to have failed — in giving to the notion of 'education as a child right' the equity element that lies at the heart of the disparities separating the education systems of the rich and the poor. Can this be done quickly enough to provide the unreached with a basic education and to help those tooling up to join the age of information management do so in an appropriate way?

Three important developments may have begun to limit future options for bringing basic education services to all the world's children by the year 2000:

The first, just alluded to, relates to the demands of the new information age and to the need for redefining the concept of basic education, since what is required goes beyond the conventional 'three Rs' and includes basic technical skills such as computer literacy and a fundamental understanding of information theory.

The second development has to do with rapid population growth combined with diminishing resources and declining economic productivity — all factors that restrict the degree of freedom nations have for delivering the kinds of services needed to achieve the goal of universal basic "Education for All" implicit in the CRC. Most affected are the nations of the developing world, especially in Africa and South Asia.

A third and largely unexpected development is the direct outcome of the 'new world order' and has to do with the recent radical shift in world power from a confrontational stalemate between two superpowers to the current atomization of nation-states. The rapid splintering of nations into smaller ethnic entities or enclaves will ultimately be counterproductive for the achievement of universal education goals. Many of the emerging new micro-nations, unable to be self-supporting and in need of reconstruction, will now begin to put pressure on donors in order to survive. As a result, the donor nations' resources may become so stretched that little may be left for helping the world's poorest, most populous nations attain the goal of universal access to basic education spelt out in the Jomtien Framework for Action and the World

Summit for Children Declaration. These recent trends may have set back the cause of child rights by several decades, especially in Eastern Europe, Africa and the Middle East where the rising waves of nationalism, ethnicity and religious fundamentalism have ignited civil strife and war.

The growing tendency towards social, economic and political turmoil challenges us more than ever before to find new ways to meet our future educational needs. In this changing situation, the nearly ubiquitous, standard Western European classroom model may be the single largest constraint to our meeting, with the requisite flexibility, the growing demand for affordable and effective basic education services. Mounting evidence suggests that formal, classroom-centred models have become the unaffordable, irrelevant and unmanageable 'albatrosses' of our learning system. Few developing countries have the resources — financial or human — to make 'Western' education work; and even growing numbers of industrialized countries undergoing unprecedented social, demographic and economic change are finding it increasingly difficult to provide equitable, quality "Education for All" using a model designed to service the needs of a pre-industrial European society.

If, as surmised, a 'new education model' is needed to match the demands of a radically different society — and to respond to the growing public awareness that, in this age of unprecedented change, learning should provide skills that contribute to the survival of both the individual and the society — then we must start to think in new ways. Learning environments (not necessarily schools) where the learning process can thrive in a flexible, well-organized and productive way will share a common set of characteristics. The facilitators (not necessarily professional teachers) who will help make this new model work may also share a distinctive set of characteristics, which will closely reflect their new role as managers of learning and not purveyors of received knowledge and nonfunctional information.

4.1. WHAT SHOULD THE CHARACTERISTICS OF THIS 'NEW MODEL' BE?

4.1.1. For Nations Seeking to Become Better Integrated into the 'Information Age'. The education systems of these nations may need to have many of the following characteristics:

- community- and home-based learning stations would be set up, closely linked to the workplace electronically via a network of personal computers, radio and satellite networks. The process would be a continuous one, eliminating the largely artificial distinctions between pre-school, primary school and secondary school levels. Children would participate as soon as they were ready to benefit from structured learning. Readiness would be determined by each individual's characteristics and needs;
- members of each community and parents would be involved in the learning process through a system of special instruction credits, which could

be earned by individuals volunteering to become facilitators of learning in lieu of their normal work;

- learning units would be modular to encourage individual access, flexibility in use and better assessment of performance. Each learner, with the help of a parent or community facilitator, would be able to choose a sequence of modules, which could be completed in the learner's own time and at his or her own pace;
- the management and assessment of learning would become a community-based responsibility, supervised and assisted by a central agency or institution responsible for overseeing norms and standards;
- the cost of the process would be borne by each local community; financial backing or assistance would be provided to poorer communities through a central financing agency or special credit bank set up to promote community-based learning;
- the content of the learning modules would be the shared responsibility of the family, the community and the private sector; and local needs and regional differences would be reflected in the learning content of the courses so as to cater more fully to the special cultural and language needs of each community.

4.1.2. For Nations Recently Coming to Grips with Their Own Industrial Revolutions

An improved schooling model with the following characteristics would probably help these nations to meet their learning requirements:

- this model would be decentralized, and owned and managed by the community;
- teachers would be held accountable for pupil performance by a system of credits based on the community's assessment of teacher performance;
- schools would be closely linked to each community and the local workplace, and curriculum content jointly decided by parents, the community and the local workplace;
- the health, nutritional and psychosocial needs of each child would be a common responsibility of the family, the community and the learning place;
- achievement would be assessed by individualized, competency-based examinations rather than by norm-based ones;
- children's learning experiences would include selected attachments to the workplace to enable them to make well-grounded career choices; and
- the contents of the curriculum would focus on the need to provide children with skills and knowledge for life as well as appropriate vocational skills.

4.1.3. For Nations Entering Their Agricultural Revolutions

Many of the characteristics highlighted above will apply to these nations, but special attention should perhaps be given to the following:

- pre-school and primary school services should be integrated under one roof, with parental and community participation as an important part of the learning strategy;
- adult literacy and life skills, together with other relevant learning modules, would be developed to encourage illiterate parents to learn alongside of their children, thus making schooling a community activity for the benefit of all;
- the curriculum would reflect each community's needs and would be jointly developed by parents and teachers;
- schools would be flexibly run to accommodate the cyclical needs of poor rural communities whose subsistence depends on working the land;
- communities would own and run their schools with the help of government advisers; and funding for the schools' upkeep would come from a special line of credit created for this purpose through a 'learning credit bank'.

The ideas brought together above are not new. Educators, past and present, have no doubt shared similar thoughts on how best to address the problems of basic education, and some may even have tried them out. The significance of these ideas here is to help generate debate and encourage a more critical assessment of the challenges now presented by the CRC, the Jomtien World Conference on Education for All and the World Summit for Children.

■ 5. Conclusion

Article 28 of the CRC — which culminates 50 years of advocating for international legislation on children's rights — unequivocally supports the notion that State Parties to the CRC must make "primary education compulsory and available free to all" and provide equal access to secondary, vocational and higher education. However, the same instrument is far less clear regarding the extent to which signatories are committed to implementing these obligations. To help address this deficiency — but also in response to the growing awareness that international organizations, conventions and declarations have in the past done little to meet the demand for quality education for children (especially those living in the developing world) — governments, educators and administrators from 155 countries met in Jomtien in March 1990 to craft a joint "Framework for Action". Through a process of consensus, this unique document, for the first time, arrives at a statement that clearly spells out how to implement the education provisions of the preceding international instruments and integrate these provisions with current thinking about basic education. The Framework for Action conceptually places learning acquisition before traditional forms of teaching. It also identifies a set of clearly articulated goals that challenge educators to find innovative and cost-effective ways of delivering basic education services to all groups of children, especially the poor, the handicapped and other children in need.

Nevertheless, if the Jomtien World Declaration on Education For All and its accompanying instruments erred, it was on the side of caution. Insufficient attention was given to the changing social and economic context and its effects (both current and projected) on the form and content of education. The rapidity of world change is affecting all societies in an unprecedented way, but not all in the same way. While the least-developed countries are barely entering their agricultural revolutions, new nations in the Pacific are well into their industrial revolutions. For their part, Western nations — once the leaders of the Industrial Revolution — are now being challenged by new technologies to restructure their economies to meet the challenges of the Information Age. In the process, substantial and increasing numbers of low-income people are seeking to migrate from the developing world to the industrialized and post-industrial worlds.

These widely differing patterns of social and economic transformation are challenging educators to think more profoundly about what children should learn, and how and where they should be learning. The unique 19th-century classroom model has failed to keep up with the challenge; it is itself in need of radical change if the goal of providing every child with a good basic education is to be achieved in our lifetimes. Part of the answer lies in the need to build partnerships and to pool resources and knowledge so as to maximize our efforts. The Jomtien Conference has challenged us all to work seriously together to develop joint plans of action in an analytical and diagnostic fashion. We have enough research results, empirical information and conceptual analyses to support such an approach in a number of regions, including Latin America, Asia and the Pacific. Similar attempts are already under way in Africa.

What is frequently missing, however, is the political will to set aside narrow group interests and reorganize priorities in favour of human needs — especially the needs of those least able to fend for themselves. For the cost of one nuclear submarine, Africa's current primary schooling could be revitalized and made more responsive to the growing demand in the majority of African countries for better-quality basic education. Well-conceived and well-designed innovative projects to reach the unreached (school drop-outs, house-bound girls, nomad children, Gypsies and other minority groups who make up the largest proportion of the unschooled) would go a long way towards reducing the high numbers of children at both the primary and secondary levels who still do not have access to basic education — and probably never will, unless we begin to think differently about how to tackle the problem.

There are many other examples pointing in the same direction as the BRAC schools in Bangladesh, Escuelas Mayas in Guatemala, and the Tostan method in Senegal (Sections 3.3.1-3.3.3). What is important about each of these experiences is not the unique solution each community has been able to find to resolve its educational issues, but the problem-solving process in itself. BRAC and Tostan, after more than a decade of activity, are now able to demonstrate positive — and apparently sustainable — results because the process that led to the outcome was developed, owned and implemented by the local community and not imposed by central governments or from abroad, as has so frequently been the case in the past.

The challenge will be how to make the education provisions of the CRC responsive to the needs of the community. It may not be enough to mandate through one more international convention the right of the child to education, if the societies being challenged are themselves run by governments that are mostly unaccountable to the people or not made legally responsible to adhere to the international conventions they have ratified. A number of possible new approaches are suggested to meet the needs of the 21st century. They will require, besides a comprehensive analysis of each country's educational needs, imagination, creativity and the courage to challenge existing Western-type classroom models with thinking that comes from within the community and is not, again, imposed from outside.

The latter observation applies, in particular, to developing countries, long held ransom by their colonial history to imported educational models that have proved to be as costly as they have been ineffective in meeting the socio-cultural requirements of communities with diverse ethnic and linguistic needs. The challenge for all today is not why or how to do it, but whether we have the political will to divert resources to what should and can be done. The new democratic consciousness sweeping the world will be unsustainable unless we all make a firm commitment to advocate real structural change to help find and mobilize the ideas and the resources needed to make the education provisions of the Convention on the Rights of the Child not just the ineffectual phrases of yet another well-meaning international convention, but a reality. It is hoped that the Convention — together with the Jomtien Framework for Action and the corresponding education goals of the World Summit for Children — will represent a new opportunity to initiate a series of radical reforms to give a basic education to every child, irrespective of race, socio-economic status, gender or creed. To some, this goal may still seem too ambitious, but many others are recognizing it as a critical investment in human development and nation building, as well as a key moral imperative of our times, essential for *all* our futures.

Notes

1 Alston, 1992.
2 Affirmative action programmes discriminate in favour of women and minority-group members, encouraging, through measures such as preferential access, quotas and financial incentives, increased representation of these categories, in recognition of past and present patterns of discrimination against such groups.
3 Alston, 1992.
4 World Conference on Education for All, 1990.
5 See also United Nations Children's Fund, 1990a and 1990b.

6 Formal education is termed the 'first channel'; non-formal education, the 'second channel'; any other means of reaching people informally or formally, such as poetry, dance, discussion groups, meetings and mass media, the 'third channel'.
7 Carnoy, 1992; Psacharopoulous, 1985; and United States Agency for International Development, 1990.
8 World Bank, 1990.
9 See Dall, F.P., 1987; and Feder et al., 1985.
10 World Bank, 1990.
11 Eisemon, 1991.
12 Stobart, 1987.
13 Naik, 1979.
14 Tronick, 1992.
15 Reimers, 1991.
16 UNICEF, 1992a.
17 Ibid.
18 See, for example, United States Agency for International Development, 1990b; Dall, K.N., 1991; Gajraj and Schoeman, 1991; and UNICEF, 1991c.
19 The following discussion of indicators relating to the education of Gypsy children in European countries is taken from Costarelli, 1993.
20 Ibid.
21 Bonfiglioli and Watson, 1992.
22 Ibid.
23 See Jacobs, 1993; Ahmed et al., 1993; UNICEF, 1993e; Lovell and Fatema, 1989.
24 Jacobs, 1993.
25 Ibid.
26 Colclough and Lewin, 1993.
27 Dall, F.P., 1992a.
28 Dall, F.P., 1993.

Children's right to protection from economic exploitation

Jo Boyden and Victoria Rialp

1. Introduction

This chapter discusses the organizational, human and economic resources that are required to meet the provisions of Article 32 of the United Nations Convention on the Rights of the Child (CRC). Article 32 addresses the problem of child labour, recognizing "the rights of the child to be protected from economic exploitation and from performing any work that is likely to be hazardous or to interfere with the child's education, or to be harmful to the child's health or physical, mental, spiritual, moral or social development" (para. 1). (See Appendix One for the full text.)

In many respects the resource needs of policy and programmatic interventions to combat the complex and elusive problem of child labour have yet to be fully identified. Although some of the resources discussed in this chapter are available and have already been harnessed, others are mentioned more because of their potential utility than their present use. Protecting children from something — in this case exploitative or hazardous work — is rather different from providing them with something, whether it be health care, education or other services. There are strong economic constraints against eliminating child labour, powerful vested interests in maintaining the status quo and widespread cultural support for the use of children's work. This situation is compounded by a lack of knowledge and concern about the problem among policy makers and government officials. Protection against injurious labour involves not just public-sector provision and monitoring, but also attitudinal change among those who benefit from children's work, including among employers who commit major violations.

Perhaps one of the most critical issues in the struggle against child labour is that governments cannot combat the problem on their own: to implement child labour policies, they must rely heavily on the mobilization and commitment of civil society. This raises an important question, however, regarding the institutional obligations to fulfil the provisions of the CRC. This treaty is legally binding only on States Parties and not on the broad range of civil-society actors on which governments depend to meet their obligations. The challenge for governments, therefore, is to create and sustain coalitions against child labour that are made up of non-statutory, and in some cases even voluntary, grass-roots bodies, the private sector and private individuals, none of whom have binding commitments under the CRC.

Because of the complex nature of the child labour problem and because approaches and strategies to attack it are still fairly new and in the process of being developed, this chapter can only draw some tentative conclusions. Much still needs to be learned about what works in the field of child labour. For example, it is perhaps paradoxical that the State of Kerala in India — one of the most widely acclaimed 'success stories' in terms of child labour — has never had an active child labour policy. Despite a low average per capita income, access to primary education in Kerala is practically universal, and evidence of child labour minimal. The exclusion of children from labour in Kerala is closely connected with the strong popular support for education that has evolved there over centuries. This case serves as a reminder that there are no ready-made prescriptions in the field of child labour and that interventions targeting child labour specifically may not always be the most effective.

■ 2. The Problem of Child Labour

Child labour occurs with considerable frequency in all the poor countries of the world and in many of the wealthier ones too. Labour prevents millions of children from attending school, exposes them to extreme exploitation and danger, impairs their health and obstructs their intellectual, emotional, psychological, spiritual and physical development. Although ubiquitous, child labour is a phenomenon largely hidden from view and often difficult to identify. This is in part because the majority of the world's child labourers are employed in small informal enterprises beyond the reach of regulatory bodies and other monitors. But it is also because many children work in a highly intermittent, casual way in activities not recognized formally as jobs. Children who attend school and work as well are most likely registered in national censuses and other official records as students and not labourers. Moreover, due to the illegality of much of what they do, child labourers are frequently concealed from outsiders by their families and employers.

Since so much child labour still remains undetected, it is impossible to obtain an accurate count of the number of children involved globally. Current estimates of children worldwide who can be classified as child labourers range from 100 million to 200 million, although their actual numbers (depending partly on definitions) are probably far greater. The dramatic economic implications of these figures, particularly in developing countries, are noted in a recent International Labour Organisation (ILO) document:

> It must also be borne in mind that some developing countries have unemployment rates of between 20 and 30 per cent and that 100 to 200 million child labourers represent 4 to 8 per cent of the world employment potential of 2.4 billion. The replacement of child labourers by unemployed adults could in theory have a major impact on employment prospects in many developing countries.[1]

According to ILO calculations, at least 18 per cent of children between 10 and 14 years of age in developing countries are working. Regional variations are wide, with about 7 per cent of child workers in this age-group in Latin America, 18 per cent in Asia and 25 per cent in Africa. Little is known about child labour trends, or indeed about child labourers under 8-10 years of age. Although it can be demonstrated that child labour in formal employment has declined markedly during this century, particularly in industrialized countries, it can only be surmised that the numbers of children working in informal activities have increased and that the vast majority of working children are now concentrated in self-employment, unpaid work, sub-contractual arrangements and unregistered enterprises.

The decline of child labour in the formal sector has been attributed to a combination of factors. First, effective systems of labour registration and inspection have been put into place in many countries, and law enforcement efficiently controls the formal sector. Second, child labour has become less attractive to formal-sector employers in the face of advancing technology, the increasing need for skilled and semi-skilled adult labour and the organization of the workforce. Third, and perhaps most importantly, higher income levels and improved standards of living in industrialized countries as well as in some developing countries have reduced families' dependence on the economic contributions of their children. Fourth, the spread of compulsory and effective schooling and changes in parents' and children's perceptions of the social and economic returns to education have provided further incentives to keep children in school instead of at work.

Despite these advances in the formal sector, the high concentrations of children in informal activities and occupations remain a serious policy challenge. This point is reinforced by ILO:

> Concern is now growing on two new fronts: exposure of children to new and greater risks and an explosion of the number of child workers in the informal, unregulated sector of the economy as a result of increasing migration, urbanisation and industrialisation.[2]

Early campaigners against child labour identified a number of specific occupations and work settings as being particularly injurious to children.

Among these, waged employment in mines, mills and factories was of special concern. Unpaid work within the home or on the farm, on the other hand, was not considered problematic. Recent policies developed by ILO, UNICEF and other international organizations similarly acknowledge that not all forms of work are harmful to all children at all ages and that clear qualitative differences exist among occupations, activities and employment relations. It is becoming increasingly evident that, from a policy perspective, a distinction needs to be made between work that is harmless or even beneficial for children and work that is hazardous or exploitative. However, the definitions of what is harmful and what is safe are as yet imprecise since the exact impacts of different kinds of work and work in different kinds of settings are not known. Even the CRC gives no definition for "economic exploitation" and work that is likely to be harmful to children — the central terms of Article 32.

Certainly, greater understanding of the true extent of children's informal-sector involvement has led campaigners to broaden their concern beyond waged work in formal work settings. They have increasingly signaled out the particularly hazardous use of children for illegal, clandestine or criminal purposes such as in narcotic drugs traffic, armed conflicts or military activities, serfdom, bonded labour, spurious adoption, prostitution, pornography and servile domestic labour. ILO argues for energetic enforcement and sanction in these cases, noting that the exploitation of child labour is in flagrant violation of the Charter of the United Nations, the Universal Declaration of Human Rights and the most elementary principles of morality.

To underline qualitative differences in the impacts of work on children, some concerned agencies use the term 'labour' to refer to hazardous or exploitative work in both the informal and formal sectors, reserving the term 'work' for productive and survival activities that are viewed as benign. Many have agreed that, as a matter of priority, action should be directed towards the elimination of the intolerable — in other words, the focus is on child 'labour' and not on child 'work'. Work is not a major problem, so long as it does not prejudice child health or development or school attendance. Some hold that, in addition, all work by children under 10-12 years of age should be a priority for policy and immediate action — on the grounds that work, even if it is neither servile nor dangerous, is not an appropriate activity for young children.

The establishment of policy priorities is expedient, especially given the limited resources presently available to combat child labour. Even with an expanded resource base, targeting the intolerable is clearly justified on humanitarian grounds. However, implementation of this policy is unlikely to be a straightforward matter. As mentioned, there are many interests vested in maintaining the status quo in child labour — many families who are dependent on their children's toil, and many employers for whom children constitute a cheap and acquiescent workforce. The unorganized or informal sector is heterogenous, vast and institutionally diffuse, and its enterprises are unregistered. Reform in this sector implies the need for new institutional arrangements and new alliances linking government and civil society in joint action. At the same time, efforts to reach informal-sector and unorganized groups need to guard against stifling the enterprise generated by such initiatives. Effective strategies require innovation and flexibility. They may also rely on collaboration among a wide array of actors: law enforcement agencies; labour, education and other ministries; cooperative forms of organization; local-level administrative and community organizations; and grass-roots movements such as women's groups and workers' organizations. Citizens' groups, non-governmental organizations (NGOs) and private-sector bodies need to be involved not just in lobbying and advocacy but in service delivery as well.

■ 3. The Historical Approach to Child Labour

The struggle to combat child labour began in the industrialized countries in the 19th century and has gradually gained momentum during this century. An early priority was to establish international norms concerning the use of child labour and to adopt national legislation in conformity with these norms. Enforcement of labour laws relied largely on worksite inspection, calling mainly on the limited resources of labour ministries. Education, a key complementary measure, was made available in most cases by expanding the formal primary and secondary school systems.

On the international front, ILO has played a particularly important role in the field of child labour, devoting a major part of its standard-setting activity to abolition. Several months after its creation in 1919, ILO adopted Convention No. 5, prohibiting work by children under 14 years of age in industrial undertakings. This was the first of more than 20 ILO conventions and recommendations touching on the issue of child labour. The most significant of these instruments is Convention No. 138 of 1973, entitled 'Minimum Age for Admission to Employment', which entered into force on 19 June 1976, and its accompanying Recommendation (No. 146). Countries ratifying this Convention agree to adopt national policies to abolish child labour and to set a minimum age for employment or work, which should not be less than the age of completion of compulsory schooling and in any case not less than 15 years. States Parties are also expected to raise the minimum age progressively to a level "consistent with the fullest physical and mental development of young persons", and set 18 years as the minimum age for work likely to harm health, safety or morals.

Apart from the standards developed by ILO, several United Nations human rights instruments cover the issue of child labour. These include the Supplementary Convention on the Abolition of Slavery, the Slave Trade, and Institutions and Practices Similar to Slavery (1956); the Declaration of the Rights of the Child (1959); and the International Covenant on Economic, Social and Cultural Rights (1966). In connection with the 1956 convention, the United Nations Human Rights Commission has created the Working Group on Contemporary Forms of Slavery, which meets regularly in Geneva to receive reports on standards, rehabilitation and violations from governments, the specialized agencies and international and national organizations. The Working Group also makes recommendations concerning the implementation of child labour standards. In 1993, it adopted a draft Programme of Action for the Elimination of Child Labour (see Section 6).

International concern about children's involvement in exploitative or hazardous work is now explicit as never before in history. The International Year of the Child, commemorated by the United Nations in 1979, brought new momentum to efforts to abolish child labour. A decade later, the CRC and in particular Article 32, reinforced these efforts. The Committee on the Rights of the Child, which is mandated with monitoring the implementation of the CRC, has indicated that child labour is one of the key humanitarian or rights issues requiring further investigation by NGOs and other institutions.

In 1990, over 150 countries represented at the first World Summit for Children, held in New York, subscribed to the Plan of Action for implementing the World Declaration on the Survival, Protection, and Development of Children in the 1990s. The Plan of Action commits governments to provide for the special protection of the working child and for the abolition of illegal child labour. It states:

> More than 100 million children are engaged in employment, often heavy and hazardous and in contravention of international conventions which provide for their protection from economic exploitation and from performing work that interferes with their education and is harmful to their health and full development. With this in mind, all States should work to end such child-labour practices and see how the conditions and circumstances of children in legitimate employment can be protected to provide adequate opportunity for their healthy upbringing and development (para. 23).

Some 147 countries are now translating the Plan of Action into National Programmes of Action (NPAs). A number of countries have included a range of goals and programmes in their NPAs that indirectly protect working children. Some 30 countries to date have directly addressed the issue of child labour in their NPAs. This is significant because in NPAs governments generally specify in detail the resources they intend to commit for implementation and sometimes even time-bound goals.

■ 4. Advances and Limitations of Legislation

Legislation has provided an important framework for action on child labour, establishing minimum standards of protection and providing a benchmark against which progress can be assessed. Also, enforcement of labour laws has proved effective in removing children from the formal sector. But two tacit assumptions were made from the outset. The first was that all children removed from the formal workforce would automatically attend school; the second, that since children could effectively be kept out of the formal sector through inspection and sanction, the problem of child labour was resolvable by legal means. However, the continuing, and in many cases increasing, incidence of child labour in the informal economies of most developing countries, and even in many industrialized countries, has now made it obvious that additional and different measures are urgently needed.

Legislative reform has fallen short of expectations for a number of reasons. A fundamental problem is the scattered and hidden nature of child labour in the informal sector. However, there are other problems as well. Labour legislation was originally developed for adult workers and focused largely on health and safety concerns. It was therefore inadequate to the task of providing for the broader welfare and developmental needs of children. National legislation and practice have generally failed to comply with the standards set in ILO Convention No. 138, in terms of the scope of coverage, the minimum age and effective enforcement. ILO Recommendation No. 146, in particular, articulates a series of measures necessary to achieve the objective of eliminating child labour, namely the pursuit of full employment, a programme of poverty alleviation, extension of social security and provision of education. However, until fairly recently at least, few countries have sought to pursue such a comprehensive policy.

In many countries, legislation applies only to people working under contract, thereby excluding informal and irregular forms of work, which is where the majority of children are concentrated.[3] Sometimes legislation only covers major industries or factories, excluding small factories or enterprises even though it is precisely there that the abuses of child labour are greatest. Legislation may apply only to certain sectors of economic activity and not to others that, as a minimum, should be covered under Convention No. 138.[4] The exclusion of agriculture is fairly frequent, for example, although plantation work may be subject to minimum-age provisions. The exclusion of children working in family concerns or employed in domestic work is also common because work in these settings is not thought to be hazardous.

Developing countries have often encountered difficulties in establishing the advisory, inspection and prosecution procedures necessary to impose the law.[5] Even when child labour laws are adequate, prosecutions may be extremely rare because of a shortage of labour inspectors, or because inspectors are poorly motivated or corrupt.[6] All too often, governments consider that, having proscribed child labour in law, they have done all that is required of them. However, legislation is not an end in itself, only one means among many. Legislation without the appropriation of the resources required for implementation can be pointless. The shortcomings of legislative reform are frequently heightened by public indifference to the problem. This means there is insufficient pressure on public authorities to bring about change. Even though NGOs have been working actively on the child labour issue in several countries, they often lack the political clout to secure change and the resources to provide for more than a small number of children.

5. New Reform Strategies

In practice, it has not proved feasible to rely solely, or even principally, on international treaties and national legislation on child labour and education to curb the exploitation and workplace abuse of children. Aware of this, ILO has long advocated the introduction of economic and social measures in support of child labour reform. More recently, confronted by the persistent exploitation of children in so many quarters, governments and the international community have strengthened their commitment to develop more comprehensive policies and measures against child labour in line with ILO recommendations and guidelines. The CRC has provided an important impetus for innovation and creativity in the field. It endorses strategies that as a matter of priority promote child welfare and protection through attitudinal and behavioural change, equity, social justice and public-sector provision rather than mere law enforcement. It implicitly recognizes that child labour can only be completely eliminated when the longer-term, underlying problems of poverty and underdevelopment have been resolved. Furthermore, it commits States Parties to introduce social, educational and economic measures as a means of gradually attaining this and other child protection goals.

Recent approaches to child labour have tended also to move beyond the narrow health and safety concerns of early labour legislation. Greater emphasis is now placed on introducing protective and promotional measures that enable children to grow and develop normally throughout their childhood years and that look at children's work principally in terms of its impact — both positive and negative — on their welfare, growth and development. Thus, the legal status of a child's work is now considered of less significance than whether or not this work places the child in jeopardy. Nor is the concern simply with work hazards that present an immediate danger, but also with those that threaten child growth and development in the long term: child labour is not only a threat to the health and welfare of children but also influences their well-being as adults.

When priority is given to child welfare, as opposed to the legal status of a child's work, the focus is inevitably on the intolerable — in other words, those employment terms, working environments and conditions that seriously threaten children's lives, health, welfare or development. Immediate and deliberate action to protect children working in hazardous or exploitative situations is the central plank of recent child labour policy. An ILO report on children in hazardous work explains the urgency and rationale for this strategy:

> ... There are three important reasons for this. First, few countries are institutionally or financially able to attack all child labour ills at once; choices must be made about where to concentrate available human and material resources. The most logical and humane strategy is to focus scarce resources first on those situations and children meriting the greatest urgency of attention.

Second, policies and programmes designed to reach the children in most need are also likely to benefit other working children. But the reverse is not true; policies and programmes targeted on the mass of children in less dramatic circumstances tend to fall short of helping the children most at risk.

Last, but far from least, a continuous focus on the most socially repugnant situations helps maintain the social commitment and consensus needed to eliminate them. It is much easier to mobilize public and political will for abolishing demonstrably injurious child labour situations, than it is for, say, prohibiting child work that is popularly regarded as traditional and safe for children.[7]

Consistent with the policy of targeting high-risk groups is the deliberate interest in a progressive, overall approach to child labour and child work. This implies gradual change rather than abrupt removal from work in all but the more extreme cases. A gradual approach is less likely than a more strident abolitionist strategy to cause economic hardship among poor families or to drive child labour underground, making it even harder to detect and eliminate. Work that is protected and safe and does not interfere with education is of no concern in this kind of policy. It may even be that in the future, when more is understood about the impacts of work, policy makers and educationalists will seek to encourage safe work because of its potential for teaching important life skills and reinforcing family solidarity, a sense of individual responsibility and personal growth.

■ 6. Implementing the New Strategies

To implement a policy aimed at progressively eliminating child labour, starting with the forms of labour that present the greatest risks to children, a series of complementary measures are required. The major components of such a policy are outlined in two key documents. The first, the recent ILO policy statement on child labour, indicates that government efforts to define and implement a national policy for the effective abolition of child labour (to use the terminology of Article 1 of Convention No. 138) involve three main types of intervention:

(a) in the first place, measures aiming to put a stop urgently to the intolerable (the use of children in dangerous types of employment, industry or occupation, as well as the use of the very young and therefore particularly vulnerable children);
(b) secondly, measures aimed at changing attitudes and behaviours about child labour;
(c) finally, measures that, without explicitly addressing child labour, attack its causes.[8]

The second document, the United Nations Programme of Action for the Elimination of Child Labour,[9] states more specifically the kinds of actions required. Measures are needed to:

Ensure...

- legislation on minimum age for child employment;
- legislation on conditions for child employment;
- application of legislation through supervisory bodies;
- regular inspection of employment conditions in the formal sector and, where possible, the informal sector;
- adequate legal protection in cases of infringement of working children's rights;
- child-specific medical care facilities at working places.

Provide...

- compulsory free primary education;
- easy access to free secondary and vocational education;
- inducements to parents for their children's primary and post-primary education;
- adequate and appropriate curricula;
- school hours adapted to family needs, especially in rural areas.

Encourage...

- widespread awareness of the international instruments dealing with child labour;
- widespread awareness of the perils of child labour;
- awareness of national legislation in the field of child labour;
- measures aimed at combating poverty and underdevelopment.

Eliminate...

- labour for children under 12 years of age;
- night work;
- excessive working hours;
- work in dangerous occupations and unhealthy conditions;
- degrading or cruel treatment of working children;
- debt bondage.

Combat by all available means...

- employment as under-age domestic servants;
- employment in the drugs traffic;
- employment in armed conflicts in military or paramilitary services;
- activities linked with prostitution, pornography and other forms of sexual exploitation.

Penalize...

- perpetrators of violations of the rights of working children through imprisonment, heavy fines and other legal punitive measures.

Rehabilitate...

- adversely affected working children through special programmes and with the help of specially trained personnel.

To comply with these guidelines, countries must first find out about the incidence and distribution of child labour within their territories. This means undertaking situation analyses that:

(a) reveal concentrations of child labour geographically and by sector, industry, occupation and activity;
(b) identify the children at most risk and determine their numbers and distribution by age and by sex; and
(c) catalogue any existing policy or programme responses, their coverage and impact.

For planning purposes, much of this information can satisfactorily be obtained through the rapid assessment procedures at present being developed by ILO and UNICEF for use specifically in determining the nature and extent of child labour at the national and subnational level.[10]

Having isolated the nature and degree of the problem, countries need to develop preventive measures. Foremost among these are interventions aimed at correcting the economic, cultural and sociopolitical conditions that generate child labour and lead to the abuse of young workers. Families need economic assistance to make the labour of their children unnecessary; and at the same time, they need to be helped to appreciate more fully that their children's health and welfare can be endangered by labour. The prevalence of child labour in many developing countries today is not just a matter of economics, since cultural attitudes and values are also contributory. Children have worked throughout recorded history, and they continue to work in all societies today. It is notable, however, that some cultures do not draw a distinction between work that is harmless and work that is injurious to children. Thus, in many cultures, child labour is tolerated in part because it is not regarded as harmful. Behavioural change, then, whether by children themselves, or by their families, communities, or employers, also entails a change in cultural attitudes.

Reducing poverty and minimizing inequality are priorities. They can be met by increasing opportunities for economic development, education and political participation; providing statutory benefits and other safety nets for families in crisis; and improving the overall quality of life for the poor. For their part, employers need to be encouraged to develop forms of production in which child labour has no role. As child labour is perceived in many countries as both normal and entirely acceptable, any economic or political interventions need to be complemented by advocacy and social mobilization to bring about attitudinal change and create popular support for reform. This should be underpinned by legal literacy and by the framing of appropriate child labour legislation, where it is lacking, bringing domestic laws into line with the CRC and the other relevant international conventions. As a 1989 ILO document states.

> The framing of child labour legislation is important not only because it places the authority of the State behind the protection of children, but also because it creates a forum within which a society clarifies its values and commitments in respect to its young.[11]

Remedial interventions are also needed to ensure the protection of working children and the rehabilitation of children withdrawn from dangerous or servile labour. Measures should target children at greatest risk in order to prevent them from experiencing further harm and to facilitate their participation in education and, when necessary and appropriate, safe work. Such measures could include legislation and enforcement mechanisms; investigative journalism and reporting of violations in the media; vigilant monitoring by grassroots 'watchdog' groups, workers' organizations and other bodies; hot lines for children who are abused or exploited; and treatment and referral of children with work-related diseases or injuries. Crisis intervention centres, shelters and social services may also be established, and school pupils and out-of-school children taught about work-related hazards and how to resist exploitation.

Given the precarious economic situation of many children who work, the provision of protected work opportunities may be a priority — although it is important to recognize that even these measures have resource implications. This strategy entails a focus on issues of employment and income, teaching children about the work ethic and the value of saving, investing and financial management. The aim is to respect the children's need — or right — to work while also stopping them from being exploited or endangered and, especially, securing their access to education. Some programmes provide protected earning opportunities, acting as labour contractors and taking advantage of employment opportunities provided by the formal economic sector; some focus on training for the workplace or job motivation; and others still are more concerned with labour organization as a means of protecting children. Many provide pavement schooling, income-generating opportunities, non-formal vocational or skills training, basic education and other services such as food, first aid and primary health and dental care. Help may be given to the children's families in the form of training in the management of money, productive adult employment, credit and family support services. Community groups may be encouraged to identify families with children who need assistance.

Securing greater access to education and other services for working children is a major priority.[12] Access to relevant and affordable primary schooling is especially important. Education may be delivered through a variety of mechanisms, including the formal schools of the public and private sectors, non-formal schools or life-skills training centres, and non-traditional alternative schools for out-of-school children. Traditional and modern media are also being used increasingly to deliver skills and general information and engage in advocacy and campaigning on child labour issues. Particular attention needs to be paid to the location and scheduling of schooling and the establishment of flexible systems of entry and exit, since these can critically influence access for child labourers. Curriculum development and the introduction of learner-centred and non-authoritarian teaching methods may be necessary in many countries if school is to be made more appealing to working or 'at-risk' children.

In sectors and occupations where child exploitation is extreme, such as bonded agricultural labour, hazardous factory or mine work, or prostitution, direct and concerted action is urgently needed. Interventions against these acute forms of child exploitation and abuse may entail recourse to punitive legal measures. Because of the high profits being made by adults in many of these cases and because of the illegality of some of the more exploitative activities, it is often necessary to mobilize and work with organizations and individuals that are not traditional partners in social action and social policy. Sometimes it even means mobilizing the groups that have the greatest vested interest in exploiting children's labour, because without their support it may be impossible to make any headway.

■ 7. Implications of Reform for Children, Families and Employers

Effective child labour reform involves a concerted effort to reduce the reliance of families, communities and employers on children's labour. Studies conducted in a number of countries indicate that in areas of marginal productivity, children's economic contributions to families, households and enterprises are critical. Data from the Philippines, Brazil, Bangladesh, India, Egypt, Indonesia, and elsewhere, suggest a high degree of dependence at the family or household level on both the unpaid and the paid work of children.[13] Most impoverished children in these countries contribute the bulk of their earnings to their families. In some households, the combined contribution of siblings is greater than that of adults. Sometimes children are earning while adults, mostly men, are unemployed (usually involuntarily, but sometimes precisely because of the availability of children's income). In one Nepalese sample, 23 per cent of the children interviewed were the sole earners in their households.[14] Even so, children's wages are rarely as significant to the domestic economy as the unpaid work they do.

A broader question remains as to whether child labour is economically efficient for households. This is an issue that has been addressed by several researchers, although the implications for families and households of taking children out of the workforce are unclear. Some studies suggest that children consume far more than they ever contribute with their labour, at least while they remain in their households.[15] The constraints on children's working or earning capacities are considerable. Children are normally paid at a lower rate than adults, reducing their economic contributions significantly. Also, their work tends to be more casual and opportunistic and less intensive than that of adults. However, much other research sustains that even if children only contribute part of their own upkeep or their school costs, to remove them from the workforce and place them in school still entails a major short-term cost to the family, since education only pays major dividends in the long run.

Quite apart from any financial implications for the family, child labour reform obviously has major implications for the children themselves. Studies from several countries indicate that many children work out of preference, not just because of the financial rewards, but also because work gives them status within the family and the community as a whole.[16] Children can obtain pleasure and self-confidence from work, even when the conditions are hazardous and the hours long. School, on the other hand, confers on children the status of dependent minor, especially when teaching is delivered — as so often is the case — in an authoritarian or even hostile manner. Policy needs to take the views of children into account if it is to be effective. This may mean providing access to education in shifts and using condensed curricula, measures that also allow for the continuance of work in activities and occupations that are safe.

In general, employers have been regarded fairly uncritically as obstructive opponents of the reform process (and, in principle, of children's rights). It is usually held that the demand for child labour is likely to remain high in the developing world because cheap labour gives employers a competitive advantage either in national markets or abroad. In industries where children currently form either the majority or a significant proportion of workers and where job functions are relatively homogeneous, hiring children may be especially profitable. Also, children are thought to be particularly useful in some activities and occupations because they are smaller, more agile and can move faster than adults. Indeed, exporters interviewed in ILO studies of the carpet industry in India and the leather-tanning industry in Egypt argued that they would cease trading rather than hire adult labour in place of children because of the serious drop in profits this would entail.[17] Similarly, a government survey of the Philippine garment industry confirmed the extremely low cost of child labour as a proportion of net profits.[18] Clearly, employers can often enhance profitability by paying low wages to children, but what role child labour plays in achieving maximum profitability is not so clear.

Recent research indicates that replacing children with adult workers is not necessarily so costly for employers. Moreover, as already indicated, cheap labour is by no means the same thing as efficient labour, and higher unit costs for adult labour may be more than compensated by higher productivity. Besides, in some developing countries many adults share with children the problems of low wages and unstable, unskilled employment; often the wage distinctions between their labour and that of children are so minor that to replace children with adults would make little difference in terms of the costs to employers. Some employers regard the employment of children as an act of charity and consider that they are doing children a favour by providing them with jobs. Sometimes they only employ children in order to retain their parents in the workforce.

Research on industrial enterprises in Indonesia found no comparative advantage to employing children, since they were being paid at the same rate as adults.[19] The researchers concluded that children were employed not because of low costs, but instead because their presence in the workforce served to make adult workers more compliant and more willing to accept lower wages. Preliminary results from an ILO investigation in India suggest that in some industries (for example, the bangle industry) children do not provide irreplaceable skills and that the use of child labour has virtually no effect on the cost of production.[20] In terms of skills, there is no overall comparative advantage to child labour in the carpet industry either, even though carpet weaving requires considerable agility. However, it appears that children do represent cost advantages to some employers in this sector.

Differences in findings from different countries, sectors and occupations indicate that, from the employers' viewpoint, assessment of the economic feasibility of withdrawing children from the workforce is best done on an industry-by-industry basis. For example, carpet manufacturers in India, fearing that unilateral action would place them at a competitive disadvantage, have been extremely reluctant to remove children from their enterprises unless employers elsewhere in the region take the same action. Garment exporters in Bangladesh, on the other hand, promptly removed children from their factories when they heard of a possible ban on the import into the United States of goods made by children. In part, Bangladeshi employers were able to respond so rapidly to that threat because children never formed more than a small proportion of the workforce — under 20 per cent — and were engaged in light tasks that were not central to the production process and that were gradually being mechanized in any case.[21]

■ 8. Institutional and Human Resources Required for Implementation

The shift in approach from the enforcement of labour and compulsory education laws to the development of preventive social and economic measures, advocacy and social mobilization, the provision of quality and relevant education, safe work opportunities and the remedial care and rehabilitation of children involved in hazardous or exploitative labour implies the need for a variety of new institutional arrangements and partnerships. This strategy requires not only many more resources than traditional approaches, but also a far greater diversity of resources. It relies on integrated or multisectoral interventions that draw on both inter-agency alliances that spread across the public and private sectors and the resources of NGOs and grass-roots movements. It also entails a devolution of decision-making and action beyond the level of central government to the local, regional and even international levels. There is a broad diversity of responses to the problem of child labour, some developed nationally and others subnationally, and the institutional and human resources harnessed in the reform process vary widely from one country to another. In many cases, a child labour policy is just now being devised and the resource requirements have yet to be properly identified.

□ 8.1. GOVERNMENT

It was once considered appropriate for central government to be the sole implementor of child labour policy. Official intervention relied heavily on line ministry resources, which were deployed largely in the development of a legal framework, worksite inspection and the provision of education as an alternative to child labour. Even today, government commitment remains highly constricted in many countries, and many governments are content with simply passing labour laws, introducing enforcement mechanisms and providing basic facilities for education. Sometimes child labour is given such a low priority that even within the Ministry of Labour there is little or no training on the issue and no provision for inspectors to dedicate themselves full time to the problem.

In other cases, an extensive policy framework on child labour may exist, but funding for implementation is inadequate. In India, for example, the 1986 Child Labour (Prohibition and Regulation) Act and the subsequent National Policy on Child Labour laid the grounds for an elaborate programme of action. The Act prohibited the employment of children under 14 years of age in specified hazardous occupations, regulated children's work in non-hazardous occupations and provided for a technical committee to advise government. The National Policy embraced measures in education, health, nutrition, integrated child development and employment. Importantly, it allowed NGOs to play an extremely active part in implementation, with the allocation of public funds to support their work in the provision of education and other services. It also provided for a system of non-formal education tailored specifically to the needs of working children, scholarships to encourage participation in education, medical inspections in areas where children work, anti-poverty programmes, and pilot schemes giving special protection for children involved in certain hazardous occupations. A serious shortage of public-sector investment in support of the National Policy and lack of interest on the part of certain official agencies, however, has resulted in very scattered provision in practice.[22]

Some governments have taken major steps to develop a strong institutional base nationally to combat child labour. Frequently these more proactive governments have been spurred into action by vigilant citizens' and human rights groups, provoked by media exposure, goaded by ILO's supervisory bodies, or, more recently, influenced and encouraged by the Committee on the Rights of the Child. NGOs have also been extremely important in influencing governments to adopt an integrated, multisectoral approach to child labour and to recognize the importance of drawing on a variety of institutional and human resources from within not only the public sector but also the civil society, and at local and national levels.

Governments may also have to call on institutional resources at the regional or international levels, such as the United Nations system, Interpol or regional or international networks of NGOs, particularly in cases involving the trafficking of children across borders for adoption, slave-employment or other purposes, or the exploitation of children within their own countries by foreigners. Intercountry cooperation is also needed to bring about legislative uniformity in the field of child labour. Solitary action in one country to ban or regulate child labour risks giving neighbouring countries that have not taken similar and concurrent action a competitive edge in the international market. Collaboration at the regional level has been given special priority in South Asia and needs to be more effectively developed elsewhere.

In many countries where alternative, multisectoral strategies are being employed, the problem has been to identify an appropriate lead or umbrella institution for policy development and implementation. At one time, the issue of child labour fell automatically under the Ministry of Labour in most countries, while child welfare issues in general fell within the mandate of the Ministry of Social Welfare. The position is no longer quite so clear, since responsibility for monitoring and implementation of the CRC is now generally awarded to the Ministry of Social Welfare. In effect, child labour is now regarded as a welfare, as much as a labour, issue — thereby requiring close coordination and collaboration in policy and implementation between the Social Welfare and Labour Ministries.

The difficulty with drawing heavily for child protection and promotion on the resources of the Ministry of Social Welfare is that this is generally the weakest of government bodies — with the lowest status among all line ministries, the smallest budgets, the fewest professional staff and the most modest premises. One alternative — the transfer of responsibility for policy development and implementation to a special Ministry for Children — may have the unfortunate effect of pushing children's rights even further into a ghetto and of attracting attention away from important specific issues such as child labour. On the other hand, the interministerial approach adopted in several countries (using a multi-agency task force for example) has the disadvantage of giving institutional leadership to bodies that have no obvious role in line management and may be bureaucratic and inefficient simply because of the many, and sometimes conflicting, interests they represent. These institutional problems have a strong influence on policy and programme development, and alternative models need to be examined for their effectiveness.

Brazil has developed a policy that starts with legislation but has far-reaching implications in terms of the human, organizational and economic resources required and the distribution of rights and responsibilities at the federal, state and municipal levels and between government and the civil society. In Brazil, the roles of government — local and national — and of the civil society are not left to chance but are prescribed in law. The problem of child labour is set in the wider context of child protection and children's rights, which are now guaranteed in the new Constitution under an article drawn up by a national commission composed of both governmental and non-governmental representatives. Civil-society support for the development of the new constitutional provisions was extremely effective, and several points developed at the grass roots were included in the final document.

The Constitution provides a general framework for child protection. Subsequent legislation, the Child and Adolescent Statute, takes this framework further. The Statute is founded on three key principles. The first is that children and adolescents are to be regarded as full citizens, must enjoy all the rights of citizens and are not to be treated as passive objects of intervention. The second is that they are recognized to be in a special condition of physical and mental development and may therefore claim exclusive additional rights appropriate to their ages. Finally, the interests of children and adolescents are granted absolute priority in the delivery of public services, the formulation and execution of public policies and the allocation of public resources.[23]

A decentralized system of administration, encompassing the federal, state and municipal levels, ensures that children and adolescents effectively benefit from resources. Within this system and at all three levels, responsibility and representation in the implementation of policy is shared equally by government and representative organizations of the civil society, working together as members of Councils for Child and Adolescent Rights. The Councils operating at the municipal level are central to the whole system, since they have responsibility for overseeing and planning the delivery of services to children and also have authority over associated Guardianship Councils which provide for children in need of special protection. The municipal government appoints half the Council's representatives; the other half are elected in open assembly, largely from among groups involved in social welfare and community education programmes. The size and procedures of the Councils are established by the municipal authorities, although parity between government and the civil society is always maintained.

Because the municipalities still control the funds for service provision, the Councils act mainly in an advisory capacity. However, the Statute has provided for the Councils to be given control of a Municipal Fund for Children and Adolescents, which is drawn from taxes and private sources. In the field of child labour, the Councils have been active in establishing special services such as health care, non-formal education, and job and psychological counselling. They have also created job placement services, vocational training, and programmes to remove children from the workplace. Another major activity is building capacity among their own number in order to cater better to children in need of protection. In a meeting in 1994 of 27 Councils,[24] virtually all reported a lack of human resources and technical assistance as being a major problem in developing effective measures for child labourers.

Attention has been similarly paid in the Philippines to the devolution of power and responsibility beyond the line ministries of central government, although the relationship between central authority and local-level implementation and between government and the civil society has not been formally endorsed in law as in Brazil. In the Philippines, an inter-agency task force, composed of both governmental and non-governmental bodies and with the Ministry of Social Services and Development providing the Secretariat, was created by Presidential Proclamation in 1986, which was declared as the Year of the Protection of Filipino Exploited Children. The following year, the task force published a National Plan of Action for the Protection of Filipino Exploited Children, in which a series of objectives and activities were specified for the prevention of child labour and the protection and rehabilitation of exploited children.

While policy formulation in the Philippines has taken place at the national level, implementation has been decentralized and incorporates both government and non-governmental bodies collaborating within the institutional framework of local-level task forces. The Philippines now has an important national programme for sexually exploited children and children living and/or working on the streets. Involved in implementation at the local and national levels are governmental, non-governmental, civic and church groups, the media and prominent political figures. The networks provide advocacy, human resource development, protection, referral and community-based, street-based and centre-based services, covering some 17 cities and comprising approximately 300 local projects in total.

In most other countries where child labour policy has been taken beyond the enforcement of compulsory education and labour laws, any coalitions between government and the civil society are far less formal than in Brazil or the Philippines, and therefore probably less sustainable. Some of these initiatives are still nascent and may well become more consolidated in the future. In Bangladesh, for example, the Ministry of Labour has joined forces with UNICEF, ILO, employers involved in exporting garments, members of the Rotary Club and a number of local NGOs to found a forum to develop national policy and programmes in the field of child labour. Agreeing that the problem of child labour in Bangladesh is far more widespread and entrenched than is indicated by recent policies that have tended to focus solely on the export sector, this forum has commenced a large-scale rapid assessment to learn what is happening to children elsewhere in the economy. At the same time, the forum has made a commitment to prioritize the removal of children from dangerous or servile labour, to advocate against child labour generally and to facilitate the development of quality non-formal education, based on models well tried by NGOs in Bangladesh, as an alternative to labour.

□ 8.2. NON-GOVERNMENTAL ORGANIZATIONS

Among the major actors in the struggle against child labour, NGOs have been on the front line, spearheading most of the initiatives and sustaining the pressure for action on multiple fronts. They have already taken the lead on this issue in India, the Philippines, Kenya and Brazil, among other countries. NGOs are active in policy development, situation analysis, identification and dissemination of information about violations, and project development. They are also assisting in the monitoring of the CRC. Although they have played a critical part in promoting and developing child labour approaches and programmes throughout the world, it is impossible to quantify the value of their contributions. Also, there is no obligation under the CRC for NGOs to play an active part in child labour reform. Yet, without the involvement of NGOs it is likely that in many countries there would have been little or no action on child labour.

ILO has recently compiled information on some 400 agencies and programmes worldwide concerned with child labour. Many of these are governmental and many others are micro-level, innovative experiments with limited outreach capacity. In many cases, with proper support from government, the more successful of the NGO initiatives could be scaled up to cover a number of children significant even at the national level. At present even the largest NGO programme for working children listed by ILO — the Underprivileged Children's Educational Programme — covers only 16,000 children in Bangladesh, a country where many millions of children are in the workforce.

Starting with the International Year of the Child in 1979, and encouraged by the momentum created today by the CRC, NGOs have stepped up their efforts at networking and building alliances among themselves and between themselves and government. They have become increasingly concerned that working in isolation and in disparate ways to provide services for only a minority of affected children is neither efficient nor effective. Most now recognize that there is a pressing need to build on collective strength, to collaborate with others in advocacy and the monitoring of violations, and to develop a wider perspective on the problems affecting children. The trend throughout the world is to form umbrella or network organizations at the international, regional and national levels. These facilitate information exchange, create solidarity around the issues and strengthen the impact of campaigning and advocacy. As indicated, in some countries NGO networks have become formally linked with government bodies in the fight to achieve children's rights and to eliminate child labour.

By working together and networking within countries and across regions, interfacing more and more with the public sector, and building alliances with media and public opinion-makers, NGOs have made progress in exposing and publicizing the hazardous and exploitative conditions in which some children work. In India, for example, the Bonded Liberation Front has identified and denounced establishments holding children in bondage and has helped remove children from their servile labour. NGOs have also lobbied for effective laws and enforcement. The NGO Concerned for Working Children in Bangalore, for example, was involved in drafting India's innovative and controversial Child Labour (Prohibition and Regulation) Act. NGOs have also created children's defence committees and other community-based monitoring mechanisms. At the regional level, organizations such as the South Asian Coalition on Child Servitude work to build public opinion and mobilize private, public and NGO support for the elimination of child labour. The organization has, for example, collaborated with the Association of Oriental Carpet Importers in Germany, child rights groups, consumer protection societies and parliamentarians in Europe in a campaign to boycott products made by child labour.

There is also increasing collaboration between development-oriented NGOs that support education, nutrition, health and other programmes for child workers and NGOs that focus on children's rights, some of which were particularly active in the drafting phases of the CRC and have participated in the Working Group on Contemporary Forms of Slavery. At the international level, these alliances include Defence for Children International, the International Society for the Prevention of Child Abuse and Neglect, the International Save the Children Alliance and Childhope. Notable at the regional level are La Red, and Child Workers in Asia. While the majority of networks have a fairly broad-based concern for children's welfare or children's rights, Childhope, Child Workers in Asia and Asianet are examples of networks that have either focused specifically on child labour or on specific target groups of child labourers or street children.

At the present time, in addition to alliances or special meetings, international coordination of NGOs concerned with children's issues is carried out by the NGO Group on the Convention on the Rights of the Child, which has a special working group on child exploitation. The NGO Group forges an essential link between the Committee on the Rights of the Child and local and international NGOs throughout the world. It aims to be an active source of information for the Committee on issues of child exploitation and on the monitoring and implementation of the CRC generally. Through the Group, NGOs can channel to the Committee evidence of serious labour violations and general information about the situation of child labour in reporting countries. The Group also supports the Committee by informing NGOs in reporting countries and international NGOs about the monitoring procedure and its role in the achievement of children's rights. Through its advocacy work, it can also help disseminate and promote the Committee's findings within the United Nations system as a whole.

□ 8.3. WORKERS' ORGANIZATIONS

Of all non-governmental bodies, workers' organizations probably have the greatest vested interest in child labour and the greatest potential for action. It is therefore remarkable that, to date, they have generally been so little involved in the issue. One explanation for this apparent disinterest is that children are concentrated precisely in the areas of the economy where union membership is weakest. Yet, unions could do a great deal not only through peer advocacy and education but also by conducting informal situation analyses to identify children involved in hazardous or exploitative occupations and tasks and referring these children for assistance. They could also work for reform by bringing pressure to bear on employers.

Some trade unions have conducted surveys and investigations that have provided important information on the conditions and circumstances of child labourers in specific sectors and occupations. Thus, for example, an inquiry by the Miners International Federation revealed that there are children working in extremely dangerous conditions in small-scale mines in several countries in Asia, Africa and Latin America. A survey by the Plantation Workers' Union in Zimbabwe uncovered information on work-related injuries and other hazards faced by children involved in agriculture. This kind of information can be extremely helpful in the development of priorities for action.

There is no inherent reason why unions should not incorporate informal-sector workers. The Zimbabwe Domestic and Allied Workers Union organizes about 50 per cent of the total workers in domestic employment, including children (usually aged 10-18 years). The membership is grouped into units starting at the local level, progressing to city and regional levels, and culminating in an elected national executive. Funds are obtained through membership subscriptions and joining fees. It is union policy to discourage child labour, although support is given to children employed as domestics. Union officials visit houses to look at working conditions and advise members; they monitor law enforcement and employment regulations; and they handle grievances, including those involving children.

Children are normally thought to represent unfair competition for adult workers and to bring wages down, so in practice most workers' organizations are probably less concerned about improving working terms and conditions for children than they are about having children withdrawn from the labour force altogether. It is not clear, however, which strategy most effectively achieves this goal without at the same time forcing children, even if they are working legally, into destitution.

Trade unions in developing countries often prefer a gradual approach, phasing children out of the workforce by retaining those already employed (and possibly giving them access to education or skills training) but limiting all new recruitment to adults, or by channelling child workers into education through sponsorship. In contrast, those based in industrialized countries tend to take a fairly hard line on the issue, lobbying for children's immediate removal from work. The American Federation of Labor and Congress of Industrial Organizations (AFL-CIO), for example, has adopted a strong position and is a major force in support of proposed U.S. legislation banning the import of products made with child labour. The International Confederation of Free Trade Unions, at its 15th World Congress in Caracas in March of 1992 and a subsequent meeting of its Asian and Pacific membership, pronounced child labour an alarming practice and called for its elimination. Another workers' organization, the Asian-American Free Labour Institute, has documented violations in Asia and promoted the application of trade restrictions on countries routinely employing child labour. For its part, the United Food and Commercial Workers Union has campaigned to persuade major multinational companies based in the United States to stop buying products from countries such as Bangladesh that are heavily reliant on child labour.

8.4. INDIVIDUAL INITIATIVE

The need to use all possible available resources in the battle against child labour is apparent, and often it is the commitment of individual citizens, professionals and service providers rather than the action of organizations that can have greatest impact. A recent advocacy document produced by the NGO Group on the Convention on the Rights of the Child specifies what NGOs, community groups and individuals, not just governments, can do to protect children from economic exploitation:[25]

> Bearing in mind that children should be consulted on affairs affecting them and that a critical factor in the enforcement of child labour laws is active public interest and concern, you can:
>
> As an individual...
> - join or set up a voluntary group for the protection of exploited children
> - write to your government representatives and your trade unions asking them to enforce labour laws;
> - collaborate with NGOs in your country;
> - contact your local media. Write articles, stories and plays, etc., suggesting ways to solve the problem.
>
> As a teacher...
> - inform parents of the advantages of education and training;
> - ensure that rural and urban children have access to literacy classes;
> - make parents more aware of their social and civic responsibilities regarding school attendance and the employment of children;
> - detect and identify abuse of working children;
> - provide support to the labour law enforcement and inspection authorities.
>
> As a journalist
> - alert the public to child labour abuse;
> - monitor and publicize the enforcement of protective laws;
> - help mobilize public opinion against the exploitation of working children
>
> As an employer
> - take care to distance children from dangerous activities; provide training, breaks and time off;
> - become less dependent on child labour;
> - lend your support to the control and abolition of child labour;
> - keep up to date about child labour laws in your country;
> - assume leadership in working with governments, other employers and NGOs to reduce violations of child labour laws.
>
> As a lawyer
> - understand and promote national and international law on children's rights;
> - help others to recognize that child labour is a violation of human rights;
> - help working children understand their rights and give them legal advice.
>
> As a non-governmental organization
> - advocate effective laws and enforcement mechanisms;
> - investigate abuses of children in the workplace;
> - work with other NGOs to promote, train and support national groups.
>
> As a trade union
> - make sure that the minimum working ages are respected;
> - document child labour abuses and denounce cases of exploitation;

- ensure that child workers receive the legal wage from their employers;
- educate children about their rights and how to exercise them;
- receive and refer complaints about violations of child labour law;
- encourage and help working children to organize in order to protect their rights.

Especially prominent roles can be played by parents, street educators or community workers, monitors, employers and employers' associations, and children.

8.4.1. Parents

In some countries, the emphasis is on the need for individual parents to ensure that their children are at school and not working. In Sri Lanka and in India in the State of Kerala, high levels of literacy among both men and women are an important protective factor, not only because parents, and particularly mothers, who are literate are a major national resource in caring for children but also because they are more likely than non-literate parents to value education for their children over work. Parental education and awareness-raising on child care, health and development are powerful disincentives for a dependence on child labour.

8.4.2. Street Educators or Community Workers

At the programme level, reaching, making contact and establishing a trusting relationship with working children and child labourers is of paramount importance. In this outreach work, street educators or community workers (many of whom are volunteers and were once street or working children themselves) have come to play a special part in several countries. The exploitation of children can be an extremely sensitive and difficult issue to deal with, and often it is best approached not by government officials but informally by people with whom the children can identify and who do not necessarily represent a threat to employers and other interested parties.

The work of educators consists in building upon the children's own realities and upon their resiliency and creativity.[26] In addition to friendship, educators may provide counselling and teach such topics as life skills, sexual health, hygiene and financial management. However, they mainly seek to facilitate rather than to teach, and encourage children to articulate their own priorities and needs and to construct their own rules of conduct.

8.4.3. Monitors

Ultimately, any strategy concerned with targeting the children most at risk is highly dependent on key informants within society as a whole. Monitors identify children exposed to hazard or exploitation, make an initial assessment of their conditions and circumstances and refer them to appropriate bodies for care and protection. They also single out abusive employers or hazardous work settings and work processes and inform relevant authorities. The people best placed to assume this role include adult workers and trade union members, investigative journalists, teachers, health personnel and law enforcement officers. Extensive advocacy and mobilization is required to establish a network of grass-roots monitors of this nature.

8.4.4. Employers and Employers' Associations

It is frequently assumed that employers oppose reform mainly because child labourers are compliant and cheap. But the evidence to support this assertion is not entirely clear. Indeed, in the present world economic and social climate, employers and their associations can be potential resources in strategies to eliminate child labour.

In some countries, the tradition of corporate philanthropy is well established, and bodies such as the Rotarians — which include many leading employers — have long been involved in sponsoring vaccination campaigns and other interventions for children. In the United States particularly, corporate philanthropy and social responsibility are believed to give companies a competitive advantage. Respect for the environment and for workers' rights, including the rights of child workers, are key components in this strategy. Several multinational corporations based in the United States are developing ethical guidelines for application with sub-contractors and subsidiaries in developing countries.

Individual employers and employers' associations are increasingly motivated to become involved in the struggle against child labour for a number of reasons: technological developments in industry; pressure from consumers in industrialized countries; the possibility of legislative intervention in the United States and elsewhere banning the import of products made by child labour; and fear of criticism, fines and even market loss. Some employers have begun protecting themselves by introducing reforms. Others are evolving marketing strategies that project an image of socially responsible trading. Thus far, the main impetus has been to remove children from the workforce, in compliance with international norms and standards, although some employers retain older children, offering them education and other services. Others still have established day care and education for the children of their adult workers.

In India and Bangladesh, employers have agreed to take concerted action to remove children from the labour force. Indian carpet manufacturers are collaborating in the 'rugmark' campaign, for example, and use special labels guaranteeing that their carpets have not been made by child workers. Bangladeshi garment manufacturers have expelled most of the children from their workforce out of fear that a U.S. ban on the import of products made by children would destroy their export production. Largely because of recent advocacy by UNICEF and ILO, there is now concern that abrupt dismissal may have had adverse impact on the children's welfare. Possible strategies for assisting dismissed children by securing their access to education are being discussed.

By adopting a series of sound business practices, larger employers can aim first to reduce and eventually to eliminate child labour in their workforce without redundancies or profit loss. As previously discussed, unilateral action may disadvantage the progressive employers in relation to those not interested in reform, which makes it necessary to work in employers' groups by industry or sector, nationally and regionally. As an important adjunct to this policy, companies in developing countries may need to promote appropriate mechanization and modernization (which generally calls for adult labour) and to capture new, non-traditional markets. Non-traditional products often require a higher level of intellectual skills and labour-efficiency than can be provided by children.

8.4.5. Children

At one time, child labourers were cast by policy makers and programmers in the role of the victim and their potential as agents of social change was disregarded. Rarely were children consulted in the planning of policies and programmes intended to assist them, and more rarely still was their capacity to engage in implementation acknowledged. A very different view is reflected in many of the more recent approaches, which build on lessons learned in adult education and child-to-child initiatives, as well as on certain key principles enshrined in the CRC: a child's right to be an active participant and not just a passive recipient is now understood to be fundamental. The roles assumed by children are diverse. In some contexts they act as monitors and in others they deliver information and services to children involved in labour. Children can also play an important part in situation analysis and advocacy and in many contexts can assist in programme management and administration.

□ 8.5. THE UNITED NATIONS SYSTEM

Governmental and non-governmental organizations in the front line in the fight against child labour have introduced their thinking, concerns and experience into the international arena. They look in turn to the United Nations system and its human, economic and organizational resources for international support and reinforcement, especially in connection with the implementation and monitoring of international treaties such as the 1956 United Nations convention relating to slavery, ILO conventions and the CRC. The organizations within the United Nations with the greatest interest in child labour are ILO, UNICEF, the United Nations Educational, Scientific and Cultural Organization (UNESCO) and the World Health Organization (WHO).

8.5.1. ILO

ILO has played a lead role in elaborating international conventions and standards on child labour, slavery and other exploitative practices and in facilitating and promoting their ratification and wider observance. It provides technical cooperation in programme and policy development, assisting Member States in the design and implementation of policies and programmes aimed at narrowing the gap between national law and practice; identifying policy options, strategies and practical measures effective in the struggle against child labour; and stimulating awareness among ILO Member States and the international community as a whole of the dimensions and consequences of child labour and national obligations under international labour law. ILO is responsible for a growing body of literature on child labour, designed for use in advocacy and as a guide to good practice. In addition, it has created several mechanisms, usually involving employers' or workers' organizations, for supervising compliance with ILO conventions. Priority has been given to preventing the involvement of children in hazardous work or employment and protecting the youngest and most vulnerable children.

ILO is at present compiling statistics on child labour globally; conducting research into the economic and social consequences of implementing minimum-age laws; and, through its International Programme on the Elimination of Child Labour, preparing a guide on the design and provision of non-formal education and vocational training programmes for working children. ILO offers technical advisory services to all ILO Member States and runs operational programmes in countries where child labour is a serious problem.

8.5.2. UNICEF

UNICEF became involved in the child labour issue in the mid-1980s when its Executive Board called for a study to be undertaken of 'children in especially difficult circumstances' (CEDC). The Organization now provides guidance and support for the NGO community and governments alike in the area of children's rights and child exploitation. It is also mandated to support State Parties in the monitoring and implementation of the CRC.

UNICEF has been particularly active in promoting awareness about street children and other CEDC groups. It has funded or helped to organize several international, regional and national workshops on child labour and related issues; provided technical assistance in programme development; and sponsored study tours and other networking and information dissemination exercises for government and non-governmental representatives working with high-risk groups of children. Globally, about 50 UNICEF country offices have CEDC programmes. In Brazil, India and the Philippines, UNICEF has worked in partnership with government, NGOs, religious bodies and the community in the development of nationwide movements on behalf of street children. The range of interventions has been comprehensive, encompassing support for legal reform, policy development, service provision, empowerment and advocacy. In Bangladesh, UNICEF is collaborating with NGOs and the private sector in the development of programmes for children employed in the garment industry.

8.5.3. UNESCO

As discussed by Dall in the preceding chapter, UNESCO has invested a great deal institutionally in the 'Education for All' policy, which received prominence at the 1990 conference in Jomtien, Thailand. Central to this policy is the argument that education has a higher rate of economic return to society than do economic development measures. The 'Education for All' policy is also viewed as being of critical importance for child labour elimination. UNESCO focuses on expanding services to children who do not have access to basic education, the majority of whom are child workers. UNESCO, unlike ILO,WHO and UNICEF, does not have country offices and about half of its staff are headquarters-based. The Organization is therefore dependent on collaboration with others for learning about issues in the field and for effective implementation of its policies.To increase its impact, UNESCO has begun to work closely with UNICEF and is also committed to strengthening its ties with NGOs. At present, it collaborates with the International Catholic Child Bureau, Childhope and other international NGOs. However, UNESCO is in practice better prepared to engage in advocacy with governments. It has, for example, created National Commissions as a way of advancing its work at the country level.[27]

8.5.4. WHO

WHO is mandated to work with children and youth in the area of health. In recent years, the Organization has developed a number of initiatives for especially disadvantaged children, one of the first being the Round Table Conference it organized jointly with the Council of International Organizations of Medical Sciences in 1985 on the subject of battered children and child abuse. WHO has sought to identify the physical and psycho-social risks associated with child labour and has sponsored research in India, Nigeria, Malaysia and Korea on the effects of work on child growth and development. With the spread of both human immunodeficiency virus (HIV) infection and substance abuse among young people throughout the world and especially among out-of-school children and youth, WHO is endeavouring to improve the quality of socially targeted health responses. One group of particular concern are children who live on the streets whose lifestyles make them highly susceptible to health problems not typically experienced by other young people.

■ 9. Economic Resources Required for Eliminating Child Labour

□ 9.1. ECONOMIC AND SOCIAL POLICIES

Cost is obviously a fundamental consideration in mounting and sustaining programmes and policies for the elimination of child labour and the protection of working children. To combat the dependence of both families and employers on children's work and to encourage children to attend school, *and remain in school*, and to protect them from exploitation and danger at work, governments must make commitments to develop fiscal, labour market and other policies and to provide greater access to affordable and relevant education as well as to essential social services and benefits. "The effective abolition of child labour requires vigorous action primarily in the sphere of macroeconomic policies, including policies aimed at improvements in specific target areas or the conditions of certain groups."[28]

Preventive measures such as social insurance and health, education and social services are all costly to maintain. However, in few developing countries is the issue of child labour a major budgetary priority, since child survival is generally seen as more critical. Moreover, in the present economic climate, there is widespread scepticism concerning the ability of governments in developing countries to provide the funds for increased state support of measures, especially when these are perceived as being orientated towards 'welfare' rather than 'development'. Military spending in many countries diverts scarce funds away from the social sector and channels labour into unproductive activities. In addition, the total debt of developing countries has multiplied thirteenfold in the last 20 years, resulting in massive net transfers from indebted developing countries to rich creditor nations and financial institutions.[29]

Yet, the problem is often less one of limited resources and more of poor distribution — much could be done with existing resources if they were more effectively allocated. In some countries a serious need has been recognized to examine the current distribution of resources and to restructure national as well as aid budgets in favour of the social sector, including by re-examining expensive public works projects, reducing arms expenditure and re-scheduling debt repayments. Because of budgetary constraints, more imaginative use needs to be made of existing financial resources, and previously untapped resources must be accessed. In fact, the governments of developing countries spend, on average, about one quarter of their budget on health and education, although the poor, who form the overwhelming majority of the population in these countries, often only benefit from half of this.[30] One of the main advantages of a policy founded on a high level of participation by the civil society is that it facilitates cost-sharing, in the sense that many costs can be spread beyond government. At the same time, though, it is important to avoid placing too much of a financial burden on grass-roots activists or on low-income families, including those with working children.

Set against the various costs of implementing a policy either to reduce or eliminate child labour are the many economic benefits that can be obtained from such action. While child labour is generally viewed as an economic resource in the short run, in practice it perpetuates poverty: child labour is not just a result, but also a cause, of poverty since it imposes many hidden costs.[31] Significant among these are the opportunity costs of child labour, most importantly the deprivation of access to education. Out-of-school children are prevented from developing intellectual and social skills that in adulthood are linked with higher earnings, greater job security and competitiveness in the labour market. By undermining participation and performance in education, child labour also impedes national economic development, since the transmission of knowledge, skills and culture through education is one of the key elements in the development process.

Because of work-related diseases and accidents, child labour also places extra financial burdens on the health and welfare sectors into the future. The health impacts of work are far more acute for children than for adults, and many work-related health problems experienced in childhood persist into adulthood, with the result that ill-health is likely to become a life-long burden.

Child labour, furthermore, exacerbates adult unemployment and depresses adult wages in many cases. The presence of children in the workforce may be used by employers as a threat against adult workers, forcing them to accept lower wages, as already discussed. The low wages paid to children act, in addition, as a disincentive to employers to modernize manufacturing processes and benefit from economies of scale. Because children's income is usually so low, their paid labour adds little to domestic income or saving. Lagging domestic income and consumption fails over time to stimulate domestic demand and production and contributes to maintaining a weak, export-dependent economy within which child labour remains an important element: a vicious cycle from which developing countries must break out if the word "developing" has any significance.

□ 9.2. SOCIAL AND ECONOMIC PROTECTION AND 'SAFETY NETS'

As has been seen, children are important as a source of additional — if sometimes only marginal — labour power and income. Child labour persists today largely because of an abundant supply of children from poor families who need to work: their families rely on their earnings and on their unpaid work within the household or in family concerns. It exists also because it serves the many enterprises in the world that remain dependent on cheap, unskilled labour for their competitiveness. Only when adult incomes are sufficient to cover household needs, small employers have revised their labour needs and children have viable alternative uses for their time will child labour become redundant. In other words, a major portion of the cost of ending child labour, and especially paid child labour, will have to be borne by the family, the employer and the community and not just by government or other implementing bodies.

It is evident therefore that efforts to withdraw children from the workforce need to take account of these economic factors, which crucially affect the decisions of children, families and employers and consequently influence the outcome of policy. It can thus be argued that since, without viable economic alternatives, the abolition of child labour would cause substantial hardship to poor families as well as to many small-scale employers, reducing to the minimum the cost to the family, the community and the employer is a key policy priority. Unless government revenue can be raised and a financial safety net created for the very poor, either through public funds or other sources, child labour will persist, even with overall income improvements and legislative intervention. With adequate protection against destitution, families would no longer need to turn to their children for their financial contribution or unpaid labour.[32]

The aim of a gradual approach built on social and economic change, with safety nets in place, rather than abrupt law enforcement, is to reduce progressively both the supply of and demand for child labour, without at the same time exacerbating poverty or undermining enterprise. Achieving this aim involves reducing the economic and social value of children's work as compared with any other possible use of their time, and lowering the value of children's work relative to that of adults. As ILO suggests, the progressive elimination of child labour also allows for the concentration of limited financial resources in targeted interventions, thereby reducing the overall costs of implementation.

The provision of economic and social support involves careful analysis of various policy options. The elimination of child labour clearly implies the need for economic development that places a high priority on the alleviation of poverty and the provision of targeted welfare support for vulnerable families. This approach entails targeting poverty eradication policies at communities and households where child labour is prevalent, focusing especially on areas and economic sectors where children engage in particularly dangerous or servile activities. There is a need for balanced regional development programmes and rural employment-generating policies designed specifically to increase the access of the poor to land, credit, improved seeds and technology as well as to better water, health and sanitation services.

The gradual expansion of the state into key areas of social insurance and social protection is an important adjunct to the stimulation of income and employment. The provision of safety nets and other family-support interventions will usually be necessary as a transitional short-term measure to compensate for income loss when children are removed from employment and being educated. Although many different kinds of models and interventions in social welfare provision exist, most fall into two broad categories: targeted interventions; and interventions providing general coverage for the population as a whole. Generally, the former have greater potential for use in child labour reform policies because they are less costly and can be tied directly to families at greatest risk.

The modern welfare state has provided essential support for families experiencing unemployment, income reduction, prolonged ill-health and other problems. Family and child benefit allowances, tax breaks, and sickness, disability and unemployment insurance are some of the approaches used. Day care is effective for facilitating women's entry into paid work and at the same time releasing older children from their child-care responsibilities. Some of these measures may seem far beyond the reach of many developing countries. But in some areas, such as community-based day care, innovative and cost-effective interventions are being expanded with considerable success, even in very low-income countries such as China, India, Sri Lanka and Vietnam.[33]

A primary consideration is the extent to which provision should be made to substitute the income of children withdrawn from labour with other sources of income for their families. Likewise, it is important to bear in mind that in cases where the differential between the wages of children and adults is significant — and especially where children form a high proportion of the workforce — employers may need financial incentives to hire adults in place of children. Already in several countries there are large-scale, income-generation and small-enterprise development and credit programmes benefiting the poorest households, often those managed or headed by women. Skills development and marketing opportunities are also important measures. Such schemes need to be analysed for their impacts on child labour in particular, since it is not always evident that they will have a positive effect. Subsidized income-generation projects, for example, are notoriously difficult to target, complicated and expensive to run and of dubious impact and long-term sustainability.

Perhaps the most promising earnings-replacement approach is the provision of cash or in-kind subsidies to maintain poor children in school, thereby offsetting at least part of their earning losses. Children may be provided with free school materials, free or subsidized food rations and school meals, or special supplementary feeding programmes. Sponsorship may be given for their care and nurture, although this is most likely to derive from private-sector rather than public-sector initiative. While a number of NGO and government programmes have found this approach effective for retaining some children in school and out of the full-time labour force, its potential for sustainability and nationwide application through government has yet to be fully explored. India and some other countries are, however, experimenting with it.

Importantly, the economic implications for government of these different schemes and approaches are extremely variable, depending largely on whether or not all or part of the costs can be transferred to the family and whether they contain an income- or employment-generation component. In the main, public-sector social protection and social security measures imply far greater cost than economic development initiatives because the latter tend to incorporate an income-generation component aimed at ensuring economic sustainability. The capacity for cost-recovery in social protection measures is severely constrained by the poverty of the client population. These kinds of interventions are therefore unlikely to be viable in countries that are heavily indebted, or without sound and reasonably progressive fiscal policies or a strong revenue base.

Another problem, mentioned already, is that 'social welfare' generally assumes extremely low priority in political strategies and government planning these days. Moreover, many governments are reluctant to introduce mechanisms to secure the redistribution of income since this could threaten their political support. This latter issue affects social protection measures more than health or education because middle- and upper-income families are generally more willing to contribute towards the costs of services that they themselves use than to those that almost exclusively benefit the poor. Even with economic development initiatives, though, impact and sustainability may be largely dependent on whether the schemes meet real needs in the local labour and other markets. Without proper market feasibility studies and planning for the gradual phasing-out of government or other sources of support, these measures may lead to a high and unsustainable level of dependency among beneficiary families.

9.3. PROMOTING SOCIAL AND BEHAVIOURAL CHANGE

It has been suggested that the elimination of child labour is dependent not only on creating an economic environment within which families and enterprises can flourish without relying on children's labour, but also on attitudinal and behavioural change. This implies the need to create widespread awareness of the disadvantages, or indeed the evils, of child labour and to form an active constituency in support of reform. Such aims can best be achieved through the review and reframing of legislation, legal literacy, extensive advocacy — both general and targeted — and the social mobilization of key actors in the field of child labour. In extreme cases, it will also be necessary to resort to law enforcement.

Quantification of the financial and other resources required to bring domestic law into line with international standards, to activate networks in support of reform and to advocate and promote behavioural change right down to the grass-roots level is clearly not possible at this point. Social mobilization, legal literacy, media campaigns and political advocacy do not involve concrete inputs or outputs that can be easily measured. Investment in these strategies depends on the degree of resistance of cultures to attitude and value change, the extent and severity of child labour, the effectiveness and outreach of the media and other communications channels, and the commitment and efficiency of activists and reformers. However, it is worth noting that social mobilization and advocacy are strategies that, possibly more than any others in the reform process, involve a major cost-sharing component since they draw widely on the resources of the civil society.

9.4. EDUCATION

Universal access to basic — especially primary — education is a central element in any policy to reduce the supply of child labourers. One of the major arguments in this regard is that when children go to school they are unable to work. Research from many countries, however, shows that school attendance does not necessarily exclude work, because many children combine the two. It seems, though, that compulsory and affordable primary education can be effective in ending full-time child labour and may therefore serve to reduce children's involvement in many of the more hazardous occupations and activities, since these often entail a full-time commitment to work. Quality education also equips children with social confidence, literacy, reasoning, accounting and other skills that can help them resist exploitation. Nevertheless, merely making education compulsory is no solution unless family poverty can be reduced simultaneously, because children will be forced to remain in the labour force, where work opportunities are available, regardless of the legal position.

For working children to be able to take advantage of 'free' primary schooling, compulsion must be accompanied by appropriate subsidies and/or financial incentives to help cover both the direct costs of education (such as tuition or other fees and, for the poorest families, books, school supplies and uniforms) and the indirect ones (such as transportation). Incentives and subsidies will also need to be sufficient to help compensate at least for part of the opportunity cost associated with the loss of the child's labour input. One approach, adopted by *Projecto Axé* in Salvador, Brazil, is to sponsor children while they attend school. The project pays street and working children a small sum for attending educational programmes and gives them an opportunity to earn additional money in programme-developed businesses involving recycled paper, T-shirts and jewellery. In Zimbabwe, the Social Development Fund, set up in 1992 under the Structural Adjustment Programme, provides support for meeting tuition and examination fees. During its first six months of operation, the Fund assisted some 8,800 primary school and 10,000 secondary school pupils. Additional support is available through a public assistance programme administered by the Department of Social Welfare. Families can apply for assistance to meet part or all of the cost of fees, although total disbursements generally fall far short of potential demand because many families are not aware of their rights or of how to obtain these benefits. Moreover, an assessment of this programme revealed that the cost of fees was actually relatively minor when compared with that of uniforms.[34]

There is a strong belief in many quarters that to ensure equity of access, the state should not impose charges for tuition at the primary level, and of course Article 28 of the CRC requires that primary education be "free". Free primary education naturally implies a significant financial burden for government and consequently for taxpayers. The United Nations Development Programme (UNDP) argues that primary education is not only of fundamental importance in itself but is also an effective way to direct resources more specifically towards the poor, since a far greater share of the benefits of primary education accrues to those who are less well off. In Costa Rica, for example, it has been found that 57 per cent of the benefits of primary education go to the poorest 40 per cent of the people, whereas only 8 per cent go to the wealthiest 20 per cent.[35] Primary education also has a more direct effect on child labour than secondary or tertiary education because children who are attracted into school when young may never become part of the child labour force.

In many countries, the economic returns to primary education are almost twice as high as those to higher education. However, too often a large share of the national budget is directed into secondary and tertiary education. According to UNDP, the primary level accounts for less than half the total education expenditure in every region. Tertiary education receives a greater proportion of government funds than primary education in Francophone Africa, in East Asia and the Pacific, and in Latin America. Restructuring is taking place in some countries, however, and the share of education budgets for primary schooling rose during the 1980s in 15 countries in sub-Saharan Africa. In Latin America, improvements have been reported for Brazil, Chile and the Dominican Republic.

As analysed more fully in Chapter Six, reducing costs in education is an essential part of increasing coverage, although it is important to ensure that this does not jeopardize quality or access. One study[36] shows that if a few selective cost-savings and cost-shifting reforms were introduced, the additional costs of achieving universal primary education could be halved. UNDP argues that recurrent costs can be reduced by 25 per cent with a package consisting of, among other things, more efficient use of community resources, multiple shifts, selective increases in class sizes and some introduction of cost recovery at the tertiary level.[37] Salaries can be reduced by expanding the use of teachers with less formal training and paraprofessionals.

School shifts in particular represent a savings on teachers and on the capital costs of buildings, equipment and other facilities. They also have the advantage of allowing children from impoverished families to combine education and part-time work. However, some studies suggest that the shift system may even encourage some children to begin or continue working, reduce the number of contact hours below a level meaningful from an educational perspective and overburden teachers.

Another way to reduce costs and increase access for working children is to make services available at mobile facilities, borrowed premises, or in the open in markets, railway stations and other sites where children congregate. The Mobile School Project in Bangkok slums, for example, delivers formal and non-formal education to children aged 8-15 years, supplying school lunch, free uniforms and educational aids as incentives. Similarly, the Department for Social Welfare and Development in the Philippines offers a variety of mobile educational, recreational and counselling services in tents located close to the workplace, with the long-term goal of attracting children away from the streets and into schools, as well as preventing child delinquency and exploitation.

Investment in increasing educational access alone is not sufficient because many of the poor find the formal education system wanting. Curricula are too academic, learning materials are lacking, and the quality of instruction offered is often very poor. Investment in upgrading relevance and quality is as important as building new schools and hiring new teachers. A growing number of both governmental agencies and NGOs have started to provide education targeted especially at working children, either by introducing non-formal or informal education or by adapting the formal system. In these programmes, attention is given to vocational and creative subjects, to training in life skills and to recreation and play, as well as to the more traditional academic subjects. Care is also taken to make schools more flexible and to adapt them, where appropriate, to children's work schedules.

9.5. REMEDIAL INTERVENTIONS

The financial resource requirements of remedial provision for children affected by labour have yet to be identified. Since only in few developing countries has a serious attempt been made to quantify the numbers of child labourers, it remains unclear how many children throughout the world require remedial care. International statistics on child labour at present compiled by ILO are of necessity based on imperfect data, although the Organization is endeavouring to develop more adequate methods of surveying child labour and of information retrieval.

Another constraint is the dearth of remedial responses from which to draw conclusions about cost. Experience internationally in remedial provision is restricted to several hundred comparatively modest programmes, few of which are of national scope and some of which service an almost insignificant number of children. The great majority of these programmes are non-governmental, although some receive financial, technical or material support from government, and many rely significantly on voluntary initiative. Most involve groups of children clearly defined as self-employed street workers, few catering to the needs of children in other types of work. Most were founded comparatively recently, and few have been fully evaluated in terms of financial input relative to impact.

Estimations of the economic resources required in remedial work must allow for the fact that the complexity and intensity of programme interventions in this field can be extremely variable. Also, some forms of intervention require a far longer-term involvement with affected children than others. Moreover, while many can function well with volunteers, some may need fully trained staff. A few programmes offer long-term residential care, whereas many simply help children obtain access to existing services or organized recreational activities. Others still incorporate a cost-recovery element, encouraging children to contribute a part of their earnings to programme maintenance.

Another important variable is the degree to which children are affected by their labour and the nature of the impact. Children who are disabled as a result of injuries sustained at work may need support into adulthood, whereas others may suffer no lasting effects. Some impacts are extremely difficult to deal with, and many — psycho-social impacts, for example — have still to be assessed through specific studies.

Despite the paucity of information on the economic resource requirements of remedial interventions and the implication that in many cases these could be very considerable, there is one clear financial advantage in this approach: remedial programmes can have a demonstrated effect on an identified group of children and so tend to attract funds with comparative ease. In recent years, a growing number of donors have begun to acknowledge the need to make more resources available to combat the widespread abuse of children's rights, and several have identified the support of children affected by dangerous or servile labour as a priority.

■ 10. Conclusion

Millions of children throughout the world work. A significant proportion of these children are engaged in activities and occupations that are in one way or another injurious to their health, welfare or development. The scale of child work and child labour internationally is enormous. The historical evidence suggests that a policy focusing on the progressive elimination of child labour — in other words, singling out those children involved in dangerous or servile work and leaving untouched those in safe activities — responds to the most urgent humanitarian need, while also avoiding family destitution and allowing for the judicious use of scarce human, institutional and economic resources.

Because of the complex nature, the extent, and the dispersion of child labour, it is a problem not readily amenable to either exclusive governmental, or single-sector, solutions. Thus, the strategies for eliminating child labour now being developed in several parts of the world depend on flexibility and creativity in resource utilization — accommodating comprehensive policies based on a diversity of programme components. In some cases, this has led to the radical restructuring of the institutional and economic arrangements upon which child labour provision has traditionally relied.

Effective reform depends on multisectoral interventions that employ child-centred perspectives. These cater to a broad range of needs and circumstances in accordance with the heterogeneity of the client-base, which is reflected in variations in age, gender, work experience, occupation, impacts of labour, together with many other factors. Policy reforms comprise both preventive and remedial measures in the areas of social and economic development and protection, education, attitudinal and behavioural change, law enforcement and the care and assistance of children harmed by their labour. It also requires consistent collaboration, drawing on the resources of government, intergovernmental and non-governmental bodies as well as of the wider civil society. There is an important opportunity to mobilize new human and institutional resources in this process, foremost among these resources being children, employers and parents, workers' organizations, grass-roots groups and national, regional and international NGO networks. As far as economic resources are concerned, it may not always be necessary to generate new funds but to distribute more effectively those already allocated.

The drawback of a reform strategy based on a high level of social mobilization and on integrated interventions is that its success depends on the creation of powerful coordinating mechanisms and the sustained commitment of key actors in the child labour field. In terms of economic resources, this kind of strategy is undoubtedly more demanding than single-sector interventions managed by line ministries, although it facilitates cost-sharing and, because of the greater coverage, is also likely to be more cost-effective. The question remains as to how to sustain enthusiasm for child labour reform among civil-society partners who have no binding obligation under the CRC, especially when reform may entail certain immediate costs for them.

Child labour is a new concern for many countries: both policy and implementation strategies are in the process of formation, and resource requirements are only now being identified. Rapid assessment and other procedures are being devised for the purpose of gauging the scope of the child labour problem. Pilot schemes, in the area of both prevention and remedial provision, have been established in several countries. One important challenge is to develop these to a scale that accommodates the needs at national levels and to ensure that they are sustainable. If child labour is to be eradicated within the foreseeable future, lessons learned from policies and programmes developed throughout the world need to be widely disseminated and full and imaginative use made of the great diversity of human, organizational and economic resources available at the sub-national, national, regional and international levels.

Notes

1 International Labour Organisation, 1992a, p. 4.
2 Ibid.
3 Bequele, 1991.
4 Ibid.
5 International Labour Organisation, 1989.
6 Ibid.
7 Bequele and Myers, forthcoming.
8 International Labour Organisation, 1993.
9 United Nations Human Rights Commission, 1993.
10 A rapid assessment has been conducted in Bangladesh, and both the findings and methods used have been documented and are expected to be published in 1995 by ILO and UNICEF.
11 International Labour Organisation, 1989.
12 Boyden, 1994.
13 Safilios-Rothchild, 1980, pp. 313-372; Cain, 1977; White, 1974; Arnold et al., 1975; Krishnakumari, 1985; Azer et al., 1993.
14 Child Workers in Nepal, 1991.
15 Mueller, 1976.
16 Szanton Blanc and Contributors, 1994; White and Tjandraningsih, 1992; Gunn and Ostos, 1992; Patil, undated; Mansurov, 1993.
17 Abdalla, 1988; Kanbargi, 1988.
18 Institute of Industrial Relations, 1988.
19 White and Tjandraningsih, 1992.
20 Anker, 1993.
21 Boyden and Myers, 1995.
22 Ibid.
23 Ibid.
24 Ibid.
25 The NGO Group for the Convention on the Rights of the Child, 1993.

26 Hart, 1992, p. 31.
27 From the verbal presentation given by Victor Ordonez, Deputy Director of UNESCO, at the Innocenti Global Seminar on Street and Working Children, held at UNICEF, International Child Development Centre, Florence, 15-25 February 1993. See also Black, 1993.
28 International Labour Organisation, 1983.
29 Boyden with UNESCO, 1993.
30 Ibid.
31 Fonseca, 1993.
32 Padmini, 1993.
33 Myers, 1992, pp. 27, 103-104 and passim.
34 International Labour Organisation, 1992b.
35 United Nations Development Programme, 1991.
36 Colclough and Lewin,1993.
37 United Nations Development Programme, 1991.

Conclusion

James R. Himes and Diana Saltarelli

1. An Overview

The United Nations Convention on the Rights of the Child (CRC), adopted in 1989, undoubtedly represents the most significant commitment to children's rights ever made. It bridges both 'human development' and 'human rights' concerns, providing for children's economic, social and cultural rights as well as for their civil rights. The CRC identifies children's basic needs and sets obligations for meeting them, but it does more than just promote needs fulfilment. It recognizes that children are entitled to society's attention and resources, that they have a legal claim or right to them.

Despite enormous progress in the past 40 years, governments in developing countries are far from meeting the basic needs of their most vulnerable populations and farther still from fulfilling their rights. This situation has demographic and economic roots, including rapid population growth, low economic productivity and the negative social impact of many structural adjustment policies. It also has political and administrative origins in many countries — ethnic conflict, political neglect and poor management. The 'thematic' chapters of this book provide some alarming global figures:

Parker and Sepúlveda report that, worldwide, 35,000 children die each day. For the most part, they are poor and from developing countries. In 1990 in the developing world, 4.3 million children under 5 years of age died from pneumonia and other acute respiratory infections, 3.2 million from diarrhoea-related diseases, and 2.1 million from vaccine-preventable diseases. In the same year, for a variety of causes, 3.8 million children failed to reach their first birthdays.

Jonsson relates that 184 million (or slightly more than one third) of all children under 5 years of age in developing countries are affected by protein-energy malnutrition, which stunts their growth, lowers their resistance to disease and impairs their learning abilities. About 190 million pre-school-age children live in areas where they are at high risk of Vitamin A deficiency, a major cause of blindness. Over 370 million women in developing countries (about 40 per cent) are anaemic. More than 1.5 billion people globally are vulnerable to iodine deficiency disorders, and 500 million people have goitre. In 1990, 120,000 iodine-deficient mothers gave birth to severely brain-damaged children; and about one million infants died because they were not exclusively breast-fed during their first few months.[1]

Dall advises that approximately 300 million children (70 per cent of whom are girls) are denied access to primary and secondary schools for geographic, economic and political reasons. In addition, 960 million adults worldwide (two thirds of whom are women) are illiterate. Costly repetition and desertion within school systems is high. Millions of children and adults fail to complete the education programmes they start. Many children do not attend school long enough to ensure literacy. Even children who do complete the primary cycle often do not acquire the basic skills they need. They find the formal curriculum irrelevant, unmeaningful or, in the case of some minority groups, culturally alien and linguistically inaccessible. Schools are underfunded and inadequately staffed. Teachers are ill-trained.

Boyden and Rialp suggest that globally there may be anywhere from 100 million to 200 million children working in hazardous or exploitative conditions. At least 18 per cent of children 10-14 years of age in developing countries, and 25 per cent in Africa, are believed to be working, either for wages or in home-based industries/enterprises. Reliable data are, however, not available because most child labour is 'hidden' and beyond the reach of monitors. There is a growing body of literature documenting the magnitude of the phenomenon and exposing the situations of children involved in drug trafficking, prostitution, pornography, armed conflicts and other hazardous activities.

Since the mid-1980s, many efforts to address these problems have been successful. Millions of lives have been saved by using simple, low-cost and highly effective strategies. Hundreds of thousands of children have been spared physical and mental impairments, including blindness and cretinism, that would have limited their lives and made them lifelong burdens on their parents and communities. Far greater numbers of children in developing countries are completing at least four years of primary schooling; and in many countries, initial steps have been taken to ameliorate the situation of working children and prevent the worst abuses of child labour.

Much still needs to be done, however, to realize the rights set out in the CRC and the end-decade goals agreed upon at the 1990 World Summit for Children.

Primary health care and basic health services must be reinforced and equitable access assured. Communicable diseases need to be prevented and controlled more efficiently. Clean drinking water needs to become more widely available and environmental sanitation improved. Starvation and deaths caused by famine must be eliminated, chronic hunger and malnutrition reduced, and the major nutritional deficiency diseases eradicated. Compulsory primary education must be universalized, adult illiteracy combated and more equitable access to schools achieved. Teachers need to be trained, learning materials produced and curricula made more relevant. Hazardous, unhealthy and servile child labour must be ended and the conditions of children in legitimate employment improved. Child labour legislation needs to be strengthened and linked more closely to measures to improve access to educational opportunities.

In addition, cultural, ethnic, geographic, rural/urban, income and gender disparities need to be addressed. Measures must be taken to alleviate poverty and provide support for 'at risk' families. Better fiscal and labour market policies need to be developed, credit schemes devised and income-generating and community-development projects initiated. Baseline data must be collected, situation analyses carried out and programmes launched with better monitoring mechanisms in place.

To make these and other essential actions possible, resources must be identified, mobilized and used more efficiently than they have been in the past. It has to be recognized, of course, that all of these needs and rights cannot be fulfilled, or even addressed, everywhere and all at once. Planning for progressive achievement of goals over time, however, and for effective sequencing of essential interventions can start now — and has in fact in a number of countries.

The preceding chapters explore the implications of the major resource-related articles of the CRC. Chapters One and Two provide a framework for resource analysis. They focus specifically on the issues raised by Article 4, which commits States Parties to undertake measures to achieve "economic, social and cultural rights" to "the maximum extent of their available resources". The concern is that this clause may provide States Parties with an 'excuse' for less than satisfactory progress in meeting their obligations. Chapter Three considers implementation of the CRC, in relation particularly to the National Programmes of Action (NPAs) for Children adopted by countries as part of the commitments made at the World Summit for Children. Chapters Four through Seven examine the resources required for implementing children's rights to health (Article 24), nutrition (Articles 24.2 [c and e], and 27.3), education (Articles 28 and 29) and protection from economic exploitation (Article 32).

In this chapter, we will return to the initial resource framework and, from the analyses provided in the 'thematic' chapters, re-elaborate its principles and highlight some of the ways that have been identified to increase the resources available and used for children. After this synthesis, we will discuss the obligations that the CRC has created not just for States Parties but also for all sectors of civil society. A few observations concerning the need for an expanded, more flexible and more creative approach to child-related issues, including resources, conclude this chapter and this book.

■ 2. Understanding "Available Resources"

As discussed in Chapter One, Article 4 was included in the CRC because governments were concerned that, without this clause, they would be legally bound to satisfy standards of children's well-being that were beyond their means. It has been shown, however, that "available resources" should not be construed as meaning just economic resources or, even more narrowly, national-level, public-sector funding. Instead, economic, human and organizational resources exist at every level of society (see Table 1.1), and all will be needed to secure children's rights. Resources can also be viewed in terms of 'stocks' (that is, the assets and endowments that society has at its disposal to conserve or use for different purposes) and 'flows' (the actual expenditures or use of these resources) (see Table 2.1). In particular:

- *economic resources* include financial resources, natural resources, physical infrastructure, technology and information. Operationally, they take the form of direct expenditure, credit, interest and profit;
- *human resources* are people, their knowledge, experience, skills, motivation, aspirations, vision, commitment and energy. Human resources are tapped at every level of society to sustain child development;
- *organizational resources* include family structure, extended family support and child-care services; municipal arrangements for education, health, housing and juvenile justice; national laws and regulations; and international monitoring systems. They are exercised in practice through decisions, mobilization, management, regulation, monitoring and training.

In terms of child welfare, the resources available at the household and community levels are the most decisive. The economic resources households can dispose of, especially income, food, shelter and fuel, are essential for children's health and well-being. But economic resources are not the only determinant. Parker makes the important point that even when individuals, institutions or countries start out with similar levels of economic resources, their ultimate success depends largely on the types and amounts of human and organizational resources that are available and developed over time.

Children are most directly influenced by their parents. The health and education of parents (and especially mothers), the amount of time they have available, their beliefs, self-confidence and energy are all factors that condition the quality and quantity of care children receive. At the community level, human resources, such as the skills of teachers and primary health care workers as well as the management abilities and commitment of municipal leaders, affect child development. This chain of influence also extends to higher levels. In fact, the status of children in any given society depends in part on the management, leadership and political skills at provincial, national and international levels.

Recent studies have underscored the importance of organizational resources at the household and community levels. Research carried out on single-parent and migrant households, for instance, has linked inadequate child care to lack of access to extended family, kinship or community support. Formal institutions at the municipal, provincial/state levels also have a significant, although often underestimated, bearing not only on child welfare but also on the use of household resources. These institutions determine the quality of health, education and sanitation services available to households. Consequently, when service provision (say of safe water) is inadequate, members of impoverished households can either do without (with negative consequences on their health, nutrition and income-generating possibilities); or they can expend time, energy or money to procure the needed service (in this case, by fetching water from often-distant free sources or paying exorbitant prices to private vendors).

Organizational resources at the national and international levels must also be considered. National policies influence provincial and municipal arrangements and resources. Moreover, national legislation and other actions affect the fulfilment of children's rights through both sanctions (against the illegal employment of children, for example) and incentives (such as free lunch for schoolchildren or subsidies for maternal and child health care). International human rights conventions can inspire national legislation; and monitoring by multilateral organizations and international non-governmental organizations can encourage governments to modify their policies in favour of children.

Parker reminds us that resources can be consumed, degrade or depreciate over time and must be closely monitored to ensure that sufficient endowments remain to support action in the future. This concept is quite clear with regard to economic resources. Obviously, household income is spent and must be constantly replenished. Schools, hospitals and physical infrastructure in general depreciate over the years and need continual maintenance to be kept up to their original levels of efficiency. It is less commonly realized that human and organizational resources also undergo the same process. Thus, Parker points out that the energy some overburdened mothers in low-income families expend to ensure their families' survival is often so great that they eventually lose their overall effectiveness. Similarly, as highlighted by Boyden and Rialp, the health, motivation and aspirations of school pupils can be affected if, besides attending school, they are also required to spend excessive hours at work, including household chores. At the organizational level, the success of volunteer organizations largely depends on strong management, new recruitment and sustained financial support, generally from private sources.

Not only must flows be monitored, but also stocks must be strengthened if progress is to be achieved. Governments, for instance, must make long-term investments in infrastructure and conservation of natural resources. More importantly, they must direct efforts towards 'empowerment', defined by Jonsson as acquiring "power over one's own life, control of resources and choices". Education and training are the most effective social investment governments can make because of their significant 'multiplier effects'. Returns to individuals include higher incomes, lower fertility rates, improved health and coping skills and higher life-long productivity. From a wider perspective, Dall reminds us that increasing "people's capacity to accumulate knowledge, communicate information, and coordinate and organize themselves productively" has historically been the basis for the social and economic development of nations. However, he warns that education should not be viewed as a "social cure-all", citing evidence that children who have suffered the "combined physical and emotional blights of poverty" are unable to benefit fully from their right to education. This point is sustained by Jonsson who reports that better-nourished children (in other words, children who have had more access than others to food, care, health services and a healthy environment) are more likely to be better students.

Our understanding of "available resources", in short, needs to be significantly expanded, particularly to recognize more fully the importance for fulfilling children's rights of the vast 'stocks' of human and organizational resources available throughout societies, including at the community and household levels. A government 'service-oriented' approach to meeting the standards set by the CRC cannot possibly result in satisfactory fulfilment of those standards. At the same time, those international and national actors responsible for implementing and monitoring the CRC cannot afford to allow the States Parties, which are national governments, to hide behind this expanded concept of "available resources", and of the responsibilities of the broad civil society, to avoid providing the political leadership, the facilitating and capacity-building roles, as well as a minimum level of essential social services, without which it is meaningless to discuss basic human rights, let alone social justice. Governments clearly have a critical role to play in catalyzing and mobilizing a broad array of both traditional and non-traditional actors in society, whose efforts are essential for effective implementation of the CRC. It is to these essential actors that this concluding chapter now turns.

■ 3. Mobilizing Human and Organizational Resources

□ 3.1. 'TRADITIONAL' ACTORS

The 'traditional' organizational actors in children's rights issues are governments, non-governmental organizations (NGOs) and bilateral and multilateral organizations.

Parker discusses in detail the evolving and interactive roles of governments, NGOs and the private sector in the financing, provision and management (or in some cases, mismanagement) of essential services such as basic education, preventive and public health, water supply and sanitation services. He identifies three models that have dominated the economic organization of services for children in developing countries in recent decades:

(a) strong central government involvement with gap-filling by the private system in the 1970s;
(b) cut-backs in government action, dictated by the economic decline and the structural adjustment programmes of the 1980s, and an expansion of the role of the private sector; and
(c) an emerging model stressing greater NGO and private provision of services, with government taking responsibility for satisfying minimum needs, providing information and management support, enforcing minimum standards and facilitating decentralization.

Besides providing services, NGOs have tended to be in the forefront of the children's rights movement and have often goaded governments into taking action on behalf of children. They also have a 'facilitating' role. The Jamkhed Rural Health Project in Maharashtra, India, for instance, has over the past 25 years promoted a community-centred approach to meeting the needs of a population that had long been poorly served by government services, by closely involving households in health matters, supporting necessary education and in other ways broadening the understanding of and response to health concerns beyond purely 'service delivery'.[2] Boyden and Rialp cite the *Projecto Axé* in Salvador, Brazil, which sponsors children while they attend school and offers them an opportunity to earn money in micro-enterprises initiated by the project.

Dall discusses a number of NGOs that have pioneered methods for empowering hard-to-reach populations, particularly girls. BRAC in Bangladesh, for example, provides part-time employment and training for married women with at least nine years of schooling who, especially in small villages, would be unlikely to find other appropriate work. These paraprofessionals serve as effective role models for the predominately female students. Parents in each community supply the school building and actively participate in the school's administration by selecting teachers, helping to design curricula and scheduling classes to accommodate children's work. The community-run and -financed *Escuelas Mayas* in Guatemala, which offer a Mayan curriculum alongside the state-approved one, have made similar arrangements. A third project, *Tostan* in Senegal, teaches students leadership, resource management and problem-solving skills that will help them bring about changes in their villages.

NGOs have increasingly joined together in networks and entered into partnerships with government. Boyden and Rialp emphasize that this is a pragmatic choice: serious NGOs have found that by uniting with others, they can extend coverage, achieve greater sustainability and provide services more efficiently. Several countries have formalized government/NGO collaboration. In Brazil, for example, government and organizations of civil society have parity representation in the Councils for Child and Adolescent Rights. In the Philippines, government and non-government bodies have formed an inter-agency task force for the protection of exploited children. NGOs concerned with child rights come together at the international level in various ways, including through the NGO Group of the Convention on the Rights of the Child, which serves as a bridge between NGO groups worldwide and the Committee on the Rights of the Child.

Bilateral and multilateral agencies form the third 'traditional' group of institutions active on children's issues that relate closely to the challenge of implementing the CRC. They carry out a number of critical functions, some of which are not always well planned and managed. Dall points out that innovative alternatives to formal education must often be financed by donors, as governments are normally wary of straying from the known path of formal education. He also stresses the role that organizations such as the World Bank and UNICEF have had in establishing priorities, and in particular in placing basic education high on policy makers' agendas. Furthermore, international organizations, and particularly the United Nations Centre for Human Rights, the United Nations Educational, Scientific and Cultural Organization (UNESCO), the International Labour Organisation (ILO), the World Health Organization (WHO) and UNICEF, create monitoring mechanisms, carry out and sponsor research, collect and disseminate information, promote awareness, network among various actors and provide technical assistance to governments on specialized facets of children's rights.

The energy and commitment of the international community as a whole is evidenced by the many human rights instruments that have been framed and ratified over the years, laying the foundation for the Convention on the Rights of the Child.

□ 3.2. 'NON-TRADITIONAL' ACTORS

The mobilization of groups and individuals not 'traditionally' involved in service provision or rights issues represents a significant trend in developing countries today and is the basis on which sustainable progress must rest.

From the vantage point of governments or NGOs, the involvement of non-traditional actors represents a savings and enables a far greater coverage than is possible using normal channels. One notable example is the highly successful Expanded Programme on Immunization (EPI). Teachers, businesses, the media, religious and social groups and communities in many developing countries actively supported both facility-based services and immunization campaigns. Many of these volunteers later became involved in the wider issues of children's rights. Likewise, child labour has been successfully combated in specific cases with the help of such non-traditional — and even improbable — partners as the employers and parents of the child labourers themselves. Sustainability is also enhanced by community 'ownership' of specific projects or even of broader public programmes.

From the perspective of the individuals themselves, the advantages of participation can be high, including, importantly, the satisfaction of contributing to, and benefiting from, improvements in the community. Participation is, as Jonsson recognizes, both a "means to empower" and a principal "outcome of empowerment". Volunteer and semi-volunteer activities can enhance individual status and, for women in particular, often represent a socially acceptable way of participating more fully in the life of the community. Moreover, these activities can open up opportunities for self-improvement. Dall, for example, describes community learning centres that offer teacher-facilitators credits towards further vocational training in addition to a small stipend. He also points out that community participation in the management and improvement of schools is an important way of reducing gender disparities in education.

It is mistaken, however, as discussed in Chapter One, to expect low-income and overburdened families to dedicate large shares of their time and energy to voluntary or semi-voluntary activities. Community volunteers, in fact, have high rates of attrition and are usually best used for short-term activities. The effective development of non-traditional responses to problems requires careful planning, new organizational arrangements and, above all, considerable lead time, particularly when training is involved.

The media are an especially valuable 'non-traditional' partner in children's rights issues. Two billion radios, 900 million television sets, 9,000 daily newspapers now keep populations in every area of the developing world informed and are essential for sustaining strategies of social mobilization.[3] The goals for children in the 1990s endorsed at the 1990 World Summit for Children explicitly recognize the media's role, along with that of other educational channels, in making "knowledge, skills and values required for better living" available to individuals and families. Education and health campaigns gain much of their momentum from media coverage. Boyden and Rialp have noted that investigative journalism and reporting of violations in the media are often effective in preventing child labour abuses. The media have also been employed to embarrass governments and others into action. And, as Ledogar points out, videos and newspaper clippings are permanent and easily retrievable records that can force politicians to be careful about what they promise.

Not all of the media's influence is positive, however. Parker and Sepúlveda, for instance, discuss the tendency of the media to emphasize "overly 'medical', curative and commodity-based solutions to health problems", which run counter to the tenets of primary health care. The media are often also seen as being responsible variously for intensifying frustrations among the poor by exalting material values; creating stereotypes and fuelling intolerance; and undermining ethnic, cultural and familial traditions.

Perhaps the least-traditional 'actors' of all are children, until recently thought of mainly as being 'beneficiaries' who are not able to reflect on their situations or to make decisions for improving it. A major point made by the CRC, and a much-needed one in many societies, is that children have a right to be consulted in matters that affect them (Article 12). Research has shown that children can make useful contributions to child-related initiatives. Dall relates, for instance, that prior to the 1990 World Conference on Education for All in Jomtien, Thailand, surveys were carried out in many countries asking pupils (as well as teachers, parents and educators) how best to solve education problems in their contexts. This 'grass-roots' input influenced the final conference declaration and framework for action. Boyden and Rialp underscore children's potential roles as 'agents of social change' and cite instances when children have served as monitors, participated in analyses of labour situations or carried out advocacy. There is, nonetheless, a risk of 'trivializing' participation or even instrumentalizing children. The validity of children's participation depends on "the age and maturity of the child" and her or his "evolving capacities" (to cite the language of Articles 12 and 14 of the CRC). Key elements of valid participation relating to civic preparedness include literacy, awareness of responsibilities as well as rights, and access to "information and ideas of all kinds", as specified in Article 13. Much greater effort is needed in these areas to empower children to be effective actors in matters that affect them.

■ 4. Making More Resources Available for Children

It has been seen that a number of strategies are available to governments, communities and households for increasing resources in support of children's rights:

The total amount of revenues can be increased. In his review of NPAs, Ledogar lists some of the many ways governments have found to draw upon private-sector resources to increase the domestic revenues available for the fulfilment of children's rights. Measures include social taxes on luxury imports, taxes on tobacco and alcohol, levies on tourists, national lotteries and proceeds from privatization. In addition, tax benefits have been offered to private enterprise in exchange for support to public schools. Ledogar finds, however, that very few NPAs assess what the resource requirements are at the level of households and communities. A rights-oriented approach to the NPA process, especially for subnational planning, could help fill that gap.

Cost-recovery mechanisms have also been established, although these measures remain controversial. Critics find that user fees for education and health services are usually regressive, inequitable, administratively inefficient, and rarely 'voluntary', even if so specified. On the other hand, it has been suggested that users may actually be spending less for 'paid' services under well-run programmes than they had to pay previously to private providers when public services were underfunded. Graduated fees according to income may be one solution in some countries. However, no entirely reliable waiver system (at least in developing countries) has been devised to exclude the very poor from payment.

Impoverished families often must devote an inordinate portion of their time simply to ensuring that they can have an adequate level of income to meet their basic needs. One of their short-term solutions is to deploy children in income-generating activities. As discussed by Boyden and Rialp, these strategies can include paid work outside the household; unpaid work in family enterprises; and child care and household chores, often not even recognized as work, that free other household members for gainful employment. In certain situations, such work may ensure the child's right to survival, yet at the same time compromising his or her right to education, leisure and even health. Families that take longer-term actions, in contrast, invest in educating their children in the hopes of increasing their future worth on the job market.

Budgets can be restructured in favour of human development priorities. Child rights advocates are pressing governments to shift allocations *between* sectors, and more precisely from defense and public works (sectors protected by powerful vested interests) to health care, education and social services (sectors that mainly favour the poor). It is estimated that military spending in the developing world during the 1980s almost equalled its expenditures on education and health combined, and was three times more than the amount received in aid.[4] Dall observes that for the cost of one nuclear submarine, Africa's primary school system could be revitalized. These are sobering thoughts indeed.

Pressure is also being applied to governments to make careful choices *within* sectors in order to favour 'human development priorities' — primary health care, basic education, nutrition support for high-risk families, rural and peri-urban water and sanitation, and family planning. The main argument for this restructuring is again equity. Low-cost and basic social services can reach the population as a whole and especially the families and children most in need. In contrast, expenditures, say, in higher levels of education and health care and in costly water supply and sanitation systems, often preferred for reasons of prestige and catering to élites, overwhelmingly benefit the wealthiest segments of the population.

Expenditure patterns can be blatantly distorted. There is a markedly inequitable distribution of health services in the United States, where, although the government spends 14 per cent of GNP on health, large segments of the population have no health insurance coverage or live in 'medically underserved' regions. Similarly, in Indonesia, according to UNICEF's *State of the World's Children 1995* report, the government spends three times more on the health of the richest 10 per cent of the population than it does on the poorest 10 per cent; in Asia, governments typically spend 50 per cent of their education budgets on the best-educated 10 per cent. This UNICEF report then states "the obvious", that such distortions are not accidental:

> The poor remain poor principally because they are underrepresented in political and economic decisions, because their voice is not sufficiently loud in the selection of society's priorities, and because their needs do not weigh sufficiently heavily in the allocation of public resources.[5]

It is not only vested interests that are a problem but also what this report terms 'asynchronism' or the 'pain now, gain later' syndrome: most measures to improve the lot of the poor will incur costs in the present but will not yield benefits immediately, and certainly not within the short time-frame of the terms of office of elected policy makers.

Budget restructuring thus involves not only ethical concerns, including inter-generational equity, but also complex strategical and political considerations. Boyden and Rialp, for instance, pose the question of whether child labour is best combated by intensifying investments in
(a) the labour sector, to enable better enforcement of child labour legislation and the adoption of measures protecting workers' rights;
(b) the welfare sector, to intensify poverty alleviation measures; or
(c) the education sector, to improve access to primary education and enforce compulsory education legislation.

Dall points out that education has only recently begun to receive the resources it has needed because health, shelter and food were even higher priorities for survival. Similarly, Jonsson observes that governments have generally marginalized 'nutrition', subsuming it under the health sector where it has been accorded vastly insufficient resources. The reason for this low priority has been government unwillingness to make the "substantial structural changes" required to address the "basically social and political" causes of malnutrition.

Budget restructuring is also required at the international level. Globally, it is estimated that only some 10 per cent of bilateral and multilateral assistance is currently dedicated to basic human needs, compared with roughly 13 per cent of central government expenditure. One innovative approach, known as the 20/20 initiative, has proposed that this share be increased to 20 per cent on both sides as a basic benchmark for meeting social-sector needs. Proponents of this initiative argue that if the formula is respected, it should be possible to satisfy minimum priority requirements in most countries, and to prepare the ground for longer-term measures to be undertaken.

Public opinion polls have shown that most people in industrialized countries favour spending aid in support of the poor. However, because of the "interlocking nature of vested interests in both donor and recipient countries", it is difficult to change the targeting of aid, especially when new priorities could result in a reduction of overseas contracts for major companies in industrialized nations or the shrinking of profitable export markets.[6]

Budgeting of resources at the household and community levels is again a political exercise. In most societies in the developing world, men control resources. This situation can have negative consequences on child welfare because women generally have the main responsibility for child-rearing and are more likely than men to allocate resources for food or in other ways that are beneficial to children. Household budgets therefore may need to be restructured on a more equitable basis. Like government budgets, household budgets can be shifted in favour of basic human needs. Financial resources can be freed for food, education and other basic needs by limiting or eliminating expenditures on, say, cigarettes, alcohol and other non-essential goods, and social events and ceremonies (for which debt is often incurred). Similarly, more time and attention can be dedicated to children if both parents take an active part in child-rearing and spend less time in non-productive activities.

Debt can be reduced. The total debt of developing nations has increased thirteen-fold during the past two decades, causing a formidable drain on developing nations' economies and a net flow of capital towards industrialized nations and their financial institutions. The cost of debt has been assigned a principal role in the deterioration of economic conditions in Latin America during the 1980s. In Africa and more particularly sub-Saharan Africa, debt reaches world records and is so overwhelming that, according to a recent UNICEF publication,[7] it "defeats development". Africa manages to repay $10 billion a year, which is only about one third of what it owes in capital and interest on loans. For significantly less ($9 billion a year), the continent could meet all its basic health, nutrition, education and family planning goals. Debt cancellation and reduction, combined with a strengthening of Africa's trading position and cuts in military spending, are the most feasible solutions for this problem.

Technologies and processes can be made more efficient. Efficiency can be augmented by substituting, where possible, less expensive resources or technologies for costlier ones; using resources to their fullest, including through recycling; eliminating waste; and taking preventive action to avoid or limit damage. For instance, networks of auxiliary nurses or paramedics can relieve doctors from the routine, less demanding aspects of their work, permitting them to treat a greater number of patients. Lower-cost facilities can be substituted for more expensive ones and can be used for multiple purposes. Existing structures can be revitalized instead of replaced. Locally available supplies can often be used instead of imported ones. Generic drugs can be substituted for branded ones. Breastfeeding can be promoted and measures taken against the marketing of breastmilk substitutes. Preventive health care can be emphasized, eliminating some of the need for more expensive curative care.

Dall discusses cost savings generated in the education sector by using resources to their fullest. Measures include introducing double shifts; increasing class size; and making greater use of self-study, teaching assistants, parents and other community helpers. He suggests, moreover, that in developing countries it may be expedient to replace the formal, classroom-centred models imported from the West — and now proving, sometimes even there, to be too costly to maintain — with less conventional models such as mobile facilities and tents.

Parker and Sepúlveda identify efforts to increase the amount of time available to women as being a decisive factor in the economic position of households. Labour-saving technologies such as fuel-conserving cooking stoves and better access to essential services (by locating hand-pumps near villages, for example) give women more time for child care and income-generating activities. A problem identified by Parker is that more-efficient methods made possible by new technologies may exist, but are often not widely known. Dissemination of information about lower-cost technologies and approaches is therefore essential. The inroads made against polio and diarrhoeal diseases in the last decades are due in large part to the efforts made to increase knowledge about vaccines and oral rehydration therapy.

Attention can be focused on critical inputs. Critical inputs are 'missing links' that constrain the level of output regardless of the availability of other inputs. Examples are the reduced ability of teachers to teach because they lack books and paper, or of health workers to care for the sick because they lack drugs and dressings. A lack of political leadership and commitment is often the main cause of inaction. Dall, for instance, blames political neglect for the failure of primary schools in Africa to function effectively. Jonsson explains how the absence of any one of the prerequisites for adequate child nutrition (access to food, care, basic health services and a healthy environment) can compromise a child's well-being. Boyden and Rialp identify "lack of information and concern" about child labour at all levels of government as one of the reasons the problem persists; they also emphasize that legislation without adequate resources for its enforcement is "pointless".

It is often possible through strategic planning, as described by Ledogar, to obtain the missing element that initially prevents goals from being realized. The principal way of accomplishing this is by enlisting the support of other forces and actors that have a 'stake' in the final outcome of the action.

Some actions can be privatized. As Parker has outlined, because of the decline of public economic resources, there is a growing trend worldwide to rely on the private and NGO sectors for the provision of basic goods and services once thought to be exclusively the domain of governments. In some instances, governments become the purchasers rather than the providers of services. For example, the private sector is increasingly responsible for the procurement of equipment and supplies needed for public hospitals or schools, for the construction of public facilities and for supplementing public water and sanitation services. In other cases, the private sector offsets deficiencies in public services. Thus, in most developing countries, NGOs have set up non-formal schools and shelters for marginalized children, and private corporations are running schools and hospitals for the better-off.

Privatization relieves governments of the burden of providing services to individuals who are able to pay for them. As a result, governments can theoretically dedicate themselves to providing broadly based services (primary education and public health care), serving as 'providers of last resort' for hard-to-serve populations and acting as regulatory agents. Parker and Sepúlveda emphasize that market mechanisms can enhance the quality of services because individuals will only use or pay for what satisfies their needs. At the same time, particularly in the case of health treatment, consumers may not be sufficiently knowledgeable to distinguish between adequate and inadequate services.

Social disinvestment and privatization can reinforce social inequities. A reorganization of the national health service in Chile in 1980, for example, resulted in a two-track system: on the one side, inadequately funded and steadily deteriorating public hospitals, which attracted few of the best-qualified physicians and health workers, catered to the poor; and on the other side, ultramodern private hospitals offered high-quality health care to the élite. Although this reorganization permitted significant cutbacks in government spending on health, it meant that "health was no longer a right but a 'commodity'", and one that a growing number of Chilean families seriously affected by recession in the 1980s could ill afford.[8]

Action can be decentralized. As central governments retreat from many areas of economic and social development, and as more private actors participate in the provision of services, management responsibility and accountability has gradually devolved to subnational levels. In the social sectors particularly, the decentralization of budgetary authority and decision-making has often contributed to making both public and private services more responsive to user demands and needs. Parker and Sepúlveda stress that district-level governments have a number of key functions, including making national policy more locally specific, financing and implementing services, and linking community facilities with the national system. Especially in countries with large and dispersed populations or heterogeneous social groups, decentralization to subnational levels makes the management of national programmes significantly easier and responds to community pressures to have more say in the direction of their own affairs.[9] Boyden and Rialp discuss the importance of devolution of decisions relating to child labour because of the wide disparities in economic and social conditions among regions, different industrial bases, and different traditions and customs governing child work. Ideally, decentralization enhances 'ownership' of programmes at the local level and encourages community participation in the management of programmes and services. Decentralization, however, is no panacea, and in countries with a highly uneven distribution of wealth and resources, it can exacerbate inequities.

Donor aid can be tapped and better used. International assistance is much sought after and is often crucial for social development and humanitarian relief efforts, especially in very low-income developing countries. Parker and Sepúlveda have noted, however, that care must be taken to integrate donor-led interventions into a coherent national framework of policies and strategies. Donors in Africa, for example, have carried out a number of "vertical" programmes aimed at reducing disease-specific mortality, which have often not strengthened health infrastructure at the local level. Some of these programmes falter as aid resources are withdrawn, not only because communities are unable to sustain operating costs, but also because they lack the technical expertise and the commitment to continue providing services previously sponsored. Many governments as well as donors are now placing less emphasis on capital-intensive, highly technological interventions, preferring to rely on, where possible, simple, inexpensive techniques that can be maintained by the community.

Many pressures are being placed on donor aid, not least of which, according to Dall, are the new nations that have emerged since the fall of former socialist regimes. For the most part these nations need reconstruction and are not yet self-sustaining. They therefore compete with the least-developed nations for available aid funds. International aid resources are also increasingly being drained to meet man-made and natural emergencies.

On the supply side, Ledogar warns that increases in international assistance are unlikely, given the current economic and political situation in most industrialized countries. Very few industrialized nations have, in fact, fulfilled their longstanding commitment to devote at least 0.7 per cent of GNP to external aid.

■ 5. Managing the Realization of Rights

In Chapter One, a four-point planning strategy for achieving children's rights is outlined consisting of situation analysis, goal setting, plans and programmes of action, and monitoring compliance and enforcement (Section 4.4). Jonsson describes a similar management tool, the cyclical and iterative 'Triple-A process', whose phases include assessment of the situation, analysis of the causes of the problem, design and implementation of resource-relevant actions, followed by re-assessment, re-analysis and better action.

Situation analysis is needed to identify as clearly as possible the problems that must be addressed and to form the basis for sustained monitoring of the fulfilment of children's rights. For projects at the community level, community representatives, households and children should be involved in this process. On the national level, what the United Nations Development Programme (UNDP) has called a "human development profile" could be developed, and it should have a strong focus on children and youth.

Goal setting, or "identifying and costing human development targets", is the second necessary step. Many rights must be achieved only progressively, as recognized in both the health and education provisions of the CRC. This approach can be supported by setting time-bound and verifiable targets. Priorities must be chosen for action, a sequencing strategy devised and resources concentrated where they are most needed.

It has been shown that careful targeting can limit unwanted dispersal and increase the cost-effectiveness of actions. One example, cited by Boyden and Rialp, is the recent trend to direct short-term efforts to removing children from specific hazardous and exploitative activities rather than instituting major programmes across the board prohibiting all child work, including some types that may actually promote children's immediate welfare, education and development. Jonsson underlines the short- and long-term efficacy of health programmes targeting diseases that can easily be prevented using low-cost methods (for instance, salt iodization to control iodine deficiency disorders). Similarly, Parker and Sepúlveda discuss the 'child survival and development' strategy (growth monitoring, oral rehydration therapy for diarrhoea, breastfeeding and immunization), four cost-effective interventions which can be linked to other initiatives, such as targeted food supplementation, female literacy and family planning, as critical *and affordable* initial priorities on which primary health care programmes could be concentrated to achieve immediate gains for children.

Costing human development targets for effective planning is complex, but should not be overly 'mystified'. Jonsson shows that projects that have simple goals (the eradication of measles or the provision of food) and tackle the immediate causes of malnutrition (disease or inadequate dietary intake) are fairly straightforward to cost. Basic data, in fact, are available worldwide on the per capita cost of measles immunization. Difficulties in costing arise when projects have more general goals (for instance, the reduction of protein-energy malnutrition) that require tackling not only immediate causes of malnutrition but also underlying and basic causes (lack of household food security and unsatisfactory feeding practices, inadequate education and inequitable control and distribution of resources). To achieve the specific objective of reducing protein-energy malnutrition, many different measures must be taken, and these measures have both obvious and hidden costs.

For example, apart from direct costs (salaries, equipment, buildings and maintenance), a project may have indirect costs (say, transportation costs paid by beneficiaries). In addition, opportunity costs may be involved. For instance, technical experts may be temporarily re-assigned to the project from other work, which in turn may suffer costly delays. These costs must be set against the long-term gains reasonably expected to accrue from the experts' interventions.

The same principles apply to NPAs. When countries define a broad goal, such as the elimination of child labour, they must, as stated in Chapter One, take into account the resource implications of "legislative, administrative, judicial, regulatory and other measures at all levels of government, needed to achieve the goals or attain the standards" agreed upon. As part of the process of setting priorities, the cost of *not* tackling a specific problem should also be estimated, however roughly.

Ledogar reports that thus far about 60 countries have included cost estimates of programmes in their NPAs and have identified the resources that are available nationally. This is one way of "laying an early claim" to foreign aid, and it is also a good indicator of the progress that is likely to be achieved should external support not be forthcoming.

Plans and programmes of action vary according to country. The World Summit Plan of Action gives a general framework of what NPAs should contain. Each NPA, to quote Ledogar, "sets goals for the decade, outlines the principal strategies and programmes for achieving them, defines institutional responsibilities, examines the costs of individual programmes and ways of financing them, and establishes indicators and mechanisms for monitoring progress towards the goals".

Monitoring mechanisms need to be both public and non-governmental. Ledogar describes some of the plans countries have outlined in NPAs for official monitoring systems. Some countries have created new organizational resources for monitoring children's rights, such as national councils, standing committees, and ombudsmen. Others are carrying out nationwide household surveys as well as specific studies on the situation of children in difficult circumstances. Many child rights advocates fear, however, that in the case of such politically sensitive issues as sexually exploited children, juvenile offenders, child labourers and child soldiers, monitoring is likely to be weakest in those countries where abuses are greatest.

Information is the "critical input" throughout this management process. Improved baseline data on nutrition, education, health and child development —especially when disaggregated by gender, age, region and income or ethnic groups — are the starting point for establishing programme objectives and realistic target dates. Moreover, only if such information exists can progress in meeting goals be measured. Information and reporting systems, however, as Parker states, are "traditionally weak ... reinforcing a lack of knowledge about actual needs and service availability, and a lack of accountability of providers and officials to the populations served". As more people have become involved in child rights issues, the demand for information has increased, which in turn has created a pressing need for the establishment of more efficient monitoring and information systems. Technological developments in recent years offer exciting new opportunities for establishing cost-effective and widely accessible child rights information systems based on increasingly affordable and portable computers and specially designed software packages.

■ 6. Meeting "Minimum Core Obligations"

Different forms of government and social organization lead to different systems for controlling and distributing resources. In most socialist regimes, central planning and strong government control of the economy have prevailed. In market economies, instead, market forces are relied upon, in varying degrees, to organize and distribute goods and services. Because markets often favour the wealthy and powerful, however, they can lead to (or worsen) a highly uneven distribution of resources among the population, a situation that democratic governments have obligations — and will eventually face strong pressures — to correct.

An assumption is often made that responsible national governments tend to ensure the most equitable, although not necessarily the most efficient, provision of social benefits, services or entitlements. As argued in Chapter One, though, much depends on whether a specific State has a strong redistributive or equity-oriented mandate in terms of the distribution of both benefits and costs. The degree to which governments, and especially States Parties to the CRC, are required to safeguard vulnerable segments of the population, including children, is the second main issue discussed in this chapter.

Phrases that could be viewed as 'escape clauses' are nearly always attached to the resource-related provisions of the CRC. The "maximum extent" qualifier in Article 4 is echoed in Article 27, which commits States to take measures "within their means" to ensure that children have an "ade-

quate" standard of living. Similarly, Article 23 provides for free services for disabled children "whenever possible". Moreover, the various measures set out in the CRC are invariably qualified by such highly subjective words as "appropriate", "effective" and "feasible". As has been analysed at length in Chapter One, however, a number of principles limiting the discretionary power of States Parties in this respect have been established through analogies with other international treaties, particularly the International Covenant on Economic, Social and Cultural Rights. More specifically, it can be said that States Parties to the CRC are committed, regardless of resource constraints:
(a) to meet a number of *"minimum core obligations"*;
(b) to devise strategies and mobilize all possible resources to fulfil these obligations "as a matter of priority";
(c) to monitor both the realization and the "non-realization" of rights; and
(d) to respond to queries by the Committee on the Rights of the Child concerning efforts made to implement the CRC.

In 1990, the heads of state and other senior officials of the over 150 countries represented at the World Summit for Children collectively decided, in political terms, what many of these "minimum core obligations" should be — at least for the current decade. Nearly all of these countries have now begun to give their own interpretations to the Summit's Plan of Action, defining their goals in NPAs, and in some cases subnational programmes of action.

The State's obligations for implementing children's rights can also be analysed in broader terms (refer to Tables 1.2 and 5.6). Governmental authorities, from the community to the international level, should *respect, protect, facilitate and fulfil* children's rights. It has been seen that "States must respect the freedom of individuals to take necessary actions and use the necessary resources ... to facilitate the fulfilment of their needs"; that they "also must protect individual freedom of action and use of resources", for instance against fraud, or unethical marketing practices.[10] The obligation to fulfil here is used more narrowly to signify the direct provision of services. The obligation to facilitate instead is used in the sense of providing 'opportunities'.

Many advocates for children place great importance on the facilitating role. Opportunities, as defined by Parker, are changes in the political, technical or social context enabling human and organizational resources to be used more fully to their potential. There are many opportunity-enhancing or empowerment strategies that governments can (and should) carry out. Community- or district-level governments should, for instance, open up credit and cooperative initiatives to women. They should facilitate community analyses of protein-energy malnutrition. National-level governments should, Ledogar suggests, involve a broad spectrum of civil society in the NPA process.

A central issue in the discussion of States' obligations is that, in theory, States Parties alone are legally bound to implement the CRC. In practice, however, the CRC cannot be implemented without the full mobilization of all sectors of civil society. The question, then, is: What are the obligations of civil society? Article 5 of the CRC recognizes the "responsibilities, rights and duties of parents ... the extended family or community". Article 18 states that "parents ... have the primary responsibility for the upbringing and development of the child". Clearly, therefore, as argued in Chapter One, from the perspective of development planning and practice, if not from a strictly legal perspective, 'obligations' must be broadly defined to include families, households, communities, the private sector and other participants in the 'civil society' as well as all levels of government.

The soundness of this argument is in a sense illustrated by the ease with which the framework for the analysis of obligations can be applied to civil society. It can, for example, be agreed that, at the household level, *parents* should respect the rights of their daughters and sons equally, including in terms of access to educational opportunities; protect children from abuse and exploitation; facilitate individual growth by allowing children to express their views freely and participate in decisions that affect them; and ensure that children are adequately nourished, protected from health hazards and educated.

At the community and national levels, there are many possible types of non-governmental actors. Boyden and Rialp cite a document prepared by the NGO Group on the Convention on the Rights of the Child specifying what NGOs, community groups and individuals *can* do to protect children from exploitation (Section 8.4). Building on that document, we can cite several examples of what a few of these actors *should* do.

Teachers should respect students and their parents without discrimination; protect students from peer intolerance and abuse; empower children by providing in-class opportunities for discussion and encouraging the free expression of ideas; and ensure that students are taught what they need to know to function well in the societies they live in, including civic values. *Journalists* should respect children by not endangering their reputations or exploiting their circumstances commercially; protect children by mobilizing public opinion against their exploitation or abuse; empower children not only by preparing articles for children about children's rights, but also by participating in educational activities aimed at developing children's skills in expressing their views; and monitor the situation of child labourers, juvenile offenders and other particularly disadvantaged groups. *NGOs* at all levels should work to ensure that children's rights are respected and protected, by governments but also by employers, parents, journalists, and others; facilitate the realization of rights by joining children in organizing children's conferences and other mechanisms for information exchange; and develop innovative strategies for the provision of services, with more family and community participation than often characterizes government programmes.

■ 7. Expanding Perspectives

One of the recurring themes in this book is that concepts commonly used in 'development' contexts need to be interpreted in a much wider sense than they have been if they are to be useful for the promotion and protection of children's rights. We have stressed that the reference to "available resources" in Article 4 of the CRC should not be viewed as a synonym for 'public funds'. 'Health' is more than just physical well-being or the provision of medical services. 'Nutrition' means more than just 'food'. 'Schooling' does not always have to take place in school. 'Children's work' is not always waged labour, and it is not always harmful.

This insistence on expanded meanings has an explanation. Using words narrowly is often symptomatic of what Dall has labelled 'bureaucratic blindness' — that is, rigid thinking, preconceptions and prejudices that have their roots both in a lack of information and, more importantly, in a lack of appreciation for the full meaning of 'human development'. These attitudes have misdirected many social development policies in the past and continue to do so today.

If 'resources' are construed as meaning public funds only, then a lack of resources can be used as a justification for what is actually a lack of political will. The resources required to fulfil children's rights are instead not just public; and they are not just economic and financial, as the many overly ambitious development projects in the past have demonstrated. Human and organizational resources are also required, including governmental, non-governmental and 'non-traditional' resources.

If children's 'health' is only a matter of their physical well-being, then the interventions needed will be mainly medical ones. But health is also mental and social well-being, and sustaining health requires interventions at many levels. Especially important is the strengthening — through information, education and institution-building — of individuals' and communities' capacities to protect and promote their own health, enabling them to become active participants in the quest for better health rather than just passive recipients of services.

If 'nutrition' is equated solely with food intake, feeding programmes will be considered the only strategies needed for combating malnutrition. Instead, it has been shown that to achieve satisfactory nutritional status, children must have access not only to food, but also to adequate care, especially in the family; appropriate health services; and a healthy environment. Far-sighted social, economic and political measures are needed to ensure that these conditions are met.

If 'schooling' means simply the teaching of academic subjects in classrooms, policy makers can feel that they have carried out their responsibilities adequately when they have strengthened scholastic infrastructure. However, the problem is much more complex as the growing numbers of 'schooled illiterates' in industrialized countries attest. "Reaching" — in the sense of providing access to schools and affecting individuals intellectually — "the small groups of traditionally marginalized children and adults wishing to receive basic education", Dall warns, "will take a special kind of determination and a sort of creativity not often displayed by Ministries of Education".

If 'child labour' is considered solely in terms of waged labour in the formal sector, then policy makers in developing countries can reasonably attempt to combat it by, to quote Boyden and Rialp, "simply passing labour laws, introducing enforcement mechanisms and providing basic facilities for education". Instead, the majority of child workers in developing countries work in the vast informal sector; or they work at home, where the time and energy they dedicate to household chores or care of siblings is not considered work at all. In either case, these child workers are for the most part beyond the reach of the law, and many are prevented by their work from attending school. Interventions preventing and abolishing child labour require, the authors reiterate, "new institutional arrangements and new alliances linking government and civil society". Strategies need to "promote child welfare and protection through attitudinal and behavioural change, equity, social justice and public-sector provision rather than mere law enforcement".

Finally, if the "obligations" created by the CRC are only binding on States Parties, then the 'problem' of children's rights is a challenge that primarily governments will have to deal with, largely through legislation and 'enforcement'. At best, legislation represents a sincere attempt by government to address issues of children's rights and well-being, and is followed by a corresponding allocation of resources. At worst, legislative actions are nothing more than cynical expressions of intentions covering up inaction. Instead, as every chapter in this book has sustained, a broader definition of "obligations", encompassing all sectors of civil society, is the only possible basis for the realization of a better future for all of our children. Only when governments succeed in providing the political leadership to guide and inspire the civil society will they have met their most fundamental obligation for the fulfilment of children's rights.

Notes

1 United Nations Children Fund, 1994a.
2 Arole and Arole, forthcoming.
3 United Nations Children's Fund, 1995.
4 Ibid.
5 Ibid, pp. 85-86.
6 Ibid.
7 United Nations Children's Fund, 1994b.
8 Sepúlveda, 1994.
9 Castillo and Akehurst, 1994.
10 Eide, Oshaug and Eide, 1991.

Main resource-related provisions of the Convention on the Rights of the Child

■ Article 2

1. States Parties shall respect and ensure the rights set forth in the present Convention to each child within their jurisdiction without discrimination of any kind, irrespective of the child's or his or her parent's or legal guardian's race, colour, sex, language, religion, political or other opinion, national, ethnic or social origin, property, disability, birth or other status.
2. States Parties shall take all appropriate measures to ensure that the child is protected against all forms of discrimination or punishment on the basis of the status, activities, expressed opinions, or beliefs of the child's parents, legal guardians, or family members.

■ Article 4

States Parties shall undertake all appropriate legislative, administrative, and other measures for the implementation of the rights recognized in the present Convention. With regard to economic, social and cultural rights, States Parties shall undertake such measures to the maximum extent of their available resources and, where needed, within the framework of international co-operation.

■ Article 23

1. States Parties recognize that a mentally or physically disabled child should enjoy a full and decent life, in conditions which ensure dignity, promote self-reliance and facilitate the child's active participation in the community.
2. States Parties recognize the right of the disabled child to special care and shall encourage and ensure the extension, subject to available resources, to the eligible child and those responsible for his or her care, of assistance for which application is made and which is appropriate to the child's condition and to the circumstances of the parents or others caring for the child.
3. Recognizing the special needs of a disabled child, assistance extended in accordance with paragraph 2 of the present article shall be provided free of charge, whenever possible, taking into account the financial resources of the parents or others caring for the child, and shall be designed to ensure that the disabled child has effective access to and receives education, training, health care services, rehabilitation services, preparation for employment and recreation opportunities in a manner conducive to the child's achieving the fullest possible social integration and individual development, including his or her cultural and spiritual development.

4. States Parties shall promote, in the spirit of international co-operation, the exchange of appropriate information in the field of preventive health care and medical, psychological and functional treatment of disabled children, including dissemination of and access to information concerning methods of rehabilitation, education and vocational services, with the aim of enabling States Parties to improve their capabilities and skills and to widen their experience in these areas. In this regard, particular account shall be taken of the needs of developing countries.

■ Article 24

1. States Parties recognize the right of the child to the enjoyment of the highest attainable standard of health and to facilities for the treatment of illness and rehabilitation of health. States Parties shall strive to ensure that no child is deprived of his or her right of access to such health care services.
2. States Parties shall pursue full implementation of this right and, in particular, shall take appropriate measures:
(a) To diminish infant and child mortality;
(b) To ensure the provision of necessary medical assistance and health care to all children with emphasis on the development of primary health care;
(c) To combat disease and malnutrition, including within the framework of primary health care, through, *inter alia*, the application of readily available technology and through the provision of adequate nutritious foods and clean drinking-water, taking into consideration the dangers and risks of environmental pollution;
(d) To ensure appropriate pre-natal and post-natal health care for mothers;
(e) To ensure that all segments of society, in particular parents and children, are informed, have access to education and are supported in the use of basic knowledge of child health and nutrition, the advantages of breast-feeding, hygiene and environmental sanitation and the prevention of accidents;
(f) To develop preventive health care, guidance for parents and family planning education and services.
3. States Parties shall take all effective and appropriate measures with a view to abolishing traditional practices prejudicial to the health of children.
4. States Parties undertake to promote and encourage international co-operation with a view to achieving progressively the full realization of the right recognized in the present article. In this regard, particular account shall be taken of the needs of developing countries.

■ Article 26

1. States Parties shall recognize for every child the right to benefit from social security, including social insurance, and shall take the necessary measures to achieve the full realization of this right in accordance with their national law.
2. The benefits should, where appropriate, be granted, taking into account the resources and the circumstances of the child and persons having responsibility for the maintenance of the child, as well as any other consideration relevant to an application for benefits made by or on behalf of the child.

■ Article 27

1. States Parties recognize the right of every child to a standard of living adequate for the child's physical, mental, spiritual, moral and social development.
2. The parent(s) or others responsible for the child have the primary responsibility to secure, within their abilities and financial capacities, the conditions of living necessary for the child's development.
3. States Parties, in accordance with national conditions and within their means, shall take appropriate measures to assist parents and others responsible for the child to implement this right and shall in case of need provide material assistance and support programmes, particularly with regard to nutrition, clothing and housing.
4. States Parties shall take all appropriate measures to secure the recovery of maintenance for the child from the parents or other persons having financial responsibility for the child, both within the State Party and from abroad. In particular, where the person having financial responsibility for the child lives in a State different from that of the child, States Parties shall promote the accession to international agreements or the conclusion of such agreements, as well as the making of other appropriate arrangements.

■ Article 28

1. States Parties recognize the right of the child to education, and with a view to achieving this right progressively and on the basis of equal opportunity, they shall, in particular:

(a) Make primary education compulsory and available free to all;
(b) Encourage the development of different forms of secondary education, including general and vocational education, make them available and accessible to every child, and take appropriate measures such as the introduction of free education and offering financial assistance in case of need;
(c) Make higher education accessible to all on the basis of capacity by every appropriate means;
(d) Make educational and vocational information and guidance available and accessible to all children;
(e) Take measures to encourage regular attendance at schools and the reduction of drop-out rates.
2. States Parties shall take all appropriate measures to ensure that school discipline is administered in a manner consistent with the child's human dignity and in conformity with the present Convention.
3. States Parties shall promote and encourage international co-operation in matters relating to education, in particular with a view to contributing to the elimination of ignorance and illiteracy throughout the world and facilitating access to scientific and technical knowledge and modern teaching methods. In this regard, particular account shall be taken of the needs of developing countries.

■ Article 29

1. States Parties agree that the education of the child shall be directed to:
(a) The development of the child's personality, talents and mental and physical abilities to their fullest potential;
(b) The development of respect for human rights and fundamental freedoms, and for the principles enshrined in the Charter of the United Nations;
(c) The development of respect for the child's parents, his or her own cultural identity, language and values, for the national values of the country in which the child is living, the country from which he or she may originate, and for civilizations different from his or her own;
(d) The preparation of the child for responsible life in a free society, in the spirit of understanding, peace, tolerance, equality of sexes, and friendship among all peoples, ethnic, national and religious groups and persons of indigenous origin;
(e) The development of respect for the natural environment.
2. No part of the present article or article 28 shall be construed so as to interfere with the liberty of individuals and bodies to establish and direct educational institutions, subject always to the observance of the principles set forth in paragraph 1 of the present article and to the requirements that the education given in such institutions shall conform to such minimum standards as may be laid down by the State.

■ Article 32

1. States Parties recognize the right of the child to be protected from economic exploitation and from performing any work that is likely to be hazardous or to interfere with the child's education, or to be harmful to the child's health or physical, mental, spiritual, moral or social development.
2. States Parties shall take legislative, administrative, social and educational measures to ensure the implementation of the present article. To this end, and having regard to the relevant provisions of other international instruments, States Parties shall in particular:
(a) Provide for a minimum age or minimum ages for admission to employment;
(b) Provide for appropriate regulation of the hours and conditions of employment;
(c) Provide for appropriate penalties or other sanctions to ensure the effective enforcement of the present article.

Goals for children and development in the 1990s

The following goals have been formulated through extensive consultation in various international forums attended by virtually all Governments, the relevant United Nations agencies including the World Health Organization (WHO), UNICEF, the United Nations Population Fund (UNFPA), the United Nations Educational, Scientific and Cultural Organization (UNESCO), the United Nations Development Programme (UNDP) and the International Bank for Reconstruction and Development (IBRD) and a large number of NGOs. These goals are recommended for implementation by all countries where they are applicable, with appropriate adaptation to the specific situation of each country in terms of phasing, standards, priorities and availability of resources, with respect for cultural, religious and social traditions. Additional goals that are particularly relevant to a country's specific situation should be added in its national plan of action.

I. Major goals for child survival, development and protection

(a) Between 1990 and the year 2000, reduction of infant and under-5 child mortality rate by one third or to 50 and 70 per 1,000 live births respectively, whichever is less;
(b) Between 1990 and the year 2000, reduction of maternal mortality rate by half;
(c) Between 1990 and the year 2000, reduction of severe and moderate malnutrition among under-5 children by half;
(d) Universal access to safe drinking water and to sanitary means of excreta disposal;
(e) By the year 2000, universal access to basic education and completion of primary education by at least 80 per cent of primary school-age children;
(f) Reduction of the adult illiteracy rate (the appropriate age group to be determined in each country) to at least half its 1990 level with emphasis on female literacy;
(g) Improved protection of children in especially difficult circumstances.

II. Supporting/sectoral goals

A. Women's health and education

(i) Special attention to the health and nutrition of the female child and to pregnant and lactating women;
(ii) Access by all couples to information and services to prevent pregnancies that are too early, too closely spaced, too late or too many;
(iii) Access by all pregnant women to pre-natal care, trained attendants during childbirth and referral facilities for high-risk pregnancies and obstetric emergencies;
(iv) Universal access to primary education with special emphasis for girls and accelerated literacy programmes for women.

☐ B. Nutrition

(i) Reduction in severe, as well as moderate malnutrition among under-5 children by half of 1990 levels;
(ii) Reduction of the rate of low birth weight (less than 2.5 kg) to less than 10 per cent;
(iii) Reduction of iron deficiency anaemia in women by one third of the 1990 levels;
(iv) Virtual elimination of iodine deficiency disorders;
(v) Virtual elimination of vitamin A deficiency and its consequences, including blindness;
(vi) Empowerment of all women to breast-feed their children exclusively for four to six months and to continue breast-feeding, with complementary food, well into the second year;
(vii) Growth promotion and its regular monitoring to be institutionalized in all countries by the end of the 1990s;
(viii) Dissemination of knowledge and supporting services to increase food production to ensure household food security.

☐ C. Child health

(i) Global eradication of poliomyelitis by the year 2000;
(ii) Elimination of neonatal tetanus by 1995;
(iii) Reduction by 95 per cent in measles deaths and reduction by 90 per cent of measles cases compared to pre-immunization levels by 1995, as a major step to the global eradication of measles in the longer run;
(iv) Maintenance of a high level of immunization coverage (at least 90 per cent of children under one year of age by the year 2000) against diphtheria, pertussis, tetanus, measles, poliomyelitis, tuberculosis and against tetanus for women of child-bearing age;
(v) Reduction by 50 per cent in the deaths due to diarrhoea in children under the age of five years and 25 per cent reduction in the diarrhoea incidence rate;
(vi) Reduction by one third in the deaths due to acute respiratory infections in children under five years.

☐ D. Water and sanitation

(i) Universal access to safe drinking water;
(ii) Universal access to sanitary means of excreta disposal;
(iii) Elimination of guinea-worm disease (dracunculiasis) by the year 2000.

☐ E. Basic education

(i) Expansion of early childhood development activities, including appropriate low-cost family- and community-based interventions;
(ii) Universal access to basic education, and achievement of primary education by at least 80 per cent of primary school-age children through formal schooling or non-formal education of comparable learning standard, with emphasis on reducing the current disparities between boys and girls;
(iii) Reduction of the adult literacy rate (the appropriate age group to be determined in each country) to at least half its 1990 level, with emphasis on female literacy;
(iv) Increased acquisition by individuals and families of the knowledge, skills and values required for better living, made available through all educational channels, including the mass media, other forms of modern and traditional communication and social action, with effectiveness measured in terms of behavioural change.

☐ F. Children in difficult circumstances

Provide improved protection of children in especially difficult circumstances and tackle the root causes leading to such situations.

Bibliography

Abdalla, A., 'Child Labour in Egypt: Leather Tanning in Cairo', in Bequele, A. and Boyden, J. (eds.), 1988.

Ahmed M. et al., *Primary Education for All: Learning from the BRAC Experience*, ABEL/AED Publication, Washington, D.C., 1993.

Alston, P., 'U.S. Ratification of the Covenant on Economic, Social and Cultural Rights: The Need for an Entirely New Strategy', *American Journal of International Law*, Vol. 84, 1990.

Alston, P., 'Revitalising United Nations Work on Human Rights and Development', *Melbourne University Law Review*, Vol. 18, December 1991.

Alston, P., 'The Article 28 of the Convention on the Rights of the Child', unpublished draft, United Nations Children's Fund, New York, 1992.

Alston, P., *Commentary on the Convention on the Rights of the Child of 1989*, United Nations, New York, forthcoming.

Alston, P. and Brennan, G. (eds.), *The UN Children's Convention and Australia*, Canberra, 1991.

Alston, P. and Quinn, G., 'The Nature and Scope of States Parties' Obligations under the International Covenant on Economic, Social and Cultural Rights', *Human Rights Quarterly*, 9, 1987.

Anker, R., 'Cost Implications of Eliminating Child Labour from Glass Bangles Production', report for ILO, Geneva, 1993.

Arnold F. et al., *The Value of Children: Introduction and Comparative Analysis*, East-West Center, Honolulu, 1975.

Arole, M. and Arole, R., *Jamkhed*, Johns Hopkins University Press, Baltimore, forthcoming.

Azer, A., Afifi, E., Mostafa, O., Abel Gawad, L. and Korayem, A., 'Training and Welfare of Working Children in Shubra el Kheima: Pre-project Survey', report for the National Centre for Social and Criminological Research and ILO, Cairo, 1993.

Barnum, H. and Kutzin, J., *Public Hospitals in Developing Countries: Resource Use, Cost, Financing*, Johns Hopkins University Press for the World Bank, Baltimore, 1993.

Bayer, R., Callahan, D., Caplan, A.L. and Jennings, B., 'Toward Justice in Health Care', *American Journal of Public Health*, 83(3), 1988, pp. 418-426.

Behrman, J., *The Economic Rationale for Investing In Nutrition in Developing Countries*, United States Agency for International Development, Washington, D.C., 1992.

Bender, A.E., 'Protein Requirements', *The Lancet*, September 7, 1974.

Bequele, A., 'Emerging Perspectives in the Struggle against Child Labour', in Myers, W.E. (ed.), *Protecting Working Children*, Zed Books in association with UNICEF, London, 1991.

Bequele, A. and Boyden, J. (eds.), *Combating Child Labour*, ILO, Geneva, 1988.

Bequele, A. and Myers, W., 'First Things First in Child Labour', ILO, Geneva, forthcoming.

Black, M., 'Street and Working Children', *Innocenti Global Seminar Summary Report*, UNICEF, International Child Development Centre, Florence, 1993.

Bonfiglioli, A. and Watson, C., 'Pastoralists at a Crossroads: Survival and Development Issues in African Pastoralism', UNICEF/UNESCO, NOPA Project, Kenya, November 1992.

Bose, A.B., 'The Disadvantaged Urban Child in India', *Innocenti Occasional Papers*, UCS 1, UNICEF, International Child Development Centre, Florence, January 1992.

Boyden, J., 'The Relationship between Education and Child Work', *Innocenti Occasional Papers*, CRS No. 9, UNICEF, International Child Development Centre, Florence, September 1994.

Boyden, J. and Myers, W., 'Exploring Alternative Approaches to Combating Child Labour: Case Studies from Developing Countries', *Innocenti Occasional Papers*, CRS 8, UNICEF, International Child Development Centre, Florence, 1995.

Boyden, J., with UNESCO, *Families; Celebration and Hope in a World of Change*, Gaia Books Ltd., London, 1993.

Brenzel, L., *Cost and Financing of EPI*, Resources for Child Health Project, Rosslyn, Va., 1991.

Brock, J.F. and Autret, M., 'Kwashiorkor in Africa', *FAO Nutritional Studies*, No. 8, Food and Agriculture Organization, Rome, March 1952.

Brown, E.R., 'Community Action for Health Promotion: A Strategy to Empower Individuals and Communities', *International Journal of Health Services*, 21(3), 1991, pp. 441-456.

Brunet-Jailly, J., *Health Financing in the Poor Countries: Cost Recovery or Cost Reduction?*, World Bank, Washington, D.C., May 1991.

Bryant, J.H., 'Principles of Justice as a Basis for Conceptualizing a Health Care System', *International Journal of Health Services*, 7(4), 1977, pp. 707-719.

Bryson, J.M., 'A Strategic Planning Process for Public and Non-Profit Organizations', *Long Range Planning*, No. 21, 1988, pp. 73-81.

Bryson, J.M. and Einsweiler, R.C. (eds.), *Strategic Planning: Threads and Opportunities for Planners*, Planners Press, Chicago, 1988.

Cain, M., 'The Economic Activities of Children in a Village in Bangladesh', *Population and Development Review*, Vol. 3, No. 3, 1977, pp. 201-229.

Carnoy M., *The Case For Investing in Basic Education*, UNICEF, New York, 1992.

Castillo, C. and Akehurst, C., 'An Overview of NPA Decentralization in Developing Countries: Basic Data', *Innocenti Occasional Papers*, DLG 6, UNICEF, International Child Development Centre, Florence, July 1994.

Child Workers in Nepal, 'Child Labour in the Tea Estates of Nepal', research report, CWIN-Concerned Center, Kathmandu, 1991.

Chowdhury, S.R. et al. (eds.), *The Right to Development in International Law*, Martinus Nijhoff Publishers, Dordrecht, 1992.

Colclough, C. and Lewin, K., *Educating All the Children: Strategies for Primary Schooling in the South*, Clarendon Press, Oxford, 1993.

Cook, R.J., *Human Rights in Relation to Women's Health: The Promotion and Protection of Women's Health through International Human Rights Law*, Document WHO/DGH/93.1, WHO, Geneva, June 1993.

Cornia, G.A. and de Jong, J., 'Policies for the Revitalisation of Human Resource Development', in Cornia, G.A., van der Hoeven, R. and Mkandawire, T. (eds.), *Africa's Recovery in the 1990s: From Stagnation and Adjustment to Human Development*, St. Martin's Press, New York, 1992.

Cornia, G.A., Jolly, R. and Stewart, F. (eds.), *Adjustment with a Human Face*, Vol. 1: *Protecting the Vulnerable and Promoting Growth*, Oxford University Press, Oxford, 1987.

Costarelli, S. (ed.), 'Children of Minorities: Gypsies', *Innocenti Insights*, UNICEF, International Child Development Centre, Florence, 1993.

Crocker, D., 'Toward Development Ethics', *World Development*, Vol. 19, No. 5, 1991, pp. 457-483.

Cury, M., Do Amaral e Silva, A.F. and Mendez, E.G. (eds.), *Estatuto da criança e do adolescente comentado*, São Paulo, 1992.

Dall, F.P., 'Education, Agricultural Extension and Peasant Farmer Marginalization', dissertation in partial fulfilment of doctorate, 1987.

Dall, F.P., 'Basic Education: An Investment in a Better African Future', paper prepared for the Organization of African Unity International Conference on Assistance to African Children, Dakar, Senegal, 25-27 November, 1992, in OAU/UNICEF, *Africa's Children, Africa's Future: Background Sectoral Papers*, 1992a.

Dall, F.P., *ICAAC Salesbook*, UNICEF, New York, 1992b.

Dall, F.P., 'Survival Skills and the Primary School Curriculum: What Should Children Be Learning in School?', *Forum for Advancing Basic Education* 2 (2), 1993.

Dall, K.N., 'The African Girl Child: Challenges and Prospects in the 1990's', UNICEF, New York, 1991.

Dasgupta, P., *An Inquiry into Well-Being and Destitution*, Clarendon Press, Oxford, 1993.

de Jong, G.A. and Rutten, F.F.H., 'Justice and Health For All', *Social Science and Medicine*, 17(16), 1983, pp. 1085-1095.

Donaldson, J.K., 'Finding Common Ground — Redefining Women's Work in Colombia', *Grassroots Development*, Vol. 16, No. 1, 1992.

Drèze, J. and Sen, A., *Hunger and Public Action*, Clarendon Press, Oxford, 1989.

Eide, A., Oshaug, A. and Eide, W.B., 'Food Security and the Right to Food in International Law and Development', *Transnational Law and Contemporary Problems*, Vol. 1, No. 2, Fall 1991, pp. 415-467.

Eisemon T., 'The Consequences of Schooling: A Review of Research on the Outcomes of Primary Schooling in Developing Countries', in *Education Development Discussion Paper*, No. 3, Harvard University, Cambridge, Mass., 1991.

Engle, P., 'Care and Child Nutrition', paper for the International Nutrition Conference, UNICEF, New York, Nutrition Section, March 1992.

Feder G. et al., 'The Impact of Agricultural Extension: A Case Study in Haryana, India', India, 1985.

Fonseca, L., 'Economic Implications of Child Labour', presentation made at the UNICEF Regional Training Workshop on Elimination of Child Labour held in Varanasi 30 August – 1 September 1993, UNICEF, Regional Office for South Asia, Kathmandu, Nepal.

Frenk, J., 'The Public/Private Mix and Human Resources for Health', *Health Policy and Planning*, 8(4), 1993, pp. 315-326.

Fuenzalida-Puelma, H.L. and Connor, S.S., 'Summary and Analysis', in Fuenzalida-Puelma, H.L. and Connor, S.S. (eds.), 'The Right to Health in the Americas: A Comparative Constitutional Study', *Scientific Publication*, No. 509, Pan American Health Organization, Washington, D.C., 1989, pp. 541-668.

Gajraj, S. and Schoeman, K., 'Primary Education: The Excluded', UNESCO, Paris, 1991.

Ginter, P.M. and Duncan, W.J., 'Macroenvironmental Analysis for Strategic Management', *Long Range Planning*, No. 23, 1990, pp. 91-101.

Goodfield, J., *The Planned Miracle*, Macdonald and Co. Ltd., Great Britain, 1991.

Goonesekere, S., *Children, Law and Justice: A South Asian Perspective*, unpublished manuscript, UNICEF, International Child Development Centre, Florence, 1992.

Goulet, D., 'Tasks and Methods in Development Ethics', *Cross Currents*, Vol. 38, No. 2, 1988.

Government of Tanzania, WHO and UNICEF, 'JNSP Iringa 1983-1988 Evaluation Report', October 1988.

Grant, J.P., 'Child Health and Human Rights', an address to the Committee on Health and Human Rights Lecture Program, Institute of Medicine, 10 March 1993, National Academy Press, Washington, D.C., 1994.

Grude Flekky, M., *A Voice for Children: Speaking Out as Their Ombudsman*, Jessica Kingsley Publishers, London, 1991.

Gunn, S. and Ostos, A., 'Dilemmas in Tackling Child Labour: The Case of Scavenger Children in the Philippines', *International Labour Review*, Vol. 131, No. 6, 1992, pp. 629-646.

Hart, R.A., 'Children's Participation: From Tokenship to Citizenship', *Innocenti Essays*, No. 4, UNICEF, International Child Development Centre, Florence, March 1992.

Himes, J.R., 'The Right to Development Vs. Development and Human Rights', *The International Journal of Children's Rights*, No. 1, 1993, pp. 81-97.

Himes, J.R., Landers, C. and Leslie, J., 'Women, Work and Child Care', *Innocenti Global Seminar-Summary Report*, UNICEF, International Child Development Centre, Florence, 1992.

Horton, S., *Unit Costs, Cost-Effectiveness and Financing of Nutrition Interventions*, World Bank, Washington, D.C., 1992.

Hutchins, S.S., Jansen, H.A.F.M. and Robertson, S.E., *Missed Opportunities for Immunization: Review of Studies from Developing and Industrialized Countries*, Document WHO/EPI/GEN/92.8, World Health Organization, Geneva, 1993.

Institute of Industrial Relations, Bureau of Women and Young Workers, 'Child Labour in the Philippines: Wood-based and Clothing Industries', in Bequele, A. and Boyden, J. (eds.), 1988.

International Conference on Nutrition, 'World Declaration', Food and Agriculture Organization/World Health Organization, Rome, 1992.

International Labour Organisation, *Report of the Director General*, International Labour Conference, 69th Session, ILO, Geneva, 1983.

International Labour Organisation, *Still So Far to Go; Child Labour in the World Today*, special report, ILO, Geneva, 1989.

International Labour Organisation, IPEC Programme Document, *International Programme on the Elimination of Child Labour: An Action Programme to Protect Working Children and to Combat and Eliminate Child Labour*, ILO, 1992a.

International Labour Organisation, Inter-Departmental Project on the Elimination of Child Labour, 'Towards Action Against Child Labour in Zimbabwe', ILO, Geneva, 1992b.

International Labour Organisation, 'Towards the Abolition of Child Labour: ILO Policy and its Implications for Technical, Cooperation Activities', unpublished manuscript, ILO, Geneva, February 1993.

Jacobs, D., *UNICEF Education Report: Activities*, UNICEF, New York, 1993.

Jamison, D.T., Mosley, W.H., Measham, A.R. and Bobadilla, J.L. (eds.), *Disease Control Priorities in Developing Countries*, Oxford University Press, New York, 1993.

Jolly, R. and van der Hoeven, R., 'Editors' Introduction', *World Development*, Vol. 19, No. 12, 1991.

Kanbargi, R., 'Child Labour in India: The Carpet Industry of Varanasi', in Bequele, A. and Boyden, J. (eds.), 1988.

Kemp, R.L. (ed.), *Strategic Planning in Local Government: A Casebook*, Planners Press, Chicago, 1992.

Kent, G., 'Children's Right to Adequate Nutrition', forthcoming in *Food Policy*, 1993.

Kiranandana, T. and Tontisirin, K., 'Eradicating Child Malnutrition: Thailand's Health, Nutrition and Poverty Alleviation Policy in the 1980s', *Innocenti Occasional Papers*, EPS 23, UNICEF, International Child Development Centre, Florence, January 1992.

Kriel, J.R., 'Social Justice and Health Care: A Theoretical Model', *Medicine and Law*, 7, 1989, pp. 567-577.

Krishnakumari, N., 'Child Labour in Bangalore City', *Banhi Series*, Joint Women's Programme, ISPCK, Delhi, 1985.

Landers, C. and Leonard, A. (eds.) 'Women, Work and the Need for Child Care', *UNICEF Staff Working Papers*, No. 10, UNICEF, New York, February 1992.

League of Nations, 'Nutrition Considered in Relation to Public Health and Economic Conditions', League of Nations, Geneva, 1935.

League of Nations, *The Problem of Malnutrition*, Vols. I-III, League of Nations, Geneva, 1936.

Lovell, C.H. and Fatema, K., *Assignment Children: The BRAC Non-Formal Primary Education Programme in Bangladesh*, UNICEF, New York, 1989.

Mansurov, V., 'Child Work in Russia', INTERDEP/CL-/1993/1, ILO, Geneva, 1993.

Marchisio, S. and DiBlase, A., *The Food and Agriculture Organization (FAO)*, Graduate Institute of International Studies, Geneva, 1991.

Mariner, W.K., 'Patients' Rights after Health Care Reform: Who Decides What is Medically Necessary?', *American Journal of Public Health*, 84(9), 1994, pp. 1515-1520.

Martines, J., Phillips, M. and Feachem, R.G.A., 'Diarrheal Disease', report prepared for *Health Sector Priorities Review*, HSPR-21, World Bank, Population and Human Resources Department, April 1991.

McLaren, D., 'The Great Protein Fiasco', *The Lancet*, July 13, 1974.

McPake, B., Hanson, K. and Mills, A., *Implementing the Bamako Initiative in Africa: A Review and Five Case Studies*, PHP Departmental Publication, No. 8, London School of Hygiene and Tropical Medicine, London, 1992.

Mechanic, D., 'Promoting Health: Implications for Modern and Developing Nations', in Chen, L.C., Kleinman, A. and Ware, N.C. (eds.), *Health and Social Change in International Perspective*, Harvard University Press, Boston, 1994.

Miller, D.S., 'Protein Requirements', *The Lancet*, October 9, 1974.

Morley, D., Rohde, J. and Williams, G. (eds.), *Practising Health for All*, Oxford University Press, Oxford, 1983.

Moseley, W.H. and Chen, L.C., 'An Analytical Framework for the Study of Child Survival in Developing Countries', *Population and Development Review*, 10, Supplement, 1984.

Mueller, E., 'The Economic Value of Children in Peasant Agriculture', in Rider, G. (ed.), *Population and Development: The Search for Selective Interventions*, published for Resources for the Future by John Hopkins University Press, Baltimore and London, 1976.

Myers, R., *The Twelve Who Survive*, Routledge, London/New York, 1992.

Naik J.P., 'The Economic Social and Family Context on the Child's Right to Education', UNESCO, Paris, 1979.

Newell, K. (ed.), *Health by the People*, WHO, Geneva, 1975.

Newell, P., *The UN Convention and Children's Rights in the UK*, National Children's Bureau, 1991.

The NGO Group for the Convention on the Rights of the Child, 'Eliminating the Exploitation of Child Labour; International, National and Local Action', mimeo, 1993.

Nigam, A. and Parker, D., 'Resources for Human Development: How Much is Needed? How Much is Available?', paper prepared for Project on Fiscal Policy and the Poor, UNICEF, International Child Development Centre, Florence, 1994.

Northrup, R., 'Oral Rehydration Therapy: From Principle to Practice', in Rohde, J., Chatterjee, M. and Morley, D., *Reaching Health for All*, Oxford University Press, Delhi, 1993.

Organization of African Unity and United Nation's Children's Fund, 'Improving the Health of African Women and Children in the 1990s', in *Africa's Children, Africa's Future: Background Sectoral Papers*, UNICEF, New York, 1992a.

Organization of African Unity and United Nations Children's Fund, *Africa's Children, Africa's Future: Human Investment Priorities for the 1990's*, prepared for the OAU International Conference on Assistance to African Children held in Dakar, Senegal, 25-27 November 1992, OAU/UNICEF, 1992b.

Padmini, R., 'Poverty Reduction and Programme Convergence to Tackle Child Labour', presentation made at UNICEF Regional Training Workshop on Elimination of Child Labour, held in Varanasi 30 August – 1 September 1993, UNICEF, Regional Office for South Asia, Kathmandu, Nepal.

Parker, D. and Jespersen, E., '20/20: Mobilizing Resources for Children in the 1990s', *UNICEF Staff Working Papers*, No. 12, UNICEF, New York, 1992.

Parmet, W.E., 'Legal Rights and Communicable Disease: AIDS, the Police Power, and Individual Liberty', *Journal of Health Politics, Policy and Law*, 14(4), 1989, pp. 741-769.

Patel, M.S., 'Eliminating Social Distance between North and South: Cost-Effective Goals for the 1990s', *UNICEF Staff Working Papers*, No. 5, UNICEF, New York, 1989.

Patil, B., 'The Working Children in Bangalore City', unpublished report, Indian Institute of Management, Bangalore, undated.

Permanent Council of the Organization of American States, 'Annual Report of the Inter-American Commission on Human Rights for 1991', CP/CAJP-862/92, 2 March 1992.

Pinstrup-Andersen, P., 'Assessing Food Security and Nutrition for the Poor', in Bell, D.E. and Reich, M.R., *Health, Nutrition and Economic Crisis*, Auburn Publishing Company, Dovar, Mass., 1988.

Pojman, L.P, *Ethical Theory: Classical and Contemporary Readings*, Wadsworth Publishing Company, Belmont, Calif., 1989.

Psacharopoulous G., 'Returns to Education: A Further International Update and Implications', *Journal of Human Resources*, 20, 1985.

Reimers F., 'The Impact of Economic Stabilization and Adjustment on Education in Latin America', *Comparative Education Review*, 35 (2), May 1991.

Rizzini, Irene, Rizzini, Irma, Munhoz, M. and Galeano, L., 'Childhood and Urban Poverty in Brazil: Street Children and Their Families', *Innocenti Occasional Papers*, UCS 3, UNICEF, International Child Development Centre, Florence, September 1992.

Robertson, R.E., 'The Right to Food—Canada's Broken Covenant', *Canadian Human Rights Yearbook 1989-1990*, 6, CHRYB, 1990.

Robertson, R.E., 'Measuring State Compliance with the Obligation to Devote the "Maximum Available Resources" to Realizing Economic, Social, and Cultural Rights', *Human Rights Quarterly*, The Johns Hopkins University Press, Vol. 16, No. 4, November 1994.

Rohde, J., 'Indonesia's *Posyandus*: Accomplishments and Future Challenges', in Rohde, J., Chatterjee, M. and Morlez, D. (eds.), *Reaching Health for All*, Oxford University Press, Delhi, 1993.

Safilios-Rothchild, C., 'The Role of the Family: A Neglected Aspect of Poverty', in 'Implementing Programs of Human Development', *World Bank Staff Working Papers*, No. 403, World Bank, Washington, D.C., July 1980.

Sarvodaya Shramadana Movement, *Sarvodaya Shramadana Movement: A Mid-term Review*, SSM, Colombo, 1988.

Sen, A., *Poverty and Famines*, Clarendon, Oxford, 1981.

Sen, A., *Resources, Values and Development*, Harvard University Press, Cambridge, Mass., 1984.

Sengupta, A.K., 'Indian Constitutional Jurisprudence on Human Rights: Creating National Conditions for Development', in Chowdhury, S.R. et al. (eds.), *The Right to Development in International Law*, Martinus Nijhoff Publishers, Dordrecht, 1992.

Sepúlveda, C., 'The Right to Child Health: The Development of Primary Health Services in Chile and Thailand', *Innocenti Occasional Papers*, CRS 7, UNICEF, International Child Development Centre, Florence, April 1994.

Shue, H., *Basic Rights*, Princeton University Press, Princeton, N.J., 1980.

Stewart, F., 'Basic Needs Strategies, Human Rights, and the Right to Development', *Human Rights Quarterly*, 11:34/3/4, 1989.

Stobart, M., 'Prologue', in Tarrow, N.B. (ed.), 'Human Rights and Education' *Comparative and International Education Series*, Vol. 3, , Pergamon Press, Oxford, 1987.

Susser, M., 'Health as a Human Right: An Epidemiologist's Perspective on the Public Health', *American Journal of Public Health*, 83(3), 1993, pp. 418-426.

Szanton Blanc, C. and Contributors, *Urban Children in Distress: Global Predicaments and Innovative Strategies*, Gordon and Breach Scientific Publications, New York, in association with UNICEF, International Child Development Centre, Florence, 1994.

Tomasevski, K. (ed.), *The Right to Food: Guide through Applicable International Law*, Martinus Nijhoff, Dordrecht, 1986.

Traylor, J.C., 'FAO and the Right to Food', in Eide, A., Eide, W. B., Goonatilake, S., Gussow, J. and Omawale (eds.), *Food as a Human Right*, United Nations University, Tokyo, 1984.

Tronick, E., 'Policy Guidelines for the Implementation of Early Childhood Development Programmes', report presented at the meeting on 'Early Childhood and Preschool Education', organized by the Education Section, Programme Division, UNICEF, New York, 25 September 1992.

United Nations, *International Action to Avert the Impending World Protein Crisis*, United Nations, New York, New York, 1968.

United Nations Administrative Committee on Coordination/ Subcommittee on Nutrition, *Second Report on the World Nutrition Situation 1992*, Vol. I (October 1992) and Vol. II (March 1993), ACC/SCN, Geneva.

United Nations Children's Fund, *Children and Development in the 1990's: A UNICEF Sourcebook for the World Summit for Children*, UNICEF, New York, 1990a.

United Nations Children's Fund, *First Call For Children*, UNICEF, New York, 1990b.

United Nations Children's Fund, 'How Child Rights Can Be Integrated in UNICEF Work: Experience from Egypt', unpublished paper prepared by UNICEF, Cairo, for the Global Consultation on Implementation Strategies for Children's Rights, Florence, 3-8 December 1990c.

United Nations Children's Fund, 'Revitalizing Primary Health Care/Maternal and Child Health: The Bamako Initiative', Progress Report, UNICEF Executive Board 1990 Session, UNICEF, New York, April 1990d.

United Nations Children's Fund, 'Strategy for Improved Nutrition of Children and Women in Developing Countries', *UNICEF Policy Review*, UNICEF, New York, 1990e.

United Nations Children's Fund, 'The Convention: Child Rights and UNICEF Experience at the Country Level', *Innocenti Studies*, UNICEF, International Child Development Centre, Florence, 1991a.

United Nations Children's Fund, 'Role of UNICEF in the Implementation of the Convention on the Rights of the Child', E/ICEF/1991/L.7, 6 February 1991b.

United Nations Children's Fund, *Challenges For Children and Women in the 1990's*, UNICEF, Regional Eastern and Southern Africa Office, Kenya, 1991c.

United Nations Children's Fund, *The State of the World's Children 1991*, Oxford University Press for UNICEF, Oxford and New York, 1991d.

United Nations Children's Fund, *Educating Girls and Women: A Moral Imperative*, UNICEF, Education Section, Programme Division, New York, 1992a.

United Nations Children's Fund, 'Bamako Initiative', Progress Report, UNICEF Executive Board 1992 Session, UNICEF, New York, 1992b.

United Nations Children's Fund, *The State of the World's Children 1992*, Oxford University Press for UNICEF, Oxford and New York, 1992c.

United Nations Children's Fund, *Food, Health and Care — The UNICEF Vision and Strategy for a World Free From Hunger and Malnutrition*, UNICEF, New York, 1992d.

United Nations Children's Fund, *Child Malnutrition: Progress towards the World Summit for Children Goal*, UNICEF, New York, March 1993a.

United Nations Children's Fund, *The State of the World's Children 1993*, Oxford University Press for UNICEF, Oxford and New York, 1993b.

United Nations Children's Fund, 'A UNICEF Nutrition Information Strategy', Draft 4, mimeo, UNICEF, New York, July 1993c.

United Nations Children's Fund, 'Links for Children in South Asia', Workshop Report, Kathmandu, April 1993d.

United Nations Children's Fund, *The Progress of Nations 1993*, UNICEF, New York, 1993e.

United Nations Children's Fund, *The Progress of Nations 1994*, UNICEF, New York, 1994a.

United Nations Children's Fund, *The State of the World's Children 1994*, Oxford University Press for UNICEF, Oxford and New York, 1994b.

United Nations Children's Fund, *The State of the World's Children 1995*, Oxford University Press for UNICEF, Oxford and New York, 1995.

United Nations Children's Fund and Government of Tanzania, *Women and Children in Tanzania*, UNICEF, Dar es Salaam, 1990.

United Nations Development Programme, *Human Development Report 1991*, Oxford University Press, New York, 1991.

United Nations Development Programme, *Human Development Report 1992*, Oxford University Press, New York, 1992.

United Nations Development Programme, UNESCO, UNFPA, UNICEF and WHO, *The 20/20 Initiative: Achieving Universal Access to Basic Social Services for Sustainable Human Development*, UNICEF, Division of Information, New York, December 1994.

United Nations Economic and Social Commission for Asia and the Pacific and United Nations Children's Fund, 'Basic Community Services through Primary Health Care: A Training Approach', *ESCAP Technical Papers*, No. 65, ESCAP, Bangkok, 1985.

United Nations Human Rights Commission, Working Group on Contemporary Forms of Slavery, 'The United Nations Programme of Action for the Elimination of Child Labour', Geneva, 1993.

United States Agency for International Development, *The Economic and Social Impacts of Girls' Primary Education in Developing Countries*, ABEL Research Study, Washington, D.C., 1990.

United States Agency for International Development, *Educating Girls: Strategies to Increase Access, Persistence, and Achievement*, ABEL Research Study, Washington, D.C., 1990.

Walsh, J.A. and Warren, K.S. (eds.), *Strategies for Primary Health Care: Technologies Appropriate for the Control of Disease in the Developing World*, University of Chicago Press, 1986.

Waterlow, J., 'Protein Malnutrition', Proceedings of a Conference held in Jamaica, Food and Agriculture Organization, World Health Organization and J. Mecy Foundation, Harvard University Press, Cambridge, Mass., 1955.

Weiner, M., *The Child and the State in India*, Princeton University Press, Princeton, N.J., 1991.

Werner, D., 'The Life and Death of Primary Health Care', *Third World Resurgence*, 42/43, 1994, pp. 10-14.

White, B., 'The Economic Importance of Children in a Javanese Village', mimeo, 1974.

White, B. and Tjandraningsih, I., 'Rural Children in the Industrialization Process: Child and Youth Labour in "Traditional" and "Modern" Industries in West Java, Indonesia', unpublished report, Institute of Social Studies, The Hague, 1992.

Williams, C.D. 'A Nutrition Disease of Childhood Associated with a Maize Diet', *Archives of Disease in Childhood*, Vol. 8, 1933.

Wilson, I., 'Realizing the Power of Strategic Vision', *Long Range Planning*, No. 25, 1992, pp. 18-28.

World Alliance for Nutrition and Human Rights, 'The Oslo Initiative', Norwegian Institute of Human Rights, University of Oslo, 1992.

World Bank, *World Development Report on Poverty*, World Bank, Washington, D.C., 1990.

World Bank, *World Development Report 1991*, Oxford University Press, New York, 1991.

World Bank, *World Development Report 1993: Investing in Health*, Oxford University Press, New York, 1993.

World Commission on Environment and Development, *Our Common Future*, Oxford University Press, Oxford, 1987.

World Conference on Education for All, 'World Declaration on Education For All and Framework For Action to Meet Basic Learning Needs', WCEFA, New York, 1990.

World Health Organization, *Primary Health Care*, Joint Report by the Director-General of WHO and the Executive Director of UNICEF, WHO, Geneva, 1978.

World Health Organization, 'Evaluation of Recent Changes in the Financing of Health Services', Report of a WHO Study Group, WHO, Geneva, 1991.

World Health Organization, 'Evaluation of Recent Changes in the Financing of Health Services': Report of a WHO Study Group, *WHO Technical Report Series* No. 829, WHO, Geneva, 1993a

World Health Organization, *Implementation of the Global Strategy for Health for All by the Year 2000*, Second Evaluation, Eighth Report on the World Health Situation, Vol. I, Global Review, WHO, Geneva, 1993b.

World Health Organization, United Nations Children's Fund, ICCIDD, 'Global Prevalence of Iodine Deficiency Disorders', Micronutrient Deficiency Information System, WHO, Geneva, 1993.

Xuan Xung, Pham, *Vietnam and the United Nations Convention on the Rights of the Child*, Su That Publishing House, Hanoi, 1991.

Zerfas, A., *Review and Analysis of National Programmes of Action as They Relate to Nutrition*, United Nations Children's Fund, New York, May 1993.

Index

[Names of United Nations bodies are set in capitals and small capitals, and names of international instruments in italics. The index draws largely on the first draft of a glossary of children's rights terminology relevant to the United Nations Convention on the Rights of the Child, dated October 1994, prepared for the UNICEF International Child Development Centre, Florence, by Sharon Detrick.]